Schools
of
Thought

REXFORD G. BROWN

Schools of Thought

How the politics of literacy shape thinking in the classroom

Jossey-Bass Publishers

San Francisco • Oxford • 1991

SCHOOLS OF THOUGHT
How the Politics of Literacy Shape Thinking in the Classroom
by Rexford G. Brown

Copyright © 1991 by: Jossey-Bass Inc., Publishers
350 Sansome Street
San Francisco, California 94104
&
Jossey-Bass Limited
Headington Hill Hall
Oxford OX3 0BW

Library of Congress Cataloging-in-Publication Data

Brown, Rexford.
    Schools of thought : how the politics of literacy shape thinking
in the classroom / Rexford G. Brown.
        p.   cm.—(The Jossey-Bass education series)
    Includes bibliographical references and index.
    ISBN 1-55542-314-0
    1. Literacy—United States—Case studies.   2. Educational change—
United States—Case studies.   I. Title.   II. Series.
LC151.B77   1991
302.′244′0973—dc20   90-19892

Manufactured in the United States of America

JACKET DESIGN BY CHARLOTTE KAY

FIRST EDITION

Code 9119

*The Jossey-Bass
Education Series*

Contents

Preface   xi

The Author   xxi

1.   Back to Basics in the Rural South   1

2.   Hand-Me-Down Literacy   31

3.   Language and Culture on the Reservation   59

4.   An Urban District: One Foot on the Gas,
     the Other on the Brakes   92

5.   The Politics of Literacy   137

6.   When Teachers Talk   164

7.   A Higher Literacy in Toronto   202

8.   Cultivating a Literacy of Thoughtfulness   232

Resource: Guidelines for Program Review from
the Ontario Ministry of Education   253

Bibliography   269

Index   284

Preface

Years ago in this country, people were considered literate if they could sign their names. As times changed, ideas about what constituted a satisfactory level of literacy also changed, and always upward. Mere ability to sign one's name gave way to the ability to write at a certain level of sophistication, higher for each succeeding generation. Mere ability to read gave way to increasingly demanding reading in a wide range of fields, and for a wide range of purposes. As our school system grew, being literate became equated with having completed a certain number of years of school. As our economic system grew and changed, school credentials played an increasingly important role in screening and selecting people for jobs. The number of years of schooling a person completed began to be correlated with potential earnings. The stakes involved in attaining the right kind or degree of literacy and the right level of education rose steadily.

The system charged with determining what the stakes would be for any individual, what life opportunities any of us might enjoy, grew haphazardly throughout this century and achieved its mature form only twenty-five years ago. Only then was it ready to be the instrument of mass education—*true* mass education—that its proponents had long promised it would become, and it was immediately clear that public expectations and economic and social changes were rendering it obsolete.

During the 1970s, critics charged that too many Americans were "functionally" illiterate—that is, not totally illiterate, but not literate enough to function productively and happily. Doubts were also expressed about whether a high school diploma still said anything about the literacy of graduates. Stories of high school graduates who could neither read nor write abounded; reading, writing, and mathematics test-score declines were chronicled year after year, with more and more public hand-wringing. Almost every state legislature passed laws requiring evidence of minimal competency for grade promotion and graduation. Almost every district developed school-improvement plans based on a burgeoning research industry that was devoted to the study of "effective" schools.

The 1980s brought new alarms about literacy in the United States, most dramatically expressed in the National Commission on Excellence in Education's *A Nation at Risk* (1983). This report was the Reagan administration's call for major improvements in education as a matter of national survival in an increasingly competitive global economy. Throughout the decade, a broader and deeper notion of literacy emerged from dozens of books and blue-ribbon reports and the words of nationally prominent speakers. The stakes involved in this more robust kind of literacy grew higher than ever, both for the individual and for the country as a whole. The decade ended with an unprecedented summit meeting of the nation's governors and the president of the United States, who issued a call for radical reform and total restructuring of the educational system.

The new literacy that requires such massive change goes beyond mere reading and writing ability, beyond the so-called basics, and beyond the current requirements for a high school diploma. It now includes capacities once demanded only of a privileged, college-bound elite: to think critically and creatively, solve problems, exercise judgment, and learn new skills and knowledge throughout a lifetime. What at the beginning of the twentieth century was a high standard for a few has apparently become, in the minds of a good many powerful people, a desideratum for all.

Background of the Book

This book is about that new, higher literacy and about whether current efforts to reform and restructure the educational system are likely to foster such literacy in all students. The book is based on a series of case studies undertaken in 1987–1988 with the generous support of the John D. and Catherine T. MacArthur Foundation. The literacy my colleagues at the Education Commission of the States and I have been investigating is one that goes beyond basic skills and includes enhanced abilities to think critically and creatively; to reason carefully; to inquire systematically into any important matter; to analyze, synthesize, and evaluate information and arguments; and to communicate effectively to a variety of audiences in a variety of forms. We have come to call it a literacy of thoughtfulness, since it involves both the exercise of thought and a certain amount of caring about other thinkers in past and present communities. A major question that underlies our study is whether the unprecedented amount of educational policy activity of the last decade is leading (or is likely to lead) to this literacy of thoughtfulness. To what degree, we wondered as we began the case studies on which this book is based, are various kinds of policy serving as positive forces for thoughtfulness, and to what degree are they discouraging it?

To find the right way to ask that complicated question, and perhaps even to suggest some answers, we interviewed experts around the country, conducted focus groups with parents and various other people interested in education, reviewed all available research and relevant policy material, interviewed state and local administrators and policymakers, and then visited schools and classrooms (mostly for grades 3, 6, 8, and 11) where thinking and problem-solving activities were supposed to be a major part of the curriculum. All told, we gathered 650 hours of interviews and observations in the case studies, about two-thirds of it based on talking with teachers and visiting their classes.

We wanted to get a good sense of the status of those policies and programs purported to be conducive to thoughtfulness (as we have defined the term). We also wanted to learn what kinds of barriers confronted people who were trying to be thoughtful or were trying to develop programs that would involve far more students in activities likely to develop critical and creative thinking and problem-solving skills.

Joining me in the interviewing and the observing of classrooms were Jane Armstrong of the Education Commission of the States; Alan Davis, now at the University of Colorado; Patty Flakus-Mosqueda of the Education Commission of the States; Anthony Petrosky of the University of Pittsburgh; Sam Stringfield, now at Johns Hopkins University's Center for Research on Effective Schooling for Disadvantaged Students; and Rona Wilensky, an independent education researcher who lives in Boulder, Colorado.

During the interviews, we explained the purpose of our research and how we intended to use the results. Our intent was to learn what people believe about students' capacities to think critically, solve problems, and become active, engaged learners. We tried to get a sense of how adults in schools and school systems interact, communicate, and model thoughtfulness for students. We inquired into the history of, and the intentions behind, reforms in the district and the state; and we probed for beliefs about relationships between policy and practice. Our interviews were conducted informally, without tape recorders, in interviewees' offices and in classrooms. We transcribed the interviews shortly after conducting them, relying on our notes and memories and often checking with interviewees to see if we had captured their remarks correctly. I have made every effort to present remarks accurately and in the spirit in which they were made.

In our classroom observations, we looked for nine general indicators of climates conducive to a literacy of thoughtfulness:

1. *The physical classroom environment.* Are reference materials and laboratory equipment available? Is the environment richly textured, with much to look at and touch, including samples of students' work? Are students encouraged to move around to gather information or to work in various groups? Are there frequent interruptions—by the public address system, for example? Is the classroom overly noisy?
2. *Interaction between and among students and teacher.* Is most of the talk "teacher talk"? How many students participate in discussion? Do students address one another? Does the teacher allow sufficient time for students to respond to questions? Does the teacher appear to be a learner?
3. *Questioning strategies.* Do teacher or students ask open-ended

questions or questions that call for analysis, synthesis, interpretation, or evaluation? Do questions drive students toward deeper understanding or comprehension of the material, or is the focus on factual recall? Does the teacher encourage students to ask questions?

4. *Amount of facilitation and probing.* Are students encouraged to clarify or expand on their ideas? Does the teacher translate or transform concepts verbally or graphically to enable different students to grasp them? Does the teacher provide conceptual bridges to help students move from their present understandings to new understandings?

5. *Discussion elements.* During discussions, do students provide supporting evidence or reasons for their comments or opinions? Do teacher or students synthesize or summarize during the discussion? Is sufficient time allowed for good discussion? Do teacher or students critique the discussion?

6. *Nonverbal indicators of engagement.* Are students alert and engaged? If so, how many?

7. *Courtesy and sensitivity.* Do teacher and students listen carefully, use polite speech, and acknowledge and support one anothers' ideas? Do they acknowledge and accept conflicting points of view? Are there signs of humor and good will? Does the teacher praise students for their responses or help lead them from incorrect to correct perceptions?

8. *Amount of reflection or self-regulation.* Do teacher or students talk about thinking or reflect on the quality of individual or group thinking? Are students able to describe their thinking or problem-solving strategies? If students take notes, what do they intend to do with them?

9. *Risk-taking environment.* Is the focus entirely on answering correctly, or are multiple perspectives accepted? Is there a general acceptance of a healthy amount of uncertainty or ambiguity? Do students explore or brainstorm? Are students encouraged to make mistakes and learn from them?

We trained ourselves to be sensitive to these indicators. After observing classrooms, we often asked the teachers why they had conducted their classes as they had, listening particularly for reasons related directly or indirectly to policy.

After studying many potential sites for case studies, we chose seven for intensive scrutiny. All seven serve substantial populations of poor and minority students, but each is addressing, via different policies and practices, the issue of achieving a higher level of literacy for all students.

Overview of the Contents

The results of our study are presented largely in narrative form, since narrative preserves the contexts without which findings are often barren and easy to misunderstand. Time after time in our studies, we found that we had to move from the particulars of daily experience in schools to lofty abstractions and generalizations about school reform, and then back again. The truth, however, lies at neither extreme; rather, it is in the going back and forth, in all our listening and all our efforts to make sense of what we saw and heard.

The story begins in the Deep South, where the major comprehensive school-reform policy initiatives of the 1980s began. The challenge to offer a much higher level of literacy to a much broader range of students is particularly poignant in many southern states because their leaders keenly feel the pinch of international economic competition but are caught up in the economic, social, political, and racial history that complicates and slows the responses they can make.

The story that unfolds in the first two chapters focuses on rural America, where teachers are educating children to leave their communities rather than remain and enrich them. It is also a story of minorities and their struggles to be both a part of and independent of a system that has long excluded them. To say that the nation needs higher literacy for all students is to say that it must do something it has not yet been very successful at doing: educating minority and poor students to their fullest potential.

The third chapter finds us on an Indian reservation. The focus is again on rural education and on a racial minority, but the story expands to address mismatches between the language and culture of schooling and the languages and cultures of a growing proportion of students. On the reservation, we find a school system that, with some help from new state policies, is finding ways to build on the language and culture that students bring to the classroom; the colonial model of education is on the wane.

Chapter Four moves the story into an urban setting. We describe the conflicts and contradictions in a troubled but typical school district, where the policy environment is not conducive to a literacy of thoughtfulness, despite a plethora of good ideas, good intentions, and good programs.

Chapter Five departs from the narrative somewhat to broaden the notion of what a policy environment is and to describe the contributions of a governor, a legislature, a state school board, and a district court judge.

Chapter Six describes a school district in Pittsburgh, Pennsylvania, where many of the problems described in earlier chapters have been addressed in positive ways. Pittsburgh illustrates what can be done to begin the kind of community conversation that undergirds a literacy of thoughtfulness. But Pittsburgh's schools also clearly reveal a fundamental conflict between contending beliefs about learning and literacy. This conflict, if not somehow resolved, will limit how deeply reforms can penetrate contemporary urban systems.

The next chapter describes the school distict where, in all our travels, we found the most advanced form of a literacy of thoughtfulness: Toronto, Ontario. How both local and provincial policy created and now sustain that literacy is the focus of the chapter that ends the narrative. Chapter Eight sums up our findings from all the schools, districts, states, and Canadian provinces we visited.

Although the chapters, like essays, can be read separately, they do refer to one another in various ways, and they do constitute a developing story. In the first five chapters, I have disguised names and places, both because I told the subjects that I would and because the situations described are intended to represent widespread conditions. Much more could be said in each chapter about the schools and districts in question, but I have tried to focus on themes that illustrate important problems or breakthroughs in creating more thoughtful policies and learning environments.

This book is for people who are interested in school reform

and in the role that public policy can play in bringing it about. I have tried to steer clear of jargon except when presenting particular examples of the language of schooling; that language, as I argue throughout this book, is part of the problem. A literacy of thoughtfulness cannot blossom for students unless it is practiced by adults. Practicing involves paying close attention to language and to the thought embedded in it.

Acknowledgments

So many people have contributed to the research project on which this book rests, as well as to the writing and reviewing of the manuscript itself, that I could not possibly name all of them here. I owe a considerable debt of gratitude to the entire staff of the Education Commission of the States (ECS) for their warm collegiality and their intelligent command of a wide range of subjects central to this inquiry. Many ECS commissioners have also provided sound advice and good ideas, and I express my general thanks to all of them.

Many thanks, too, to the John D. and Catherine T. MacArthur Foundation for its generous support of this entire project, and to Peter Gerber at the foundation, whose encouragement, tireless networking, and thoughtfulness about so many matters have added immeasurably to the substance of the study and to the pleasure of conducting it. Thanks also to Hayes Mizell of the Edna McConnell Clark Foundation for his support in researching and writing sections of the book.

My deep appreciation goes to Zaretta Hammond, Tim Cowhick, and Kim Moyer for their tireless efforts as research assistants; to Iris Fontera for her help and advice on our focus-group meetings and Aspen retreats; to Sharon Plucker, Anna West, and Edie Romansky for organizing my information and my mind; to Xavier Patricia Callahan for her meticulous and thoughtful copyediting; and to case-study compatriots Jane Armstrong, Alan Davis, Patty Flakus-Mosqueda, Anthony Petrosky, Sam Stringfield, and Rona Wilensky for their insightfulness and camaraderie.

I am grateful to Catherine Canney, Roberta Hartman, Mary Jo Lorenz, and the students at Prairie Middle School for their willingness to take risks in the name of literacy research, as well as to the hundreds of students, teachers, and administrators who shared their valuable time and their even more valuable feelings and ideas with yet another group of researchers (who visit the front only to retreat to lives more distant from the action).

Finally, deep gratitude and love to my wife, Sharon, for her insights, patience, and steady encouragement.

Denver, Colorado   Rexford G. Brown
January 1991

The Author

Rexford G. Brown is director of communications and a senior policy analyst for the Education Commission of the States (ECS), a national nonprofit education policy and research organization based in Denver, Colorado. He is also the director of a five-year, million-dollar project called Policy and the Higher Literacies, funded by the John D. and Catherine T. MacArthur Foundation. He received his B.A. degree (1963) from Middlebury College in American literature, his M.A. degree (1965) from the University of Iowa in American and British literature, and his Ph.D. degree (1971) from the University of Iowa in English literature and modern letters. Brown has been a high school and college teacher, as well as an adult educator. He has been with ECS since 1971 and has published many articles and reports on a wide range of education and policy issues. *Schools of Thought* is his first book.

Schools
of
Thought

CHAPTER ONE

Back to Basics
in the Rural South

Coming into the state, Sam Stringfield and I drive through seemingly endless swampland until we reach higher ground with sandy soil and long-needled pines. Heading toward the state capital, there's not much to see but woods. It is an outdoorsman's paradise in these parts, not much changed from its original frontier condition. We haven't reached the great plantations yet.

As we drive along, Sam describes this Deep South state as a place that is in competition with the third world . . . and losing. For most of the state's history, economic development has meant attracting business and industry with the promise of low-skilled, low-paid, nonunionized labor. But, however low the wages in the state, they are far higher than wages in Mexico or Puerto Rico or Korea.

Sam works at the Northwest Regional Educational Laboratory. He has been visiting places like Japan and China and is troubled by the implications for Americans of a rapidly growing global economy. An intense, bearded man who talks quietly, he emphasizes his points with fierce eye contact, even while he is driving.

"There are three categories of countries," he tells me. "First, there are those that are developing a cutting-edge economy and will invent the new technologies and machines. They're followed by the cloners, the imitators, the people who, because of exceptionally low

1

labor costs and because of information and expertise transfer, can quickly imitate what the cutting-edge economy creates and can produce it at a much lower cost. Behind these two, locked right now in neck-and-neck competition, come the endangered economies. Their labor isn't cheap enough to compete with the cloners, nor is it educated enough to compete with the cutting-edgers. They're living on borrowed time."

He gestures at the countryside around us.

"This state is like one of those bottom countries," he says. "In fact, much of the South is like that: living on borrowed time."

He has a point. This state is among those with the lowest per capita incomes, lowest employment rates, and lowest literacy rates. The largest source of income in the state is welfare payments. The state was among the last to make education compulsory and has the largest proportion among the states of adults with less than eighth-grade education. It has been having trouble attracting high-tech, cutting-edge industries and has been losing low-wage work to foreign competitors.

What do you do to catch up with the rest of the country, and with much of the industrial world, in a state whose primary economic virtue has been, for two hundred years, cheap labor? What do you do when much of the talent has left, and what remains is woefully dependent or undervalued, and you do not have a tradition of developing talent? The answers, according to the state's current leaders, lie in massive educational reform and in "basic, drastic change," as one leader puts it.

That's why Sam and I have come here in the spring of 1988. This state, near the bottom in so many other things, was among the first in the nation to pass comprehensive school-reform legislation (which it did in 1982). We want to see if the reforms are having the desired effects. Many more fortunate states have followed this state's example, impelled by the same economic fears. We want to see if the school-reform policies these states have been pushing will actually lead to what many business and political leaders are calling for: a much higher level of literacy for a much broader range of students—a literacy that includes a better ability to think critically, solve problems, make judgments, and tackle complex challenges creatively.

Sam and I leave the main road and drive into the sticks. Sam, who says he is still struggling with the contradictions of his southern upbringing, is impressed by the disappearance of so many sharecroppers' shacks in the past twenty-five years, since his family last drove through this part of the world.

"They used to be everywhere," he says. "I'll never forget them."

We still see a few, and we see off the road, back in the woods, the chimneys where burnt-down shacks once stood.

"That one over there was the kind they used to call a 'shotgun,' " Sam says. He points to a long, narrow, abandoned tin-roofed shack with fallen porches front and back. "They called it that because a 'good old boy' could fire a shotgun through the front door, and the shot would come right out the back door."

We pass a number of small, neat brick homes and churches, clustered together in tiny communities of blacks who probably work in the capital city, twenty miles away. Here and there we come across modest farms with modest, freshly painted wooden houses and white wooden fences. We turn down a dirt road into the woods and pass several well-kept mobile homes with little white wire fences around scruffy yards. Some black families are walking down the road to a small bungalow that serves as a church. After a while, the road ends at a couple of plywood-and-tarpaper shacks perched on the edge of a garbage dump. Colorful laundry flutters on clotheslines above the garbage, where black children chase one another in play. The modest farms, the neat brick houses, and the well-kept mobile homes testify to a changing South. But the garbage dump, the shacks, and the chimneys are reminders that this was the seedbed of much that has troubled the American conscience and shaped life for people far beyond this place.

What brings us to this state needs a little more explanation. For some years now, a growing number of governors, business leaders, futurists, economists, and educators have been worrying aloud about America's competitiveness in world markets. They are alarmed that, in a few short years, the United States has become a debtor nation, importing more than it exports. They are concerned about the consequences of foreign manufacturers' capturing larger and larger proportions of markets once dominated by American companies.

It may be that the United States has been enjoying an artificially high level of economic success since the end of World War II, and it may have been inevitable that other countries would eventually challenge us, whatever we did to improve our productive capacity; many complex factors undoubtedly have contributed to our current situation. But attention has focused increasingly on productivity, not on technology, as the source of our woes and the key to any American comeback. "Human resources," as they are called—people, in plain language—are what will make us competitive or not (see, for example, Berryman, 1987a; Schlefer, 1989; Zuboff, 1988). Accordingly, policymakers and businesspeople have taken great interest in schools, where "human resources" are most self-consciously developed. The nation has been undergoing a school-reform "movement" for most of the 1980s, and the movement shows no signs of letting up.

At first, the call was for "basic skills." The term means different things to different people, but what all definitions entail is something like the good old "three R's": basic reading, writing, and arithmetic skills—a focus on fundamentals, not on frills. Throughout the 1980s, however, a growing chorus of people has been expanding the definition of *basic* and calling for more sophisticated achievements. A group of businesspeople I met with in Denver, Colorado, represented this point of view spontaneously. When I asked them what kinds of things they thought about when they were hiring, firing, and promoting people, the first word someone mentioned was *creativity.* Then someone else mentioned flexibility. As we moved around the table, people added problem-solving ability, skill in dealing with customers, adaptability to change, ability to work with others, good attitudes toward work, and willingness to learn. Although someone eventually mentioned basic skills, it became immediately clear that no one wanted to hire a person who had no more than basic skills. What they wanted were employees who could think, workers who could make independent judgments, people who did not have to be told everything all the time.

Most of these businesspeople worked in the service sector, not in manufacturing. It is easy to see why service workers should have to be good communicators, able to do a lot of paperwork and deal effectively with unanticipated problems. Service jobs are people-intensive. The only edge you really have over your competitor is better people—people who are more competent, easier for customers to talk with, more considerate.

What surprised me, however, was that some manufacturing people are just as interested as service people are in having more thoughtful employees. A good example comes right out of the Deep South: the textile mills. Tom Bailey, of Columbia University's National Center on Education and Employment, has been visiting mills, observing the work, and talking to workers and managers about their jobs. What he finds is that the global market has been forcing textile mills to stop making the long runs they used to make and to make many shorter runs now, of different materials and patterns. The business involves much more customization than it used to; it entails filling more small orders and doing less bulk production. As a consequence, mass-production techniques are giving way to "flexible production" techniques—more shifts, more equipment changes, more sophisticated machines—and these techniques have altered the workplace. It is more dynamic, less routine, more complex, and more unpredictable. That kind of environment requires a different kind of worker than the assembly line does. It requires someone who can think quickly, be flexible, and work well with others to retool and solve problems. Some of the new machines are mysteries to most of us; it takes a special kind of imagination to figure out what is going on inside. Thus, "brainless" assembly-line jobs in the textile industry and others are increasingly giving way to jobs that require some thought.

A third work-force reality behind the call for workers with higher literacy is the centrality of information in any business—service, manufacturing, or even agricultural. Everyone has become dependent on information and its attendant computer technologies. Acquiring information, sifting through it, synthesizing, analyzing, interpreting, evaluating, communicating it to different audiences for different purposes, using it to plan—these kinds of thinking and action consume large and crucial proportions of everyone's resources. The "information age" has become the "information glut," and employers need people who can sort the wheat from the chaff.

In the early 1980s, state governments responded to the call for a more skillful work force with an unprecedented outburst of policy actions, carried out through governors, special blue-ribbon task forces of business, educational, and political leaders, and state boards of education and their legislatures (Pipho, 1983, 1984; Education Commission of the States, 1987a, 1987b). They are still very much occupied with administering all the reforms. The question is whether these reforms (or any reforms that come from state political and business leaders, for that matter) lead to a much higher level of literacy for a broader range of students.

On a sunny Monday morning, we walk from our hotel to the offices of the state department of education, passing the state capitol on the way. High atop the capitol dome, the American and state flags flutter in the breeze. The state superintendent of education, Jim Harris (names have been changed throughout this chapter), is a distinguished looking white-haired northerner who came to the state a few years ago and has not yet picked up a drawl. When we ask what brought him down to the Deep South from a pretty good job and the promise of retirement in a few years, he says, "It was the challenge. This is probably one of the most powerful superintendencies in the nation. If you want to make a difference, which I do, then this is a good position to be in. Things had gotten pretty easy for me up north, too. I needed something tough. And I was getting awfully tired of winter."

Harris outlines the central elements of the state's 1982 education-reform act. The act reorganized the state department of education, eliminating a number of curriculum specialists. It required the appointment of a nine-member state board of education and a state superintendent. It aimed to establish a statewide kindergarten program (the state had no kindergarten requirement) and called for placing assistant teachers in the first, second, and third grades, to lower the pupil-to-adult ratio and improve reading. It called for assurances that students would have mastered one level of course work before becoming eligible for promotion to the next. It created compulsory school attendance and suggested dropoutprevention programs. It established statewide achievement testing in grades 3, 5, 8, and 11. It called for new requirements in teachers' and administrators' certification (which would include allowing people to become teachers without going through the usual programs), establishing a commission to oversee the process. It demanded better preparation of teachers and administrators and called for on-the-job performance evaluation. It also called for massive in-service staff development and instituted performance-based accreditation (I'm not sure what that is). It required an "instructional management" system (a series of tests, given every nine weeks, to tell teachers exactly how students are doing on certain state-mandated objectives) and established an executive-management institute. It raised high school graduation requirements and called for state mathematics and science scholarships and for a state-funded residential school focusing on science and mathematics. It ordered studies of ideas for reorganization of schools and school districts and authorized higher salaries for teachers. Finally, it established a schedule for implementing these reforms by 1990.

The story of how such a comprehensive package of recommendations was put together, placed on the legislative agenda, and passed in spite of vigorous political opposition would constitute a book in itself. There are still many places in the South where it is politically smart to castigate opponents for being educated—or, worse yet, for having been educated in the North. The governor who eventually championed this reform package learned that the hard way, when he first ran for governor on an education platform and lost. He made it to the statehouse only when he downplayed his interest in the schools. The current governor's interest in education is well known, as is the fact that he has an advanced degree from a northern university; two-thirds of the white voters in the state voted against him in the last election. Educational reform is controversial here, and many of its political advocates have had to take risks with their constituents to move it ahead. Politicians who have done this successfully have had black voters' support more often than not. Thus have the civil rights and voter-registration drives of the 1960s paved the way for the school reforms of the 1980s.

Jim Harris is acutely aware of the "top-down" nature of the reforms, and he is not the least bit apologetic about it.

"Reform may not have begun at the grass roots in this state," he says, "but that's where it's really going to take place. This state believes in mandates. It's a southern tradition to hate government and yet to place all responsibility for getting things done in the hands of a few politicians."

He reminds me of something a southern friend once said: that southerners idealize local control so much because they've never practiced it.

"It may be somewhat paternalistic," Harris says, "but it's how you get things done here. There's too much at stake, in terms of the state's economic development, for us to rely just on the locals to move ahead. Too often in the past, local control meant the autonomy to operate poor, mediocre, or discriminatory schools."

Harris tells us that a great many teachers and curriculum people from around the state have been involved from the start in designing all the changes that are required by the reform act.

"We have to use local people in order to do all of this, because the state simply doesn't have the manpower to do it by itself. So in that respect, the top-downness of the reforms is deceptive. The state can say what it wants, but it only knows what to say because local school people tell it, and it can only carry out the policies if local people help it.

"I know the teachers' union wasn't happy when we started the teacher testing," he continues. "I know some people will tell you the basic-skills test and the literacy test and the curriculum guides and all were foisted upon them by bureaucrats, even though lots of teachers were involved in developing all of those things.

"But let me tell you this," he says, his face coloring and his eyes hardening as if he's had this argument many times. "The system just wasn't working. We have had a lot of very bad schools. A lot of kids have been getting shortchanged. When that stops, when all of our schools are at least providing the fundamentals, the minimum kids need to have a chance, then no one will be happier than I will to turn over more power for them to keep improving any way they want."

In our travels, Harris will not be the only policymaker we will talk to who is a little hot under the collar about accusations of the state's heavy-handedness. It is a common criticism, especially among teachers' unions and professional organizations, that the reform movement in every state has been dictated from the top down by politicians who have too little regard for or understanding of local control and school realities. This is a traditional American disagreement, stemming more from differences of principle than from differences of fact. Bill Chance, an education policy analyst who looked closely at reform in seven states, says that in every state there was much more local and professional involvement in the reforms than was commonly known (Chance, 1986). But if you have not participated in the planning or carrying out of reforms that are going to affect your livelihood, or if you are naturally suspicious of government's actions in a sphere long associated with local control, you may understandably be skeptical about such reports. Harris is right, however, about where the policy ideas that upset educators come from: other educators. Not being experts in many things, policymakers depend on professionals in various fields to help them figure out what will help and how to make it happen. Criticisms of educational policies often arise, not because policymakers have not consulted teachers or administrators or researchers, but because they have consulted the wrong ones.

We ask Harris about the state's interest in a literacy that goes beyond the basics and the minimum competencies, to include problem solving, inquiry, and various higher-order thinking skills (or HOTS, as they are often called).

"Well, down here, HOTS means 'hold our top soil,'" he says, laughing. "But, seriously, we are interested in thinking skills, and the state board is talking a lot about that issue. The problem is that we have to have first things first. People have been criticizing our basic-skills tests because they emphasize minimum competencies and don't pay heed to higher-order thinking skills. That's a fair criticism, but you have to remember that the testing program here was designed precisely to measure those minimum competencies, because it was evident that many students were not achieving even that very low level of performance. In order to acquire higher-order thinking skills, it is first necessary to acquire the basic skills."

These were assertions we were to hear many times, and they have several levels of meaning. Politically, they rest on an assumption of the state's obligation to assure citizens that certain minimal standards are being maintained. Educational standards, in this sense, are analogous to hygiene standards for restaurants—for example, that there will be no rats in restaurant kitchens. The idea is to protect the public interest at some basic level (assuming, to pursue our example, that many restaurants will go much farther than the minimum standards, more because of self-interest than because of the government). Thus, to assert the priority of basic skills over more sophisticated aspects of education is first of all to say that this, constitutionally, is where the state's responsibility to the public interest most clearly lies. Practically speaking, minimum standards are the easiest ones on which to get widespread agreement, and they are usually the easiest to measure and enforce, and so they are very appealing to policymakers in all matters of public interest, not just in education.

To say that basic skills come first is also to say that it would be politically foolish to start reform somewhere else. Reform is a matter of building coalitions. You start with the simplest ideas that are likely to muster the broadest support. When you have accomplished something at that level, you move on to the next level. In Harris's state, it certainly would have been impossible to start anywhere else.

Harris's statement—that students cannot acquire higher-order thinking skills until they have learned basic skills—is more political than educational. The fact is that children can practice various kinds of thinking and problem solving at any age, regardless of whether they have mastered the basics. Unfortunately, however, this educational reality has had to yield to political reality here, in order to get anything done at all.

Before leaving the state department of education, we talk to Mary Aims, the state's curriculum coordinator. Aims is a determined-looking woman who thinks her job is as much "to get out of the way" of interesting developments as to spread the word on the state's curriculum guidelines and on how to meet them in the classroom. She is very excited about the kindergarten program developed to meet the reform act's requirement. Because it is brand-new, she believes, it is based on the best available knowledge about how children learn and about what they need developmentally.

"Right here in this supposedly backwater state," she drawls, "we may have the most advanced kindergarten program in America."

It is based on Montessori principles and whole-language approaches to learning, she tells us (Kahn, 1990; Goodman, 1986). The Montessori philosophy emphasizes hands-on learning experiences that begin with the child's basic interests, rather than with the teacher's. Montessori children take responsibility for their own learning, make choices, and exercise their minds more fully than children tend to do in traditional classrooms. The whole-language philosophy emphasizes active, thoughtful learning and immerses the child in rich reading, writing, listening, and speaking experiences.

"This has been a revolution in the state," Aims says. "And it may work itself up the ladder, into the first grade, then the second, and so on."

Is this a conscious strategy, I wonder—to talk about minimum basic skills politically, all the while sneaking a more robust literacy into the early grades? Or is the reform package just a grab bag, parts of which are very different and even at odds with one another? The people who designed the kindergarten program, it turns out, have a strategy very different from the state's. While the state tries to reform schooling by imposing new mandates, the kindergarten people aim to reform schooling from within. They envision children so empowered by their early education experiences that they will not tolerate minimum-focused instruction in the later grades. This is an interesting idea. Which side will win—the basic-skills curriculum, or the kids who have already gone beyond it at an early age and will not settle for the old routine?

Aims believes that the schools in this state will be very different ten years from now: more exploratory, less textbook-oriented, more interesting. At the same time, the state has had to issue three hundred emergency certificates in special education to teachers with no background in that area at all, and it clearly faces a challenge in training its current corps of teachers.

"The only thing we don't have," Mary says, "is money. But we're going to give it everything we've got, with every dime we can get our hands on."

Sam and I have been joined by Anthony (Tony) Petrosky, a poet and professor at the University of Pittsburgh. We leave the capital and set out for Southland County, believed to have some of the best rural schools in the state. After twenty or thirty miles of rolling countryside, the land begins to flatten out as far as you can see: plantation country. Field after field of plowed-under cotton rolls by. More sharecroppers' huts and shacks are in evidence, although sharecropping itself disappeared when the big cotton machines came in after World War II. With the disappearance of sharecropping began the mass migration of uneducated rural blacks to northern cities like Chicago and Detroit. It has been argued (Lemann, 1986) that they brought with them a history of dependency and abuse, which has kept them as exploitable in the city as they were on the plantation; the "permanent underclass" of northern cities began here among the descendants of slaves.

At the county seat, we catch up with Bobby Johnson, who has been superintendent of Southland County's schools for twenty years. He is an elected superintendent, serving out his last four-year term. About half the superintendents in the state are elected and tend to stay in office for a long time. In rural areas, school districts can be major employers. Superintendents control contracts in many areas—food service, construction, and bus driving, for example. They are powerful people.

Southland County School District is long and narrow, covering almost sixty miles and including 2,500 students in pockets around the plantations. Almost all the students are black children. Public schools in rural areas tend to be black schools; white children attend private "academies" in old buildings, church basements, and private homes scattered across the county. The city schools are integrated (although they almost always have white majorities), but out where the black population is the majority, successful efforts at integration are rare.

The economy is shifting in the plantation country. People who left years ago to go north have been trickling back. The catfish industry has been a shot in the arm for the region, although it is not altogether predictable. The area also has a manufacturing plant for health-care equipment, a fastener plant, some auto-trim industries, a manufacturer of parts for lawn mowers, a giant grocery chain, and other businesses (generally small ones) that offer a range of openings, from minimum-wage levels up to management. Most of these businesses came here because this was a right-to-work state, and it had cheap labor. People are trying to develop some unions in the catfish industry and in the health-care-equipment plant, and this effort is causing serious concern: if there are unions, it is believed, industry will go away. Rural life in the South, as elsewhere, is a constant struggle to hold on to people and businesses that seem always on the verge of leaving.

Bobby Johnson is a white-haired, very pleasant white man who presides over a school district attended almost entirely by black students. He has a tolerant, long-term view of education in the state and believes that Southland County has been more or less ahead of the state for some time. He also believes that the reform act of 1982 has had a powerful effect on his schools, and he tells us that expectations about children's being able to learn have changed in positive ways. He says many teachers, who did not really believe that all kids could learn, have had to see it to believe it. He sees the teachers in this district as very much in need of techniques for doing something besides drill and practice, and he would like to see them challenge kids to think more and become better questioners. The state's teacher test, he believes, helped "raise consciousness" and got his teachers thinking about what is important. Johnson strikes all of us as a conscientious, fair-minded, dedicated superintendent.

It's late in the day and we are tired, but we talk for a while with his energetic assistant, Julia Driver, who is in charge of curriculum and instruction, staff development, testing, and "anything else that needs doin'." Rural districts are usually short-handed, and it is clear that Southland County is lucky to have such a resourceful person. Driver is a white woman who was brought up on a plantation and decided to go to graduate school only after she had brought up her children. She has just received a Ph.D. from the nearby state university and is well versed in all the lingo about reform. She demonstrates her Scantron machine, and she shows us her computer program for recording children's scores on the tests that she has created and administers every nine weeks, in keeping with the state mandate. She feels that many teachers still do not understand this system and still think of the tests as "Dr. Driver's tests," not as their own.

"You see, this is really for them, not for us or the state," Driver says. "They don't quite believe that yet. But the whole idea is to give them some objectives to focus on and some regular information about how their kids are doing on those objectives. Teachers made up the objectives for the state, and I made up the questions, using the guidelines that came with the objectives. But the tests really belong to them, and the information is supposed to help them know their students better and be better able to help them."

She adjusts some punch cards that have jammed in the scanning machine and then says, sighing, "Now, if I could only find the time to do the staff development, I could help them do that. . . ." As she talks to us, the machine behind her beeps, repeatedly and annoyingly, as it processes the 2,500 cards that track each student in the district on each major objective of the state curriculum being emphasized during this nine-week period.

To understand what is going on in American education today, you have to know about *objectives*. The word is used to denote bits of knowledge or skills that students are supposed to acquire and that they will demonstrate as a consequence of their instruction. An objective is something you aim to achieve ("My objective was the top of the mountain"), but the word also suggests that whatever you are trying to achieve is an object of some kind—that is, it is somehow tangible, concrete, and measurable. Use of this term also assumes that knowledge, skills, attitudes, and behaviors are certain kinds of objects, which can be understood and described in the same ways in which physical objects can be understood and described. To believe, for instance, that world history can be described in terms of a number of specific instructional units, you have to believe that world history is like a large object, composed of many smaller objects that in turn are composed of even smaller ones, any one of which can be removed and studied by itself.

Almost all American schools describe curricula and instruction in terms of goals (broad aims), objectives, subobjectives, and subsubobjectives. When people propose new courses of study or new programs, they explain the goals and objectives and how it will be proved that they have been achieved. When people make up tests, they tie them to various objectives. When teachers plan lessons, they lay out the objectives to be achieved. When teachers are evaluated, they are judged according to their ability to achieve certain objectives. When state departments of education carry out legislative orders to establish and maintain minimum levels of competency, they do so in terms of measurable objectives. Exhibit 1.1 shows some of the sixth-grade objectives that Julia Driver was keeping track of with her instructional management system.

School people around the country have different ways of writing objectives, but these are typical. Julia Driver's guidelines are typical, too, in that they provide instructional advice (usually to look at the teacher's manual) and testing specifications that spell out exactly how to measure the achievement of the objective. For example, consider this sample item, testing a passage's main idea:

> Jack woke up early, with excitement. He had to take the jack-o-lantern to school for the party. Mother had made cupcakes, with orange-and-black icing. The class had made witches, bats, and ghosts to decorate the room. Everyone was going to have fun!
>
> What is the main idea?
>
> 1. Jack was a good boy who liked school.
> 2. Jack was happy and helpful.
> 3 Jack's class was to have a Halloween party.

Through such objectives, state policy is turned into action; through such measures is the quality of education assessed, progress gauged, and instruction fine-tuned.

The next morning, Tony Petrosky, Sam Stringfield, and I begin to visit schools. The first teacher I talk with is Ms. Wilson, a sixth-grade social studies teacher at Southland Elementary School. She tells me that the reform act has been very helpful to her. She has her students dramatizing and acting out parts of the Constitution because, through state-encouraged staff training, she has become aware that different students learn things in different ways.

Exhibit 1.1. Learning Objectives for Grade 6.

Reading

Identify selected written abbreviations and symbols
Identify the change in meaning of given words when affixes are added
Use a dictionary to define a word
Recognize selected written words (taken from the vocabulary list for basic skills)
Given a paragraph, select the implied main idea
Identify supporting details
Identify a paraphrased statement
Determine appropriateness and accuracy of information
Distinguish between fiction and nonfiction

Mathematics

Divide up to a three-digit number by a two-digit number, with and without remainders
Simplify proper fractions
Multiply a whole number and a proper fraction
Solve a two-step word problem involving whole numbers

Language Arts

Recognize misspelled words from a given list of words
Define *simile*
Define *metaphor*
Recognize plot
Summarize plot
Given a sentence, identify the correct form of a singular or plural noun
Select the correct form of an adjective or an adverb to complete a sentence
Select a complete sentence from a set of alternatives

Social Studies

On a map, locate Canada, the United States, Mexico, Central America, the West Indies, and South America
Identify the definition of each of the following terms: *isthmus, delta, bay, island, peninsula*
Given a definition, identify *import, export, dictator, dictatorship*
Identify the U.S. Constitution as the highest law in the United States
Identify the Declaration of Independence

"Not everyone can learn through reading," she says. "Some children need to see what's going on and hear about it."

She has taken a writing workshop, where she learned how to get her students to write more and how to respond to their papers.

"I did not like being tested," she said, referring to the state-mandated competency test. "I thought it was an insult and felt that

I was already doing the right thing. But I guess I did learn from it—
you know, what to call some of the things I was doing."

She believes that kids don't particularly like to read. She tells
me that the PTA is active, the parents are behind the teachers and
support them, and that, because they live in a rural area, a lot of
parents are pushing for better education.

I also visit Ms. Burden, a third-grade teacher. She has a dry,
authoritarian approach to teaching and walks back and forth in
front of the class, clasping a teachers' guide to her chest, now and
then eyeing it as she goes along. She is hard to understand: she
seems to have a minor speech impediment. Moreover, because this
is a classroom with a divider drawn across it, you can hear the
children next door chanting multiplication tables. But the children
in Ms. Burden's classroom clearly know what she wants. She has
posted today's lesson objectives on the wall. Every desk has a dictionary and an open textbook. The pupils are reading, with apparent enthusiasm, a story about the Great Houdini. One student reads
aloud, and then the teacher calls on other children to state the main
idea. The children are always right on the money, or close.

Ms. Burden asks, "What do you notice about Houdini and
Boudini?" The students make some guesses, and finally one says,
"The words sound alike," and she says, "Yes, they rhyme." She says,
"Someone who does tricks is a . . ." and the students all chime in
at once: "Magician." When she gives directions, she says, "Do you
have any questions?" The class replies in unison, "No, ma'am."
Her instruction is dictated by the teachers' guide. To the extent that
it asks questions based on students' use of higher-order skills, she
uses those questions. But, regardless of the questions Ms. Burden
asks, there is only one answer, and there is no discussion.

She moves on to teaching the concept of sequence. She asks
the children, "What do you do when you get up in the morning?"

They seem confused. They look at their books for an answer.

"No," she says. "What do you do when you get up in the
morning?"

A child describes his routine: he washes his face, puts on his
clothes, eats his breakfast. She uses this recital to introduce the
concept of putting things in order. She gives the class a handout

called "Putting Things in Order," reproduced from the same text-book series that contains the Houdini story.

The children begin to work in their seats, and Ms. Burden and I chat for a while. She says that she likes the state curriculum, but that it doesn't cover everything and she has to do "lots of research." She points with pride to a thinking-skills book that she is studying. When Julia Driver comes in, Ms. Burden compliments her for having told her that it was unnecessary to read all the directions to the children; what Ms. Burden does now instead is be sure that the children read the directions themselves and ask her questions if they don't know what words mean.

"It saved me a lot of time," she says. "It's made my job a lot easier."

I visit Marie Miller, an energetic teacher who is also covering sequence because it is on the state curriculum. The children have been given a handout about why the bear has a stumpy tail, and the sentences of the story have been scrambled. The children have to put them in order. A child goes up to the board and puts down the number in the sequence that one of the sentences should have, and Ms. Miller asks the class, "Who agrees?" Most do. One girl does not, and Ms. Miller asks her where she would put that sentence. The girl replies, and Ms. Miller says, "That's wrong." She moves on and asks someone else to go up to the board. Again, there is some disagreement about what sentence order the child suggests, and Ms. Miller calls for a vote. The majority disagree with this child, and Ms. Miller says he's wrong. On it goes—sometimes disagreement, but never discussion of why an answer is right or wrong.

"If you don't have this order," Ms. Miller says, "change it on your paper to get it right."

Then she has a girl read the sentences aloud in the proper order, but there has been no discussion of alternative sequences, and it is not clear whether anyone knows why a particular sentence should be first, second, third, or fourth. The sentences all have key transition words and markers, like *so* and *then* and *but* and *once upon a time,* and there could easily be some discussion of these markers and of how they help us determine the way in which things are ordered, but there is no such discussion.

The next lesson is the same. Instead of a narrative, however, it consists of directions for making a hot fudge sundae.

"Here are some sentences," Ms. Miller says. "They are not in the right. . . ." The class replies, "Order." She asks them to take down the sentences, rearrange them at their desks, and then draw the sundae. Because she does not make it clear that the sundae should be drawn to match the words in the sentences, there is some confusion later on. Ms. Miller moves around the classroom. As the children raise their hands, she inspects their sentence order and makes sure that they have left enough room to make their drawings. When the sentence order is wrong, she either says, "It's wrong" and changes it or says, "It's wrong, you'd better change it." Students keep moving the sentences around until they get the sequence right, but there is no discussion of why any particular order is better than any other, nor is there any discussion of the wrench thrown into the works—a sentence that begins with "finally" but is not the final sentence.

As I chat with Ms. Miller, she says that she believes the state objectives have been very helpful to her.

"We know where we're going, and mastery is very important," she says. She believes the children are doing well, "given their background." Unlike Ms. Wilson, she believes that parents do not pay much attention to their children. She is very supportive of the state-mandated instructional management training, and she appreciates the training she had on "assertive discipline," a means of controlling students' behavior. She thinks that the mastery testing is helpful, and she goes back after she gets the test results from Julia Driver, reteaching until the students have mastered the skills. She believes that she is learning a lot from the reforms and that they are making her a better teacher.

Between observations, I talk to William Watkins, a science teacher. He is currently having his children build a model of a volcano. Mr. Watkins grew up on a farm in this area and had to milk cows in the morning before going to school. He would like to take children on field trips, but it is difficult because the school district does not carry enough insurance. From a scientific standpoint the catfish industry has very interesting machinery, but he cannot take the children to the processing plants because of the insurance problem. Nevertheless, he has taken children to the planetarium at the nearby university. He has textbooks but no supplements or workbooks, and he has to make the most of his own equipment in teaching science. Mr. Watkins is very supportive of the reform act.

"I feel monitored, I feel watched," he says, "but that just means I have to be competent, I have to plan a lot. I like that pressure."

He thinks the teacher testing has been helpful. In his opinion, the most important thing the teachers have learned is that the lower-ability groups can learn the same things as the higher-ability groups.

I visit with Ms. Ferris, a third-grade teacher who has five years' experience. She, too, believes that staff development has been very helpful, and she feels that she learned more about teaching in her first year of teaching here than in her entire college experience. She has observed other teachers during her breaks and has found that activity helpful. She truly believes that all kids can learn and thinks that most parents have been supportive. Last year, at the principal's suggestion, she visited kids' homes and found it a moving experience that helped her as a teacher. She does not believe that children have to read first and only then learn how to think; she thinks you can do the reading and thinking at the same time. She is grateful for the nine-week tests. "Now we know exactly what to do and what to drill into these kids," she says.

When I observe her class, she is transformed from a somewhat nervous young woman into an authoritative and vigorous teacher. She is reading aloud about Harriet Tubman. She leaves a word out now and then, and the students, who have been reading along with her, call out the missing word. When she has finished, she asks questions from the teachers' guide.

"Do you think Miss Tubman was brave?" she asks.

"Yes, ma'am," they say.

"What does it mean to say Harriet Tubman was 'the Moses of her people'?"

A half-dozen students have never heard of Moses.

"Suppose Harriet Tubman lived today," she says. "Would her life be different?"

A child replies, "Everything done changed, and it ain't no slavery any more."

She asks another child, "If you had lived then, would you have been a slave?"

The child says no, she would not have been.

She turns the discussion to Martin Luther King. She asks the children, "What do you already know?" The kids appear not to know how to answer questions about their opinions and real knowledge. They thumb through the text, and they give her parroted answers about Martin Luther King. Even when she tells them to close their books, they give her received wisdom, not answers based on their own experience.

"Raise your hand if you think Martin Luther King was brave," she says.

They all raise their hands. The questions she takes from the guide lead her from the main idea to factual questions to questions about sequence. But again, when she gets to inferential questions ("Why did blacks think the boycott would work?"), there is no real discussion, and she seems displeased with some of the answers she gets. She is good at driving the students back to the text again and again, and she is good at making them rely on their memories, but neither she nor the class seems to know what to do when it is time to move away from the information that is directly in front of them.

With ten minutes to go, Ms. Ferris shifts to science and teaches a very delightful lesson about the classes of animals. She has taught them about mammals, reptiles, amphibians, and so on, and she creates fictitious animals—the snufflaphagus, for example, and the puffaspifflus. She asks them, "If it's a mammal, what do you know about it?" And the children reply, "It has hair," or "Its babies are born alive," and so on. The children, charmed by the names that she makes up for these creatures, show that they have a good sense of the definitions for the classes of animals.

Ms. Ferris does try to push beyond facts and immediate recall, to get students to think, because the teachers' guide encourages her to do so. When a student says something that sounds like a pat answer, she says, "What did that mean?" or "He wanted freedom from what?" But without their texts, the children are uncertain about what to say; and, much to her obvious consternation, she cannot get discussions going.

The problem is that she is stuck in a recitation format. To recite is, literally, to cite again ("to repeat," the dictionary says, "from memory"). The teacher is in charge during a recitation, and everybody understands that the idea is to show the teacher what you have learned. As Cazden (1988) points out, during a recitation the teacher exercises total control over the right to speak, tends to ask questions to which students already know the answers, tends to move fast, and tends not to show any tentativeness or doubt. These conditions—plus the fact that people are in rows, not face to face— make thoughtful discussion and inquiry next to impossible, and yet our observations (as well as a good deal of research) show that such conditions dominate in classrooms across the country (for example, see Goodlad, 1984; Sizer, 1984; D. K. Cohen, 1988). So pervasive is this recitative way of talking that it seems natural, and its limitations are invisible to the people caught up in it. They try to get a discussion going, without realizing that a discussion would violate all the unspoken rules of discourse to which they are habituated. They get frustrated, decide discussions cannot take place, and remain stuck in recitation.

Tony Petrosky's notes record a typical recitation dialogue that took place at Southland County Junior High School:

> *TEACHER:* What kinds of books are on the back wall?
>
> *STUDENT:* Periodicals.
>
> *TEACHER:* No. Cox, what kind of books are on the back wall?
>
> *STUDENT:* Fiction.
>
> *TEACHER:* What else, Misha?
>
> *STUDENT:* Biographies.
>
> *TEACHER:* If I wanted to know where George Washington was born, can I find that out from the encyclopedia?

CLASS: [in unison] Yes.

TEACHER: How many encyclopedias can you think of?

CLASS: [in unison] *World Book. Book of Knowledge.*

TEACHER: Dictionary. You all know what a dictionary is, right?

CLASS: [in unison] Yes.

TEACHER: Give me five things you use a dictionary for.

CLASS: [silence]

TEACHER: Write that down. Look it up for tomorrow. Give me examples of special subject dictionaries.

STUDENT: Bible. Sports.

TEACHER: Atlas is next. What is an atlas, Cannon?

STUDENT: Maps.

And on it goes. We are all familiar with this kind of discourse, and we would probably all agree that there should be a certain amount of it in the classroom: memorization is important, and drill is helpful for learning certain kinds of things. But if this is the primary way you talk, opportunities for thoughtful exchange, extended inquiry into substantive matters, and collaborative undertakings are all going to be rather rare.

I meet next with Ms. Green. She is leading a class on sentence parts. The objective for the day is written on the blackboard: *The student will identify subject and predates* [sic] *in sentences.* She has put some sentences on the board and asks students to go up and circle the subject and the verb and to describe the subject, the verb, and the predicate in each sentence. One child seems to get stuck at the board. "I can see that you are thinking," Ms. Green says.

She has written some of the words on the board in scrambled order, to allow for more than one correct sentence. As in all the other classes, children seem eager to go to the board and participate. Now and then, when a child has found one order for a sentence, Ms. Green asks, "How can we turn this sentence around, so it doesn't need a question mark?" She has the students write their own sentences and then read them, telling the class what is the subject and what is the predicate. One boy creates a compound complex sentence, and Ms. Green does not deal well with the fact that there is a subject and a verb in both parts of the sentence; she hasn't counted on that. She tries to correct him, but he is not sure why his response is wrong, because he has found a subject and a verb, only in the wrong parts of the sentence. We chat while the children work in their seats, and Ms. Green tells me that the state competency test will be given in two weeks. She likes the mandated curriculum and says it helps her know what she's doing. She also likes the opportunity to use the nine-week test to confirm her own judgments. She likes mastery testing, too, because it makes her think critically. Like about half the other teachers, Ms. Green feels that there is practically no parental involvement. She points out that the majority of the students in the district do not have telephones, and she can't just call up the parents.

After the students have finished their work, she moves to a unit on American history, about the right to worship. She asks if the British law about going to church was fair, and one child says yes. Ms. Green disagrees, but there is no real discussion. "Why did the pilgrims come over?" she asks, and on the class goes, a class filled with the great-grandchildren of slaves, the grandchildren of sharecroppers, discussing the questions of rights in terms of freedom of religion in 1688.

Ms. Green refers students to earlier chapters for answers to questions about rights, and she does seem to give each child a certain amount of time to answer a question before inviting another child to come in and help out. She also shows some reflection in front of the students. At one point, she says, "What is being violated here?" There is silence. Then she catches herself and says, "Maybe you don't know what I mean by 'violated.' Let me think about this." After a moment, she rephrases the question, and then, when she has done it, she explains what the word *violated* means. Thinking aloud and changing her mind in front of the students is a good way for her to break out of the language of recitation. Overall, however, Ms. Green's approach leaves me with the impression that many opportunities for learning have been overlooked.

I visit another third grade. The teacher, Ms. Pierce, is authoritative and dynamic, and, like all the rest, she is running a recitation with a drill sergeant's firmness. The recitation is on food groups, and it's well done. Ms. Pierce has laid out some menus and is asking the students to critique them in terms of the number of servings and the number of food groups represented. Having done that, she invites the students to create and draw their own meals. Like the children in all the other classes I visited, these children seem to prefer recitation to open-ended, think-for-yourself kinds of activities. They are tuned in to looking for the right answer, filling in the blank. They get confused by other types of questions. Even when asked for their opinions, they scan the textbook and look at the blackboard. They look for the answer outside themselves. The teachers seem as frustrated as the students do, but nobody knows quite what the problem is or what to do about it.

In another building, Tony Petrosky has been watching a teacher break out of the recitation formula. Here are excerpts from his notes:

> Mrs. G., an eighth-grade teacher, presents math through writing and problem solving. She is also the assistant principal of the elementary school, a one-story green cinderblock building that looks like the government housing surrounding it. Everything in the school—the books, the overhead projector, the electric typewriters, the podiums, the flash cards, the desks and file cabinets—is worn and gray, like the vast winter fields that encompass these tiny communities. But Mrs. G. brings an enthusiasm and a set of high expectations to her students that seem to physically push against the grayness. She's black, a veteran teacher in the district, and all but three of her students receive free lunches. She describes her students as average kids. The lesson for the day is a review of computational skills, in preparation for one of the basic-

skills tests. She arranges her twenty-one students into four groups, and they quickly cluster their desks into circles. Mrs. G. writes the figure $9,980 on the blackboard, along with a set of directions for using computational skills on the figure by making up stories to explain how each of the groups would use the money. The groups must also use separate sheets of paper to show the computational operations discussed in their stories. They have thirty minutes to do this. The groups work well together. I watch two in particular, and every student gets to speak at least four times. The group leaders appear skilled in asking questions about the computations and the stories. Mrs. G. and her student teachers walk around from group to group, answering questions and making comments. After a number of false starts and revisions, the groups I observed came up with stories that the leaders read aloud to the class. Here is the first one:

The Fortune from the Wheel

Fourscore seven years ago the Fabulous Freebirds played the Wheel of Fortune. Fabulous Frankie won $2,480, Terrific Jerry won $5,600, and Magnificent Marvin won $1,900, which gave us a total of $9,980. We bought three plane tickets to come back [to the state]. We bought the old ghost town of Blaine that cost us $50 and left us with $9,930. Then we sold the town for $2,030, which added our fortune to $11,960, and then we bought three limos for $3,000 apiece, when multiplied by three that hit our fortune for $9,000, which left us with $2,960. With some of the money we had left, we bought us some clothes to wear that added up to $2,040, after that we bought three plane tickets to go back home where our daddy was. We had only $10 left so we sold our three limos for $9,970, plus our $10, we had $9,980 again.

I don't want to make any claims for this piece of writing, other than to say that it gets its job done in a coherent narrative that the kids had fun putting together. Nevertheless, it stands as an example of an approach to math review that does not rely on recitation and that does allow students an opportunity to solve a problem through collaborative work, in a discussion whose end products are the discussion itself and practice in computation and writing. Mrs. G. has told the class that these are to be first drafts and will be edited tomorrow. She has also shifted some of the responsibility for classroom work and management to her students. Apart from the groups, which she uses frequently, she has a "Look What You Missed in Math" bulletin board. There are three large envelopes on the board, one for each of the past three days, and each one contains a student's narrative, which explains what happened in class that day so that students who have missed the class can read the report and complete the work. There is a different reporter every day; each row of five students is responsible for a week's reporting and for making sure that the reports are done on time. Mrs. G. says that she has shifted from being a recitation-oriented teacher to being a "math-writing" teacher because of her participation in a writing-across-the-curriculum project at a nearby state university. She feels supported and appreciated by her principal and does workshops for other teachers whenever she can. She thinks it will take a long time to get her kind of teaching implanted in the district, since there is so little time or money available for staff development.

By and large, near the end of our day of visits, I am impressed by the energy of the children and the number of volunteers. Hands are always up, and students are always volunteering, whether they have the answers or not. They are quite attentive—and they are experts at recitation, just as their teachers are. I'm impressed by the mutual respect, too, and by the students' admiration of their teachers. But I've seen heavy reliance on teachers' guides. The teachers, although they say they have learned much in recent years, are cautious. They follow directions literally, seldom venturing beyond the letter and into the spirit of instructions. Questions that deal with inference and analysis, like others that are potentially very interesting and may lead to insights, appear briefly, are given very short shrift, and disappear as quickly as they arise. It is clear that the children can do far more than they are being asked to do, but few teachers know how to ask them for more.

I go on to chat with Ms. Barnes, the elementary school principal, who has been a very kind and helpful guide. Like so many of the teachers here, she has local roots. Her office is also the photocopying center, and so people wander in and out as we talk. Ms. Barnes says that the state-mandated teacher competency test has helped the teachers, and she believes they have discovered that doing the things they will be tested on makes the test easy. She also says that reform has focused the teachers, made for consistency, and prompted them all to talk to one another and move along together. She feels that state-sponsored executive management training has helped her as an administrator. She knows now what to look for when she goes into the classroom and evaluates her teachers.

She is proud of her kindergarten. Because Southland Elementary was a pilot school for kindergarten, it is far ahead of kindergartens elsewhere in the state. Some elements of kindergarten instruction, as its proponents had hoped, have spread to the higher grades, in particular the "learning center" focus, which is a way of giving students more responsibility for their own hands-on learning. More and more first-, second-, and third-grade teachers are setting up learning centers of their own. Studies have shown that over the last nine years the kindergarten has made a major difference: test scores are higher, and children who have gone through the program have low dropout rates.

When I ask Ms. Barnes what her priorities are, she says her first priority is reading. Reading skills are not what they should be, and she wants to bring every child at least up to grade level. Her second priority is parental involvement.

"We don't have much parent support at all," she says. "The PTA meetings are sparse. The majority of children do not have telephones, so it is hard to contact their parents."

Last year she sent her teachers out to visit homes, and it was a revelation for them. This year they do not have the time to do that, but she thinks it is an important thing to do.

Another high priority is staff development. She wants to get high expectations even higher. She wants to see enthusiasm for children. Her reflections on school reform are philosophical and optimistic.

"We're being asked to do a lot," she says. "But once we get everything going, it gets easier for us. Once this state gets people on the same track, we're going to have better education for these children.

"People have been looking at this state for a number of years," she continues, "and looking down at it. I think one of these days, someone's going to say, 'Let's do what *they* did.'"

Ms. Barnes has no illusions, but she tells me that she has seen things happen over the last twenty years that she thought she'd never see; her becoming the principal of a public school is one of them.

What we have seen in Southland County, and in similar rural school districts in similar states, is poignant. On the one hand, policymakers and business leaders sense that something drastic must be done to raise the literacy of the work force, in order to compete in a new and threatening economic order. On the other hand, the state has little history of investing financial capital in such areas, and even less history of upper-class whites investing in the futures of lower-class and black citizens. Clear and heartening signs of progress are everywhere, but the magnitude of the task is daunting.

Teacher after teacher has told us how discouraging it is to "educate the kids to leave their homes." The rural population dwindles as the rural economy withers and the quality of life declines. Recent studies show that rural students fare even worse than inner-city youth on many major indicators of stress (Helge, 1990). They have higher levels of substance abuse, depression, and criminal activity. A higher proportion have been abused. Help for them is farther away and harder to get. Evidence of a payoff for staying in school is harder for them to find.

Also poignant is the distance between what the state has done, virtually exhausting its available money, and what it has yet to do. Time and again, we have seen very modest accomplishments pointed to with pride. "You should have seen it before," people often said, and we were glad we hadn't.

I'm reluctant to second-guess the approach the state has taken. People have worked hard to do what they can with what little they have. Many parts of the system undoubtedly needed repairing and have been fixed. Many people needed and have received encouragement and leadership to improve schooling. The vision of a higher level of literacy for a broader range of people has been vigorously expressed and made politically salient.

I can only observe what this chapter's glimpses of our visits suggest: that none of the school-reform initiatives, with the possible exception of establishing the kindergarten, has yet changed the way students and teachers read, write, talk, and think. In other words, no reform has penetrated to the heart of the literacy question.

The state has reorganized departments, changed educational appointments, set up programs, added personnel, lowered various ratios, created more tests, strengthened compulsory-attendance laws, improved certification requirements, developed new procedures for performance evaluation, trained people in instructional management, raised graduation requirements, offered more scholarships, mandated new studies of school organization, and raised teachers' salaries. States can do these things. But can they change what really matters—how people read, write, talk with each other, how they discover and wrestle with ideas, how they strengthen, broaden, and deepen their literacy?

We now leave the county seat and head out toward Daviston, an all-black, virtually separatist town, whose schools post scores higher than those of any other black schools on the state's tests of basic skills and functional literacy.

CHAPTER TWO

Hand-Me-Down Literacy

Before describing Daviston, let me back up and provide more context for these case studies. For more than a year before going out to visit schools, I had been talking with people around the country about literacy and about how definitions of it are rapidly changing. The word *literacy* has certainly been used widely these last few years. We hear about cultural literacy, civic literacy, computer literacy, media literacy, information literacy, and scientific literacy, for instance. In these contexts, it means much more than the simple ability to read and write; it seems to mean something like "to know a certain amount about"—to know a certain amount about one's culture, for example, or about computers. Usually when we read about one of these kinds of literacy, there is an accompanying assertion that young people do not know enough about the subject in question.

But literacy is clearly more than knowing, even with these uses of the term; implicit is the notion that you should be able to use this knowledge with some degree of proficiency. Knowing about computers, for instance, is not enough; you should know how to use computers to do various things. And to get from knowing about something to knowing how to use it, you have to bring something else into play: you have to be able to think in certain ways. Many definitions of literacy entail assumptions about the ways in which literate people think. To be computer-literate, then, would be to know about computers, know how to use them in various ways, and be able to think and solve problems as people typically do when they work with computers.

With their frequent mention in the press and on television, these subject-focused literacies have popularized the assumption that literacy means something more than knowing how to read at the sixth-grade level (a common definition). At the same time, even people who have kept their notions of literacy confined to reading and writing have steadily raised their standards for adequate performance, in and out of school. Literacy research has revealed that the concept is far more complicated than we used to think it was. Individuals can be literate with respect to some materials, and in some contexts, but illiterate or only marginally literate with respect to other materials and contexts. Levels of literacy that were perfectly adequate for a productive life fifty years ago will no longer suffice in a world that has become more dependent on information technologies.

The vast majority of young adults now surpass the literacy standards of twenty-five years ago, but as many as half of them are "midlevel" literates, who are not very good at finding information, adding to it, transforming it into new knowledge, and communicating it to others (Kirsch and Jungeblut, 1986). The definition of literacy on which that determination rests (the ability to use written information to function in society, achieve goals, and develop knowledge and potential) expands the traditional concept of literacy, as a simple decoding process, by making it inseparable from a number of complicated thinking activities, which take place in contexts of personal and social purpose.

In an effort to understand what was happening to definitions of literacy, I asked a number of people with deep experience in literacy-related work to come to the Aspen Institute of Humanistic Studies and talk about it for a few days. Their comments helped determine the questions we asked and the things we looked for when we went out to visit schools in Southland County and elsewhere.

Nancy Hoffman, of the Harvard Graduate School of Education, said that literacy definitely encompasses more than just the ability to deal with texts.

"It has to have something to do with thinking and with the ability to think about thinking, too," she said. "Literate people should have ways of knowing when their thinking is not going well. Their thinking has to be systematic, too, and replicable. They should be able to define the values that underlie their thinking and be able to tell you why it is good to think that way and not some other way."

Hoffman added that a literate thinker must be able to live simultaneously with relativism and certainty.

"You have to be sure that the way you're thinking is right," she said, "but also you have to know that not everyone is going to have the same view."

Bill Chance, a policy analyst who has been studying school reform, probably spoke for many people when he said that higher literacy is indistinguishable from higher education. He suggested that it means the capacity to read and understand at an advanced level, to understand the mechanics of grammar and be able to express oneself well in writing, and to understand the critical dimensions of American polity, society, and Western civilization.

Michael Apple, of the University of Wisconsin, cautioned against defining any kind of literacy as simply an individual capacity.

"Thinking is social," he said. "It's a dialogue, both with the past and with others at the same time. If you teach it as an individual thing, you miss the whole point. A higher literacy would be one that was eminently social."

Richard deLone, author of *Small Futures* and consultant to the Committee to Support the Philadelphia Public Schools, approached the topic by asking what a person who had higher literacy would be like.

"We're talking about someone who enjoys the workings of his or her own mind, someone who is able to grapple, with a reasonable degree of tolerance, with ambiguity and indeterminacy," he said, "someone who can think critically, someone able to communicate with and also interpret a variety of levels of language and other symbolic systems. I'm also looking for people who have attempted to grapple with great texts, great ideas, great disciplines, and to master them, in the hope that they are used to make some sense out of the world, whether they do that collectively or individually. Finally, somehow schools should produce people who learn how to learn."

Donald Graves, of the University of New Hampshire, pointed out that literacy is not just something for a child's future; it is for living now.

"It's too easy to put it into terms of 'someday,' whether you're in preschool or whether you are an adult," he said. "It's not a skill for someday. It's a way of being, right now."

Graves said a higher literacy would have to include "problem finding" as one of its components, and he agreed with others that it is not an individual thing.

"You can't really acquire it alone, and you can't use it alone," he said. "It dies if it is not a way of making contributions to others."

Guitele Nicoleau, who works with illiterate people in many communities, defined literacy in terms of the tools for participating in the processes that can reveal and change the conditions of one's life.

"I think literacy is a kind of action," she said. "It is not of much value unless it can lead to something that would promote some kind of change for people who are afflicted by conditions over which they do not feel they have much control."

Matt Lipman, founder and director of Philosophy for Children, agreed.

"I think reading and writing are forms of action because they are forms of inquiry. And all inquiry transforms the situations it works in. I don't go along with this idea that we first have to learn to read before we can read to learn. You can be exposed to ideas and values as you learn to read just as well as you can after you've supposedly learned."

Judy Langer, of the Center for the Learning and Teaching of Literature at the State University of New York at Albany, encouraged a broad view of literacy, seeing it as "the ways of thinking that people use in a literate society." For her, "literacy involves not only the uses of reading and writing but also many of the reasoning behaviors that people often use when they're engaged in reading and writing, such as interpreting, responding to, building meaning from or thinking about language—even when no reading and writing are taking place."

As our conversation went on, it became clear that, for many of these people, literacy is first of all a process of *making meaning* and *negotiating it with others.* It is not just a set of skills useful for understanding the works and ideas of previous generations; it is a way of creating, here and now, the meanings by which individuals and groups shape their lives and plan their futures. I was reminded of something that Dennie Wolf had said when I visited her at Harvard earlier in the year: that literacy is not merely the instrument of recording what we know; it is the grasp of a whole domain of knowledge and of the values that affirm the goodness of knowing this or that.

We saw, then, that in our visits to schools we would be looking for a literacy that was imbued with the value of knowing and that engaged people in making meaning and negotiating it with others through reading, writing, discussion, and performance. We began to call this a *literacy of thoughtfulness* because standard definitions of the word *thoughtfulness* could be used to convey both the reasoning and collaborative aspects of literacy, the caring about and working with others. Some such literacy would be a necessary (although perhaps not sufficient) basis for any education that would be likely to produce many more of the types of workers and citizens so many leaders are calling for in the name of national survival. We knew, of course, from the work of many who had gone before us, that we would not find much attention to this newer literacy in schools, and we knew that this would not be an uncontroversial goal of schooling: quite a few parents do not want young people to be critical and creative thinkers, collaborative learners and problem solvers. But we wanted to estimate where on the continuum, ranging from "no thoughtfulness" to "great thoughtfulness," certain kinds of schools for certain kinds of children were. We also wanted to know more about how much the current schooling and school-reform policies were likely to engender or inhibit a literacy of thoughtfulness.

Daviston is in a southern county that, like Southland County, is among the very poorest in the United States. Founded by slaves after the Civil War, it was incorporated before the turn of the century. It has always been a town of black citizens, for black citizens, run by black citizens. Because the ex-slave who cofounded the town was highly literate, the town has always had a library and an interest in offering high-quality education to its children. The biggest day of the year in Daviston is graduation day at the high school, when not only mothers and fathers of graduates but also their grandmothers and grandfathers and aunts and uncles come back from all over the United States to celebrate.

The average proportion of people with a high school education in this part of the state is about 45 percent; in Daviston, however, over 80 percent of the parents of children in the local high school have at least a high school diploma. There is a tradition of finishing high school, and there is parental pressure to do so. Here, black children grow up seeing black doctors and lawyers and chemists and certainly teachers, the largest group of professionals in the town, more than half of whom have master's degrees and many if not most of whom are themselves Daviston High School graduates. This no doubt accounts for the fact that the Daviston students had the second-highest passing rate on the functional literacy exam and exceeded the state average on the basic-skills assessment.

Daviston appears no more prosperous than the other rural towns sprinkled around the county. Its professionals live in the suburbs around the county seat. Main Street is a motley collection of shabby buildings and broken-down homes. The most attractive buildings, besides the large Victorian house of one of the town's founders, are the schools. The school district's offices are in a somewhat dilapidated frame house.

Richard Vann, the superintendent, arrives. We have gotten off on the wrong foot because of an article about us in the county newspaper, which did not mention that we are going to visit the Daviston schools. Vann's pride is hurt, and he is no longer sure he wants us to visit. I called him yesterday to apologize, and I arranged for the newspaper to set up another interview so that there can be a separate story on our visit to Daviston. I make a mental note not to do newspaper interviews when I'm doing research in a state whose politics are unfamiliar to me.

I ask Vann and Harold Roberts, one of his assistants, how they account for the performance of the Daviston schools, given the economic conditions of their students. They attribute the students' success to the community.

"Expectations," Vann says. "You're expected to go to school. You're expected to do well. You're expected to go to college. Sixty percent of the students go on to college because that's what their parents have done and that's what's valued."

Everyone I talk to will say more or less the same thing. The notion that what you expect from children is what you're most likely to get is one of those commonsense ideas that get lip service all over the country but, perhaps because it is so commonsensical, little serious attention. Down here, though, it is not just another abstraction.

Vann says right away that higher-order thinking skills are high on his priority list. He feels that his teachers are not trained to teach these skills and that it will take time. He thinks their training as undergraduates and graduate students discourages thinking because it's all lecture and recitation. He himself is working on a doctorate and writing a dissertation on learning styles.

Roberts worries that too much emphasis is being placed on basic skills. He doesn't want to focus too much on those because he's worried that such an emphasis will show up later in declining scores on college-entrance exams. I think he's right.

Vann says he is worried about getting a false sense of superiority just because his school is a leader in test scores based on minimal competencies. He believes that the school-reform act has been good for the children of this state but not necessarily good for Daviston, which was already doing many of the things that the basic-skills assessment focuses on.

We meet with the high school's counselor. He tells us that 97 percent of the children here receive free lunches. Most qualify for Pell grants, and that's why the schools are able to place 62 percent of them in postsecondary schools. He says that the community's high expectations, the school's good staff, and the fact that there is not much turnover are big contributors to the school's success. Daviston, he points out, already had standards above the state's. A student needs twenty-two units for graduation, to include four years of English, three of math, three of science, four of social studies, and four electives (which will include French or Spanish).

The school-reform act has certainly put a burden of paperwork on the counselor because he does not have a computer. He tracks all the objectives, as well as all reteaching and retesting for 1,200 students, by hand. Like Vann and Roberts, he believes that thinking skills are an important priority and need work. The pre-college-entrance tests show that students lack reasoning skills, and he thinks this deficiency needs to be addressed.

Daviston High School looks much better from the outside than it does inside. As you enter, the first thing you notice is the trophies, hundreds of them, in a case that takes up most of the lobby, with more trophies in cases on the adjoining walls. Most of the trophies seem to have been awarded to the band. The school is in bad repair. It needs paint, and many things are dirty. Ceiling tiles are missing. Several large windows are broken and clearly have been for a long time.

Tony Petrosky and I meet William Meers, a former coach with twenty-seven years in the system. Like fifty-two other teachers in the district, he is a Daviston graduate. He took over for Richard Vann as principal of the high school several years ago. Meers has not worked any observation plan out for us; he says it's not necessary, because visitors should be able to drop in on any teacher at any time. As he shows us around he says, "We don't worry about the halls, the broken windows, the floors. We're here to educate children. That's where we put our money and our time."

Meers takes Tony and me to an eleventh-grade English class. The teacher, Ms. Bledsoe, is doing a recitation on the uses of *this* and *that* and on other points of usage. She's working on material that I suppose kids were taught years and years ago; the students have been given usage rules, which they then illustrate.

Ms. Bledsoe says, "This is to help us improve our written and oral *what?*" The class isn't sure, and so she says, "*Speech,* our written and oral *speech.*"

The students go up to the board and illustrate the rules that they have learned from the book. They are obviously used to writing on the board. They are polite about having to do this, even though it is very boring and remote and abstract. Ms. Bledsoe drills them.

"What does a predicate adjective do?" she asks.

Someone replies. She turns to another student and gets the same reply. She turns to another. I'm reminded of how much I hated teaching grammar: it was so clearly uninteresting to my students, and I didn't know what to do about that.

Anyone who watches a teacher drill teenagers on grammar and usage will be forced to conclude that it's a monstrous waste of the students' time and that they tolerate it only because they have no choice. These students are no different from students anywhere else, although perhaps they're more polite and more tolerant. (As Tony said later, "Inner-city kids wouldn't tolerate this. They'd turn the class into chaos.") Classes like these figure among the most poignant memories of schooling for many people. You find that out when you're an English teacher and talk to people at parties. As soon as they discover that you are an English teacher, they start stammering and apologizing for their grammar. "I wasn't too good at that stuff," they tell you, even though they are doctors and lawyers and successful businesspeople. Yet there is no subject to which they were more exposed than this one—relentlessly, year after year. This exposure seems to have had the opposite effect from the one intended. It appears to have created a nation of people insecure and unknowledgeable about their native language—which, by the way, they had all learned by the age of three, without schools.

Thus it is no surprise to see a black teacher in an all-black school meticulously drilling students in the particulars of standard written English. She knows what kinds of grammar questions are on the college-entrance examinations. She also knows what kind of language college professors want to see in student papers, and she knows what dialect employers want to hear: the dialect of power in this country, the dialect spoken by television newscasters and presidential candidates. In fact, that is the dialect of Daviston, allowing for some southern variations. Blacks in other counties say you can always tell when a black person is from Daviston from the way he or she talks, which they describe as "educated" or "more northern." When kids come down here from Chicago and Detroit and talk their street talk, no one knows what they're saying. As one student told me, "That's city stuff, not black stuff."

Now, in the classroom, a student is struggling with the difference between *there* and *their*. Ms. Bledsoe pushes him to use *there* in a sentence. He seems unable to, and yet she knows—and all the other students know, and he knows, and I know—that of course he can use the word *there* in a sentence. Ms. Bledsoe keeps saying, "You know. I *know* you know. It's so simple. You use it all the time," and so on, which is true, of course. She pushes until it's embarrassing and frustrating for everyone, until he blurts out, "There goes nothing!" Everybody laughs in relief.

This episode is interesting because it raises the question of how someone could *not* know something that he and everyone else *knows* he knows and has been taught at least a hundred times. My guess is that what the student was struggling with was not the rules of usage but the rules of classroom discourse: the rules of "teacher talk" and recitation, the hidden rules of the relationship between students and teacher. When you have been out of classrooms for a while and then come in as an observer, you see these things. Questions that purport to be about one thing are really about something else, often something that can't be discussed or clarified because it's invisible to everyone involved. Social contexts, which heavily govern how we talk to one another, tend to be invisible because everyone is perceiving what is going on from a personal point of view; only an outsider can see them. Something about the social context of this exchange about the word *there* made it difficult for the student to answer; it was not the student's ignorance of the language. How much of what is interpreted as ignorance is really failure or unwillingness to play a particular kind of language game, refusal to enter into a particular kind of social relationship and obey rules whose presence you can intuit but may not acknowledge? I wonder.

After her grammar class, Ms. Bledsoe has a speech class that she invites me to sit in on. The students are doing oral presentations. There are no rules, and there doesn't seem to be a context for their presentations, as far as I can tell. A kid reads, with relatively no expression, and then there is silence. The next kid reads: unresponsive and bored looks, heads on hands, glazed eyes; "Casey Jones," Masefield, "Casey at the Bat," Langston Hughes, "Kim,"

"Chicago," "The Raven," Marc Antony, Juliet, all the usual stuff; no sense here of the great southern black rhetorical tradition, no rhythms of the great black church leaders and speakers.

These students might as well be in middle-class classrooms in Des Moines. That's why this school is a high performer in the state, I decide. Out here, in one of the most impoverished rural areas of North America, we have this little traditional suburban school, going through the motions of what used to pass, in the 1950s, for a standard college-preparatory program. The faces are all black, and the vast majority of the students are dirt-poor, and yet they walk the way suburban kids walk, and they worry about suburban things like college-entrance exams, and they are as polite and well behaved as the best of suburban kids.

Good as this school is, especially in comparison with surrounding schools, I can't help wondering how good it *could* be if it weren't sleepwalking through this conventional and (to me) inappropriate dream of schooling, nor can I help contrasting what I see in this class with the idea of a higher literacy. Where is the active making of meaning? Where is literacy as a kind of socialization?

It strikes me that these students are acquiring a hand-me-down literacy. Embedded in it are values affirming that it is good to know these kinds of things, but they are someone else's values, someone else's affirmations, and they go unacknowledged and unquestioned. Passivity is also embedded in this hand-me-down literacy, as are conformity and notions about the relevance of grammar and English literature to success. I'm reminded of what the great black writer Ralph Ellison said many years ago, when he visited my college: that black intellectuals have essentially two choices. The first is to learn everything that white middle-class Americans learn, in which case you have to deny so much of yourself and be such a "good Negro" that you can't criticize the system effectively. The second is to embrace the powerful literacy of black rebellion, in which case you are an outcast and can't influence the system effectively. The great black writers and intellectuals, Ellison concluded, all seem to have found yet a third choice, but at great personal cost.

I can't judge what is best for these kids. What I call a sleepwalking education may look very different to southern blacks, who long ago learned how dangerous it is to do anything particularly dramatic. This slow, steady, modest, middle-class college-preparatory training has served many a student well in these circumstances. I wonder, though, whether the circumstances have now changed enough to give a broader and more empowering literacy the chance to unfold. If so, can it unfold in the climate of reform this state has created?

I talk with Ms. Bledsoe about school reform. She believes that it has been good and has raised standards across the state. Reforms are making her work harder now, she says, but things will get better. She feels the most pressure about trying to prepare her students for the basic-skills test in April, and she feels a strong responsibility, too: students have approached her and said, "Make sure we don't have to take it again." She thinks that she would be teaching more literature, as she used to do, if it were not for the basic-skills test. She also worries that the students' college-entrance exam scores may suffer because she is aiming too low and leaving out important material.

"The basic-skills test is not a full curriculum," she says. "There are other more fulfilling things that are just being left out."

Efforts toward staff development have been helpful, she thinks; but, in general, there has not been much training, and there is little sharing of ideas. At the monthly departmental meetings, the talk is more substantial than it used to be, but it's talk about the basic-skills assessment, and conversation across departments is rare.

Ms. Bledsoe believes that the secret of Daviston's success is very concerned, hardworking teachers and their good relationship with students.

"For most students, you know their brothers, their sisters, and their parents, and they're here for a long time. That makes a difference," she says.

It certainly is different from most city schools, I reflect, where student turnover can be higher than 100 percent per year. Ms. Bledsoe worries that the school needs high test scores, to avoid a merger or a consolidation that would lead to Daviston's loss of identity.

"This school is the center for the community," she says. "It's used for all kinds of functions. If the school goes away, there won't be a community here anymore, not in spirit."

She intends to work on higher-order thinking skills in the

future, but it's difficult right now, she says: "I have to make sure these young people pass the tests and that this school has the highest scores around." She does what she does, it appears, because she feels that the students' and the community's future is at stake. I agree. But which future does she have in mind: the future as it might have been cautiously imagined twenty years ago, or the future visible today?

Tony and I visit Mr. Bass, who is teaching advanced math. First he goes over the homework. He is an easygoing, good-looking guy with a nice, relaxed style. He basically does the work himself on the board, where he has written the day's objective: "converting pi fractions to radian." He seems to be doing well until a student asks him to explain why a sixty-degree angle is pi over three. He goes back to reviewing fractions, he talks about allusions to pi in the Bible, but he doesn't answer the question. A couple of students seem very smart. They could easily handle this question, but instead of turning it over to them, Mr. Bass tries faking it.

When I talk with him, I find out he's a second-year man and very nervous about our presence. He is a graduate of Daviston who went to Memphis and became a chemist. Now he's working on a doctorate at the university while teaching here. When he gets his degree, he will probably move on. It is not at all clear that he is a certified math teacher, or that he has had much training as a teacher of anything else. It occurs to me that he may be doing this to help the school out and make some money, and that it may not have been his idea to teach advanced math. Teaching chemistry would certainly make more sense—if, indeed, he really wants to be a teacher at all, at least in the traditional mode.

Mr. Bass seems to be the kind of person who relates well to young people, but he also seems extremely uncomfortable lecturing to them on topics he is not too sure about or turning the class over to students who probably know more than he does about certain things. He could be an ideal adult to have in the building as a mentor of some kind, or as a chemist who lets kids learn by watching him work—but not as a teacher of the state's chemistry curriculum; that would be a different role. The trouble is that most schools do not have such positions, and so people like Mr. Bass either do not get used at all or are asked to do things that they are not good at. It is widely believed that a large proportion of teachers in the average school—perhaps as many as 20 percent to 30 percent—are teaching outside of their fields (National Education Association, 1987).

Between observations, I chat with Mr. Meers, the principal. He believes that tradition is very important in Daviston. But while high school graduation remains a big event, he believes that the younger parents are not as committed to discipline in the schools as parents were twenty-five years ago. He also thinks that kids twenty-five years ago had to work, and now they don't; they don't have as much responsibility as they used to.

On his desk is a paddle made from a strip of old tire. Mr. Meers still calls parents, most of whom he knows, and tells them, "I'm going to paddle your child. Is that all right with you?" Some parents, he says, have called him up and instructed him to paddle their children.

Mr. Meers thinks that the school districts will have to be consolidated sooner or later: the county has six school superintendents, one of whom doesn't even have any schools to look after. If the districts were consolidated, the county would save at least half a million dollars. He thinks this is the only way for Daviston and its schools to survive, and he hopes they can find a suitable district to consolidate with—that is, a district with money. He says that the state desperately needs a school-finance equity law, and he is thinking that it may be necessary to go to court in order to get one.

Unlike the superintendent and his assistant, the principal believes that if the school concentrates on the basic-skills and functional literacy exams, college-entrance examination scores will automatically go up. He doesn't think that a stronger emphasis on basic skills, functional literacy, and remediation will hurt efforts to develop a higher literacy.

Mr. Meers wants to get all paperwork, including the grading of papers, out of the classrooms. He's not sure why the college-entrance exam scores are going down. He thinks the decline may be due to the parents, or it could be that the kids have lower goals and less motivation. Across the board, Mr. Meers gives the state school-reform act good grades. He thinks the training for executive management was helpful, and the competency test made a very notice-able difference in his teachers.

I visit an eighth-grade math class. The teacher is very dapper and intelligent. He is showing students formulas for finding area and volume, and he keeps making sure that they understand what to do if they're given a formula. I see a lot of boredom, a lot of staring off; the inefficiency of it all is obvious. One clear conse-quence of having large classes is that the teacher feels the need to go over things again and again, to make sure that every student is reached. But many things that take fifty minutes in a large class could be done in ten minutes in a smaller class. Mass education is necessarily inefficient because it requires so much repetition and review. Most people think it is most efficient to educate large numbers of students at once; but when you sit through classes like this one, you see clearly that it is an appallingly wasteful approach and should be used only sparingly. All over the school, we see the need for training—not, as in Southland County, to wean enthusi-astic but underprepared teachers from their teachers' guides, but rather to show articulate, fairly well-prepared teachers how to move away from basic skills, away from boring, conventional materials and recitations, and how to draw much more out of themselves and their students.

During this math class, it dawns on me that the Daviston schools are surpassing state norms without even trying. They're living off their history, their wonderful community faith and spirit, their racial pride and independence, their parental support, their teachers who want to come back here and repay the community, their low turnover of students, the fact that there are no drug prob-lems here and no gangs. The Daviston teachers and principals can virtually sleepwalk through a tired pedagogy and an uninspiring curriculum and get away with it because, poor as they are, they're blessed with conditions that many an urban superintendent or prin-cipal would give his eyeteeth to have behind him. In the cities, there are money and technology and ways of attracting the best available teachers, but education flounders because it is so difficult to create the one indispensable, fundamental thing: a community. I try to imagine what could be done here if the schools were really cranking, really adding something to the students' momentum in the world.

I go to a remedial reading class. It's in a split classroom, with a partition down the middle—but not all the way down the middle, and so we can all hear the loud teacher on the other side. I look at the reader they're using. It has stories followed by "fact" questions and "thought" questions. It presents "main idea" questions and "thinking for yourself" questions—for example, "Why do you think people in India can't read?" and "Do you think TV would help?" It has a section on "reasoning about what you read."

As I examine this book and watch what is happening in the classroom while the teacher moves from child to child, I cannot help wondering if all this elaborate reading technology totally misses the point about the nature of reading. It seems as if clever adults have backtracked from the experience of reading to some abstract, linear, sequential model of how it must occur; from that standpoint, they have blown the reading experience into a million different bits that somehow get reassembled into textbooks like this one. Why anyone would ask these questions, or why a teacher would be doing this or that, are things that are never explained. On page after page, much is taken for granted, and much is unclear and unspecific. It is hard thinking just to read through this book, just to fill in the blanks of the discourse and cogitate about everything left unsaid but lurking between the lines.

I watch the teacher go through the "thought" questions that follow a story about a boy in India. Each child reads a question in sequence and then answers it, usually in one or two words or sentences. There seems to be only one answer to each "thought" question, and there is no impetus to discuss or debate the issues it raises. Many of the questions are disingenuous: even these so-called slow learners can see that the questions are not designed to make them think, but rather to test whether they have the story's facts right.

Tony tells me that a good contrast to this class is one he visited at Southland High. Here are some excerpts from his notes:

> The state-mandated literacy exam takes a writing sample from students, and this year (1988), the eleventh graders must pass the exam if they're going to go on

to twelfth grade. Last year, 27 percent of the state's eleventh graders failed the pilot exam; 40 percent of the state's black students failed the writing sample. This has caused a lot of teachers to drill students on grammar and usage (which passes for writing instruction in most places), but it has also legitimated Mrs. S.'s approach to writing instruction, which requires a lot of writing. Mrs. S. is a teacher from out of state who began her teaching in this area at a white academy, which she didn't like. She says the academies are "very conservative—they do grammar drills all the time and have students writing sentences, then paragraphs, then three-paragraph themes in the twelfth grade."

Mrs. S. conducts her classes as workshops. Students write, work in response groups to discuss their writing, read books and write about them, keep journals, and write to each other about the books they're reading and the videos they watch. Samples of students' writing cover the walls of her room, and their portfolios and journals are stacked on shelves along the windows and the back of the class. During the classes I observed, students read to each other from drafts of the Family History Project papers they have been working on for the past two weeks. The three pairs I pay attention to spend all of their time responding to each other's papers, especially to the content and organization of the work, and when they finish responding, they begin to rewrite.

I have read through ten folders of her eleventh-grade students' writing. Each had twenty-six pieces of writing in it. Thirteen of those were two to eight pages long, with multiple revisions; the rest were one-page letters, or comments on books and movies. Of the ones I read, three were far above average and two were below average (mostly because of surface errors); the rest were of general quality and would have stood alongside my own writing students' beginning papers. Here's a twelfth grader's paper that Mrs. S. rated as above average:

The Secret Is Together

My family is very special because we are together no matter what. I cannot say in words the magic that keeps us together. I can only show it my way.

When my sister was in high school, she was the star of the basketball team. While exercising at practice one day, she got sick. It was not any illness that the coach could figure out. He offered to take her to the doctor, but she insisted that she was all alright. She didn't practice that day. When the coach brought her home that evening, he told my mother what happened. My mother talked to her and found out that she was pregnant. My sister said that she was scared to tell anyone. She thought that no one would understand. I was too young to understand at this time, but everybody else in the family understood. They made her feel comfortable at all times. They knew that this wasn't a time for scolding, but a time for understanding and caring.

Another basketball event happened when I was in ninth grade. I was playing basketball [for the school team]. One day when we were practicing for a game, I went up for a rebound, came down real hard, and hurt my right leg. Although I couldn't walk much on it, the coaches and I thought it was just a sprained knee. Later on we found out it was broken. I didn't know how to handle it, for this was the first time that I had ever been injured. I thought that this was the beginning of a totally boring time. I was wrong. My mother made sure that I got my medicine and that I would eat my meals. My older brother and the two youngest of my older sisters would play games with me. My oldest sister, who lives in Houston, comforted me the most on the phone. She showed me that having a broken leg isn't bad at all. Actually, it was kind of good. Because of my broken leg, I got more attention than I usually get.

These two events show that when one person in my family needs understanding and help, the other members do not hesitate to be there. That makes my family special.

This is a decent paper. The narrative proceeds smoothly, with some detail, and the paper is almost error-free.

Here's a paper that Mrs. S. rated as average. This would be placed either at the low end in general writing or at the top in basic writing at my university.

Another World

In my children's life I want the best for them, the way most parents do. I want to pass down good morale, strong religion, good health, and a strong educational background.

My children are going to be raised totally by my husband, if there be one, and me. I want to be the one to teach them right from wrong. Good morals will always help them when they're down, and once there to boost them up.

Strong religion is very important for everyone. I want them to take all there problems to the Lord in prayer. Don't let the world crush you when the Lord is there for you, just keep on praying and fighting back.

I know I want them all to take good care of there body, don't abuse it. Don't take drugs and smoke. You can cope without dope.

An education will take them far, especially for a daughter being a woman and black, she'd really have to have a strong education background. I don't want them to play off in school like I did. I want them to get it the first time.

The only and the most important thing that I don't want to leave to my children is a violent temper that runs through my family. Sometimes the violence would run into problems that must cause no communication between sisters and brothers for years at a time. I don't want that. I want them to learn to control their tempers.

Although this student is having slight problems controlling her narrative, her writing is coherent and it has few surface errors—nothing that I would consider serious (for example, many sentences that aren't sentences).

The final paper of interest is one that Mrs. S. rated as below average. It would be a basic-writing paper at my university.

What Makes My Family Special

To me, I have a very good family. They are extra special to me because I am the youngest of the bunch. I guess that's why we are so special, because we care for one another. Our mother raised us to treat each other all the same and not cruel.

My family is very religious. We all go to church together on Sunday and serve God, and if there's anyone that my family knew and needed some help, they help.

For instance, the little girl who has cancer and needs money, our family and the church got money from the post and sent it to her. We also helped lots of children at christmas time.

This student is having problems creating a detailed narrative, and some of the sentences run into snags and become what my students call "crazy sentences." But the problems aren't very serious; with a semester in one of our basic-writing courses, this student would most likely move on to general writing.

The point is that Mrs. S. has been able to take these students, who have had very little writing instruction in their eleven years of school, and in two years help them to write well enough to place in college composition classes. Only 3 of her 145 students failed the state functional literacy test last year, an accomplishment for which she was rewarded with a smaller class this year, of 100 students. Mrs. S. tells me that her greatest fear is that her students will not do well on the multiple-choice questions on the literacy exam and she will be compelled to drill them in grammar, like other teachers.

Sam Stringfield, too, had a good experience visiting a third-grade class. His notes read as follows:

Mrs. Jones teaches third grade. Her class has twenty-five kids, seated in short rows that are arranged in a semicircle facing the teacher's desk. The walls are covered with kids' work, including a lot of writing.

The class was going through a spelling/word-power lesson. Instead of drilling, however, Mrs. Jones rolled out a piece of heavy paper about three feet wide and twenty-five feet long. It had big squares on it. Kids took turns rolling dice and moving stuff around the squares. As they landed, there were understood rules that governed which new word they were to make up a sentence or short story about. The sentences and stories operationalized the definitions. Part of what impressed me was that the words were hard for third graders—for example, "cooperation." The kids obviously knew and enjoyed the game and put energy and creativity into it for the entire forty-five minutes.

I was also impressed by the integration of subjects in the answers—for example, "Level: it was above sea level." This led to a discussion of sea level among the kids, most of whom have never seen a sea. Another word was "evidence." They had a hard time reading it. She got a group of them to work at sounding it out, and eventually they, not she, got it. Most were unsure how to generate a sentence using it. Mrs. Jones then asked, "Which one of our stories used *evidence*?" Hands shot up. Examples were given. Eventually the class generated a definition and some additional sentences using "evidence."

It wasn't enough in this class to memorize the spelling and a definition. The kids were being taught to sound out hard words, to think through what their meanings might be, and to generate stories. Once the kids figured out that "antidote" was a remedy against poisoning, they couldn't wait to use it in little stories. Maybe this isn't an example of higher-literacy instruction, but it seemed to me to create a highly literate climate for the kids. Everything was used to make kids think.

Mrs. Jones said to me, "I'm basically a three R's person, but I want children to learn how to think, to cope with the real world, to challenge me. Like yesterday, we were discussing the treaty between Reagan and Gorbachev. Would the Senate ratify it? I think they need to think about things like that."

In some classes, a literacy of thoughtfulness is there for students to grasp; I suppose it always has been. But these dribs and drabs of it do not seem adequate to outweigh experiences, far more frequent, like the ones I had in my classroom visits.

The southern states, particularly those that were most involved in the plantation economy and culture, have a unique regional history that accounts in large measure for their current economic, social, and educational situation. No one who considers the concrete, day-to-day realities of slavery can doubt that its effects on blacks and whites alike were profound enough that many more generations will have to pass before they will be expunged. Many people alive today remember knowing emancipated slaves; thousands more are their children or remember their children. Their grandchildren and great-grandchildren number in the millions.

The Civil War took place only a little more than one long lifespan ago. It was a devastating war, whose debilitating effects on the region lasted for forty years after Appomattox and can still arouse anger and tears. People talk about the New South, born between the two world wars, and about the newer South, which arose from the civil rights struggles of the 1960s, and now about the latest New South, being forged in bustling southern cities whose trade delegations fan out across the world. But the Old South is not dead and gone, and its effects continue to influence our national life in countless ways.

One consequence of its history is that the South has long seemed to lag behind the rest of the nation; it started toward modernity much later and with greater burdens. It is true that southern states have been leading the educational reform movement of the 1980s, but it can also be argued that they have had more to reform, with more at stake than other regions of the country. One conclusion we reached from our visit to this state is that its school-reform efforts have helped organize and focus what had been a fairly disorganized and unfocused educational system. I can't count the number of people who said things like "Well, I was really upset about the reforms in the beginning, but it turned out that the reform program helped me a lot."

Teachers especially, in spite of the fact that their union forcefully opposed the teacher-testing aspects of the reform, were almost unanimous in their belief that the objectives have helped them focus, that the competency exam has given them ideas about what good teaching entails, and that the inservice training has improved them as teachers. When I observed some of them, it was clear that they still needed considerable training to move beyond a dependency on materials developed by publishers, by the state, or by others who are undercutting teachers' opportunities to be creative.

People who argue against the reforms because they were imposed in a top-down fashion are missing two essential points: first, the capacity to bring the reforms about from the bottom up simply was not there; and, second, in a peculiar way, change in the South has always come down from the top. The plantation model of social and economic organization was about as rigidly hierarchical as any has been since the Middle Ages; everybody knew his or her place and deferred to higher authority. Weak state governments went hand in hand with powerful families and charismatic leaders, who made decisions for everyone else. In this region, there is a long tradition of being told what to do; to outsiders, it sounds worse than it is (Cash, 1941), with this exception: a part of that tradition is whites telling blacks what to do.

As Jim Harris told us, "No one gave a damn about whether black teachers were well prepared until their children suddenly had a black teacher." The South's transition from having a racially segregated school system is incomplete, especially in rural areas, but white children do have black teachers now in urban, integrated schools, and a problem that could once be swept under the rug— the miseducation of black children—can no longer be ignored. Thus, pressure for competency testing of teachers and for teacher-education reforms comes partly from contempt for or worry about black teachers, not all teachers.

Race also enters into school reform in that many of the state's reform leaders were elected by blacks, who in many parts of the rural South constitute the majority, both in the public schools and at the ballot box. Black voters are saying that they want better public schools, and they often elect white politicians who pledge to see that they get them. Whites go about improving the schools in the southern tradition of white overseers: by telling black teachers what to do. We encountered few black educators in either Southland County or Daviston who openly objected to this situation, but we might have heard more candor if we had stayed around longer. Everyone seemed to agree that something had to be done to improve schooling, and no one cared much whether whites or blacks called the shots, as long as they led to improvements.

Tony came away from the Deep South studies with the feeling that instruction in the all-black schools we visited is conducted in a "language of authority." He speculated that it derives from a history of authoritarian relations between whites and blacks, but this claim would be difficult to prove. We all remarked on the prevalence of a certain type of black teacher we called the "drill sergeant" type: firm voice, stern face, strict enforcement of classroom behavior, total confidence in the truth of what he or she is saying, and an attitude of "You'd better listen to me, or I'm going to come over there and shake some listening into you." They seemed deeply caring of their students but hard on them, too: they know the world will be even harder on them, and they'd better get these kids toughened up or they'll never make it, they'll give up like too many before them. When the teacher asks you the "what" question, you'd better know what, and you don't just say "Yes"—you say "Yes, ma'am" or "Yes, sir."

Blacks have learned the language of authority the hardest way of all—by being at the wrong end of it—and many a successful southern black man will tell you that he achieved his success only by being tougher than those who were trying to keep him down.

Again, whether and to what degree this teaching style derives from regional and racial history is something we can't really say. What interests us is whether this style is so closely bound up with authority relations and control, and so compatible with mandates, recitation, and lecture, that it inhibits teachers and students from carrying on the more open kinds of conversation necessary for developing a literacy of thoughtfulness.

The visit to Daviston also dramatizes some differences (which the chapters to come will elaborate) between rural and urban education for blacks. Daviston provides its young people with a concrete context for their lives and their learning; a sense of history, however bitter; and a sense of community, however endangered by the steady erosion of the rural way of life. Black children in all-black schools in all-black rural communities seem to behave differently, as a group, from how black children in city schools behave. The rural children seem more self-possessed. When we talked about this with various people, we got different interpretations. For instance, Jim Moffett, who grew up in the Deep South, has written a great deal about education and has taught all over the country. He cautioned us about the "natural compliance" of southern children.

"We were bred to be compliant," he said, "taught early on how to please people and show deference. In some ways, this makes an authoritarian kind of education work better than it should. It presents an illusion of success."

Judy Alnes, director of public relations for Control Data Corporation, said that the students she observed in South Africa were also compliant and well behaved. Was their behavior a reflection of some inner peace, or was it an indication that they were well controlled and "knew their place"? Estus Smith, of the Kettering Foundation, grew up near the schools we studied and said he believed that the students really were more self-possessed than many urban children and could be so because they knew they were part of coherent, sustaining communities.

The question of how to interpret the learning behavior of the children we observed is important to us because the kind of literacy we are looking for is one that empowers students to be creative and independent thinkers rather than compliant, docile ones. It may be that thoughtful literacy cannot be fully mobilized without a strong sense of community—without widening circles of meaning, through which individuals can understand themselves and their condition and construct coherent, purposeful lives. If rural communities like Daviston are providing the encouragement for such lives, then at least one of the primary conditions for thoughtful literacy exists; and if the urban environments of many black children lack that encouragement, then we have a clearer idea of the challenge that urban educators face: to go beyond the mere technology of education, to build and sustain coherent, vital communities in and around their schools.

The teachers we observed in Southland County will need considerable help from each other and from outsiders to meet the challenges that a higher literacy presents. But they know that. They soak up suggestions like sponges; they want to know more, they want to be better. By contrast, the teachers in Daviston are more worldly and somewhat better educated, but they seem more complacent. Content to mimic what teachers in northern and suburban schools do, and sheltered by community conditions that make up for mediocre teaching, they seem to lack any zeal to improve. Both groups of teachers could benefit immeasurably from intensive staff development centered on developing school and classroom climates conducive to critical thinking. Both groups could profit from a deeper understanding of literacy in Guitele Nicoleau's sense: a means of grasping and changing one's condition. Unfortunately, the state has run out of money for staff development. It spent everything on training teachers to deal with the basic-skills objectives and tests and on helping them manage their classrooms. What little money remains is earmarked for raises in teachers' salaries (and even the raises are going to mean a fight with the legislature). Moreover, while higher salaries may be important in the long run, they will not change the way teachers teach.

When we left the state, Jim Harris and his assistants were in a position that seemed to us symbolic of the situation that many other states face: they were dealing with media attention from the U.S. secretary of education's annual ranking, which ranked this state very low in absolute terms but very high in its rate of improvement. Reporters were calling and asking why the state ranks so low, what is going to be done about it, and why the school-reform act, after five years, has not brought about more dramatic changes. Our friends were replying that much lost ground has been made up, that minimum standards are finally being met, and that now everyone in the state is at least "on the same page." The state is closing the gap. Given its poverty and how far behind everyone else it has been, that is remarkable progress.

At the same time, however, they are painfully aware of the limits of such reforms, the long road ahead of them, and their dwindling supply of political and financial capital. They know that minimum standards are not going to be enough and that the state's attempts to focus people on minimum standards run the risk of getting people stuck there. They know that if the state tests basic skills, people will teach basic skills, and they worry that some people will not teach much else. The state board is already talking about higher-order thinking skills, but no one knows where the money could come from to teach teachers how to exercise these skills themselves, much less pass them on to students. Furthermore, people in the state department of education are of different minds about whether this or any other state should be pushing beyond a commitment to minimum standards.

"States can't make people nice, can't make 'em love one another," Harris's assistant told us. "States can't make people good and they can't make 'em scholars, either. States make laws, that's all. That's all they're supposed to do, and it's not a hell of a lot. Most of the good things we want to get accomplished have to be done by people all over the place, certainly not by people here in the state capital. There's nobody here but politicians and bureaucrats, God love us, and we're just doin' what we know how to do.''

CHAPTER THREE

Language and Culture on the Reservation

It's a warm, sunny day. The classroom door is open so that the third graders can go in and out, gathering material for birds' nests. Through the open door I can see the brilliant blue sky above a red-orange mesa dotted with juniper bushes. I am visiting a public school on an Indian reservation. Six students are making nests at the moment; another half-dozen are sitting and lying on a carpet in the corner, reading *Black Beauty*. One girl listens raptly as her long, shiny black hair is slowly combed out by another girl kneeling behind her. In the opposite corner of the room, six more students are composing a joint story about volcanoes.

I am watching a group of five boys and a girl in the "sentence corner." Sentences have been written on construction paper, cut into "subject" and "predicate" halves, and scattered about the table. The students' job is to put halves together in any way that makes correct sentences, and then to write the sentences down on a piece of paper. One boy matches *The man* with *aren't hungry*. The girl watches him write it down but shakes her head. Another boy writes it down, too. A boy matches *The duck* with *laugh every day*. Again, the girl seems doubtful, but the boys write it down, with no discussion. Someone matches *A horse* with *wasn't inside,* and they all write it down. Then *A prisoner* is paired with *see very well*. This is rejected without discussion.

As I puzzle over the group's decision-making process, two Indian women enter the room. One, very old, goes to a chair in the "native language" center, greeting no one, while the other, younger woman gathers four children together for a lesson. The older woman speaks only the native language and looks at no one in particular; the younger woman translates what she says. The children need instruction, it seems, both in their native language and in English. In this part of the reservation, about 78 percent of the students come from homes in which the native language is spoken. In more and more homes, the parents speak a functional version of the native language but are no longer fluent in it and cannot read it (it has a very short history of being written down). Thus, many children, perhaps as many as one-third, come to school illiterate in two languages.

Critical, creative thinking and problem solving in English require fluency, not just a functional grasp of the language, and so we have come here to observe efforts to develop a literacy of thoughtfulness in a bilingual, bicultural environment. The challenge here is to cultivate fluency in English and at the same time nurture and sustain students' contact with the native language and the culture it carries. This task is made more difficult by the tribe's ambivalence about its language and culture.

Some tribal leaders talk of the economy, the kinds of jobs they must develop on the reservation, and the need for the tribe to leap from the nineteenth into the twenty-first century. Since there are so few jobs on the reservation (the unemployment rate is officially at 44 percent, but unofficially estimated to be at about 60 percent), these leaders see schooling as training for competition in a white world. Many of them attended Bureau of Indian Affairs (BIA) schools, where they were punished for using their native language, even on the playground. Other leaders, from the more remote and conservative parts of the reservation, say that an Indian who loses his language and culture is no one. The tribe, they say, must develop economically on its own terms and in its own ways, not the white world's.

The job of getting these children fluent in English is further complicated by the native language itself and by the lack of any books for teachers to use in understanding how radically different it is from English. It sounds somewhat like Chinese: one sound, uttered in different tones, can take on different meanings. One night during our visit, a medicine man gives a fifteen-minute invocation before dinner. I ask a companion what the medicine man has said. She responds, "He said 'Bless this food.'" I insist he must have said more. She thinks about it and then says, "Not really."

"We have no words," a native teacher explains when I ask him about his language.

"Well, you must have words," I reply.

He thinks about it and says no, there really aren't any words in the sense in which I am probably using the term.

"It's a descriptive language," he says. "There's no one word for anything. It all depends on what's going on and what you're trying to describe. We don't have subjects and objects, direct or indirect. We sort of have verbs, but we don't have nouns in your sense, and the relation between them would be the opposite of what it is in English, anyway. The same action—say, handling something— might have many different verbs, depending on the objects involved or where it is performed or how the hand is being used. We don't have a past tense, and we don't have all those perfect tenses. We don't have auxiliaries. We don't have articles. We don't have prepositions. We don't have synonyms, to speak of. We don't have pronouns and gender, in your sense. We don't have sentences, in your sense. We don't have comparatives and superlatives. Things can happen in our language that can't happen in yours, strictly speaking. Rocks can talk, for instance, and it's okay, it makes sense."

There are no books that could tell English teachers what to expect from speakers of the native language, in terms of understandable confusion and language interference. No courses are offered in any of the surrounding state universities to teach about the language and how best to build bridges between it and English. This problem has been known for over a century. A few linguists and anthropologists have written about it, and famous federally sponsored critiques of Indian education have again and again called it the central problem in the education of American Indians (see, for example, Kennedy, 1969). Yet no instructional remedies exist, nor are there any tests for screening children or for diagnosing specific strengths or weaknesses in their use of their own language or English. The English as a Second Language (ESL) tests used around the reservation were designed for speakers of Spanish. On the basis of these tests, students are routinely labeled fluent and subjected to an English-language curriculum that is largely incomprehensible to them, while their problems in both languages either go undetected or are labeled unremediable by teachers who simply do not know what to do. No wonder, then, that in a nearby district, a test of supposedly fluent students in grades 1, 3, 6, and 9 found that one-third could not use the present perfect tense, 80 percent could not use the past perfect tense, half could not produce past participles for verbs like *eat*, and 40 percent could not pluralize or change tenses. And in the school I am visiting on this sunny day, the key to the kind of critical, creative thinking that will lead to academic and occupational success is an old woman who has not yet surrendered her past. . . .

The consequences of the Indians' failure to become fluent in reading and writing are low test scores and low expectations among educators and Indians alike. Mr. Williams's eleventh-grade social studies class is typical. Mr. Williams is legendary as the "winningest" football coach in the area's history. He's a small white man from Texas who has not lost his drawl even after twenty-two years on the reservation. When I ask him what has kept him here so long, he says it's laziness.

"I hate lookin' for jobs," he says. "I'm sure not here because I'm a missionary."

Mr. Williams says his students read at the seventh- or eighth-grade level; nevertheless, he uses a textbook with an eleventh-grade reading level because he thinks it is the best history text. He says many of his students do not write in complete sentences, and so he doesn't assign much writing.

"These kids need a lot of structure," he says. "The more you structure things for them, the more at ease they are. They wouldn't take well to progressive, do-what-you-want, independent-study kinds of things. That makes them uneasy. It's an SES [socioeconomic status] thing. Their parents don't see a lot of value in education. Never did."

I ask him if he does anything to help the students improve

their reading and writing, and he says no, it would be too much work and would probably be hopeless.

"These kids have a combination of ignorance and arrogance," he continues. "There's a lot they don't know—and they're proud of it. They probably hate me because I'm white. They don't want to learn from a white man."

As the students file in, he lowers his voice somewhat but still talks loud enough for someone to overhear.

"Every teacher here has lowered standards," he says, "whether they'll admit it or not. We all bend over backwards to get these kids through. But they don't know much."

I watch Mr. Williams conduct a lecture about county government: lots of facts, names, figures. The kids write it all down in notebooks. Steadily, boringly, he plods through the material, occasionally calling on a student for a one-word answer to a factual question. Once, he works through a simple calculation about how much money a mill levy would raise. The kids do not respond to his question, and he says, "Come on, you can't be failing *all* of your courses!" You can see how he must have been as a football coach.

Mr. Williams's attitude toward his students raises some troubling questions. He believes that most of them can neither read nor write at the high school level, but he carries on as if they could. He makes no effort to help them; thus, they do poorly, and he lowers his standards. It is apparently easier to lower standards than to teach what students need to know in order to do the work.

It occurs to me that lecturing and recitation make a lot of sense when you are pretty sure your students can't read and write very well, and you don't feel that it is your job to address those deficiencies. You identify yourself as a "content" person, not a "skills" person, and you try to cram some knowledge into them and then test quickly, before it disappears from their short-term memory banks. Then you go on to the next lesson and do the same thing. You give students an oral education.

Before I leave the high school, another teacher gives me a new reason for not demanding much of these students.

"For a lot of these kids," he says, "excellence is being a witch. I don't feel I'm doing a kid a favor by singling him out. In fact, I've never recommended a student for special-program recognition because when you do, their grades go down."

Perhaps white people exaggerate the influence of the more exotic elements of the culture, such as belief in witches, but some students did tell me that academic success brings on a decline in popularity.

"When you do good," one of them said, "kids call you a schoolboy. Since I got in the academic decathlon program, my grades have been going downhill." He indicated that he was letting this happen because he wanted to stay popular.

My colleague Alan Davis has observed classes at the reservation's intermediate school and found the instruction to be much like that in the high school. The following excerpts are from his notes:

> The intermediate school is housed in a building designed in the late 1970s to facilitate team teaching and flexible grouping. The floors are carpeted, the walls painted in light, warm colors. There are no hallways. Instead, each grade occupies a pod, a cluster of pentagonal rooms circling a central planning area, like a section of a honeycomb. There are at least four teachers for each grade, and their shared planning room and coordinated planning periods give them ample opportunity to maintain communication.
>
> The principal of the intermediate school spends much of his time outside of his office. In the morning, he drops in and out of classrooms, seeing that the day is smoothly under way. When teachers are absent, he sometimes fills in as a substitute. He is accomplished in music and crafts and teaches woodworking and pottery part-time. He wants to strengthen the emphasis on fine arts in the curriculum, and he reminds teachers of the importance of writing and basic math skills. Beyond these curricular priorities, however, there is no articulated theory of instruction to guide and define the process of education in the school. Teachers report that they are given considerable autonomy to develop their own instructional

techniques. What they have come up with largely relies on the use of textbooks and seatwork exercises to
convey knowledge and develop basic skills.

Students are grouped by ability for language-
arts and math instruction. Today, the high-ability
sixth-grade language class is learning about irregular
verbs. They sit in rows facing their teacher, a man in
his early thirties, who is standing in front. The walls
are decorated with commercial posters showing football players, the Statue of Liberty, the solar system,
and a list of class rules drawn up by the teacher. Textbooks are taken out, and the teacher reads aloud.

"Some irregular verbs change one vowel to
form the past participle. What is the past participle of
'begin,' Adrienne?"

Adrienne looks at her book and doesn't say anything. The teacher continues.

"The past participle is what we use with 'has'
and 'had.' He had . . . what? Adrienne."

"Begun."

"Okay."

He continues.

" 'Drink' in the past tense is what, Marvin?"

"Drank."

"Okay. And the past participle is . . ."

"Drunk."

"When we drive home from town, what do we
see on the highway sometimes? Drunks. Yes. But it's
not as bad as it used to be. There's less drinking."

The lesson continues through the exercise in
verb forms. Nearly all the students participate in the
recitation, one at a time, proceeding slowly down the
page. When the exercise is completed, the students
write a sentence employing each verb in its participial
form. As they work, the teacher leaves the room for
several minutes. The students continue to work, some
talking quietly

"When I taught in Detroit, it was very different," the teacher confides. "There, there was enormous energy. You had to work to keep the lid on. Here, the students are low-key. If I stand in front of the class without saying anything, they sense something is wrong, and they immediately become quiet. If I did that in Detroit, they would ignore me and talk all the louder."

In an adjacent sixth-grade class, the middle-ability language-arts students are studying complete sentences. Their teacher, a Native American woman in her forties, has explained the difference between a phrase and a sentence. The students are working in groups of three, taking a list of phrases and changing them into complete sentences. They take turns. One child adds a missing subject or predicate to complete the sentence. The next reads it aloud, and then all three agree whether it is correct before going on to the next.

In a sixth-grade math class, middle-ability students are reviewing yesterday's assignment: thirty word problems from the arithmetic textbook. The problems involve using multiplication and addition to compute costs—for example, "If apples cost $.40 each and oranges cost $.50 each, how much would five apples and three oranges cost?" The students, seated in traditional rows, compare their answers as the teacher calls upon one student at a time to read aloud the answer to a question. After each answer, the teacher asks how many got it right. About half the class raise their hands. Some work on assignments from another class. Some look around, seeking distraction.

After all the answers have been given, the teacher goes back over the problem missed by the largest number of students.

"If movie tickets cost $4.50 for adults and $2.50 for children, what is the cost for twelve adults and five children to attend the movie?"

He begins by simplifying.

"Say it cost $1.00 for each person in this room

to go to a movie. How much would we have to pay? Write it down."

Students stand and count the class. Some walk around for a better view. After a minute, talking begins to build. The teacher walks around and checks for answers.

"Now, let's say it costs $1.00 per student, and $2.00 per adult. How much would it cost?"

Students figure briefly at their seats and then begin to file up to the teacher to check their answers. In no time, the teacher is surrounded by students. The teacher asks them to return to their seats and poses the original problem from the book. The rest of the period is spent demonstrating the solution at the board.

These vignettes are not fully representative of instruction at the intermediate school, but they capture its emphasis. In most classes, instruction is based on the textbook. The teacher explains a new skill, and students read about it and then practice it in exercises. Assignments occasionally involve creative writing. In science, the textbook includes activities, and many sixth-grade students prepare projects to enter in the science fair. Overall, teachers report that these latter activities constitute a small proportion of class time by comparison with seatwork exercises on basic skills.

No consciously articulated philosophy or vision of education motivates instruction in the intermediate school. Teachers speak of their autonomy and describe their principal as supportive, but they do not describe any particular set of goals or beliefs underlying their approach except to identify areas of emphasis: "We emphasize basic language skills," some sixth-grade teachers report.

Thinking is not a central goal in the intermediate school. Children do spend time learning how to solve applied math problems, but most teachers do not tell us about any efforts to develop critical or analytical thinking, encourage the expression of ideas, teach the tools of investigation and inquiry, or have children reflect on what they have read or done, nor do we observe any fruits of such efforts in classrooms or students' products.

What goes on in the reservation's schools is also going on in schools across the nation; but is this the right curriculum, and is this the right kind of teaching, for children whose language and culture are so radically different from mainstream language and culture? At first glance, the situation appears logical. If people from other cultures want to cash in on the opportunities available to people in the mainstream culture, they should have the same instruction that mainstreamers have. They should read the same books, study the same grammar, work on the same worksheets, listen to the same lectures. After all, if it works for white middle-class children, it should work for anyone else.

The problem is that here, as in many other parts of America, it doesn't work very well. At least one-third of the students never graduate from high school. Their scores on nationally standardized achievement tests are usually in the lowest quartile. Ninth graders on the reservation are estimated to be about three years behind ninth graders elsewhere in the state, and twelfth graders are estimated to be five years behind. The reason dropouts most often give for leaving school is that they find it boring. Of all Native Americans who begin higher education of some kind, only 2 percent finish. Tribal education officials bemoan the fact that the lack of language proficiency interferes with students' ability to think, reason, and solve problems; yet, by and large, people here keep plugging away at the same kind of schooling, year after year. Instead of blaming this approach itself, they point to the many reasons why it doesn't work: schools have been widely available on or near the reservation only since 1950; 80 percent of the people on the reservation are on some kind of welfare; alcoholism is a serious problem across the reservation, as is fetal alcohol syndrome, which seriously limits learning ability (Dorris, 1989); many parents do not know how to help their children adjust to schooling; some students have to travel fifty miles by bus to get to school; teachers are hard to get and harder to keep. With so many plausible excuses for low performance, why question the current approach?

Nevertheless, with schooling so alien to their ways, the wonder is that these children learn anything at all. A number of Indians told me they thought they were "right-brain" people forced into "left-brain" institutions. They meant it in a loose, metaphor-ical way: a right-brain person is more holistic, more spatially and artistically oriented, while a left-brain person is more analytical, more linear as a thinker. Some research seems to confirm this view of Indians, but other research casts doubts on it (Rhodes, 1988). More to the point are observations about the ways in which children in the tribe learn naturally, before and outside school. Robert Rhodes, a researcher at the University of Northern Arizona, has studied natural learning in southwestern tribes. He finds many contrasts with formal schooling.

"To begin with," he told me, "these kids naturally have a lot more responsibility at home than they are given in the typical school. They take care of brothers and sisters. They take care of herds, often for days at a time, and at very early ages. They take care of animals. They learn in contexts that make them responsible for their learning. But at school they are not given any responsibility."

The children on the reservation learn naturally from each other, Rhodes said. They observe adults and then go off and practice alone. When they feel they have a good start on the skill, they show a friend and then a group of friends, who work together on the skill. Only when a child has achieved a degree of mastery does he show an adult. The adult usually just observes quietly and approvingly or perhaps performs the skill himself, without comment. A child's natural learning is self-initiated and involves adults only at certain times and in certain ways. The contrast with formal schooling is sharp. Particularly important, Rhodes believes, is the aspect of performance. Indian children do not naturally perform on cue, in public and at an adult's bidding.

"Indians take a long time observing a situation and thinking about it," Rhodes said. "Sometimes they seem to cogitate forever before acting. The trial-and-error approach to problem solving makes no sense on the reservation. If you're a long way from home with the herd, and the weather is looking bad, and you're running out of food, you have to decide the right thing to do the first time. There's little margin for error."

Schooling is not set up for long cogitation or delaying action. It means action first, and then improving the action. This seems unnatural to Indian children.

These Indians' language and religion assume that everything

is connected to everything else in some way. They learn naturally when they have a complete picture in mind of where they are going, what the outcome will be, and why they are doing whatever they are doing. They are purposeful. For them, as for many other children, schooling lacks coherence, wholeness, and purpose. Teachers themselves generally don't know why they are giving a particular lesson at a particular time. Everything has been broken into so many small parts and steps that the larger goals or purposes are obscure at best.

"Teachers often encourage action without understanding," Rhodes said, "so that students can then learn from their errors. But a lot of Indian children want to know what the ultimate outcome will be before they even start."

Indian culture is far more oriented to people and relationships than to products and things. An environment in which talking and working with your friends is seen as cheating, or in which you are expected to shame your friends by showing off knowledge or skills they don't possess, just doesn't make sense, Rhodes said.

"The Native American student has to hear and understand a teacher's question in English, sometimes translate that to his own language, determine what the question really means and how it relates to his reality, develop an answer, sometimes translate that into English, and finally determine if it is appropriate to volunteer that answer out loud to the teacher or if the volunteering of the answer will make him less than a team member. All of this takes about forty-five to ninety seconds. Teachers are very reluctant to wait longer than five or eight seconds. The result is that there is little interchange between student and teachers in the classroom, where the teaching style is one of presenting material and trying to discuss it through questioning.

"Native Americans prefer to let things happen, where Anglos like to make things happen."

This attitude, often coupled with distrust of white people, language insecurity, and boredom, creates the so-called passivity and apathy that frustrated white teachers often attribute to Native Americans.

It could be objected that many children, not just Native Americans, learn differently in natural environments from the way they do in school, and the contrast does not seem to hold them back. Moreover, some would argue that schooling is closer to the kind of experience most young people will face as adults—doing what they are told, whether they like it or not—and so they may as well get used to it, regardless of whether is it "natural." The only reply to such objections is simply to point out that this kind of schooling is inefficient and ineffective, does not work for a large number of students, and does not really prepare them to be productive, happy adults. As one superintendent likes to say, "If your horse is dead, for God's sake, dismount!" What can we lose by trying something more attuned to the students' experience, when it is so obvious that current practice doesn't work?

This thought led some educators on the reservation to begin a project, centered in the primary school, that is transforming the school district and may one day transform education across the reservation. The nine stated goals of the primary school reflect a strong effort to attune curriculum and instruction to students' natural learning styles, language, cultural experiences, and everyday realities:

1. To implement an integrated, holistic approach to learning, and to develop programs that reflect and enhance real-life interests and experience
2. To implement development of essential skills as they benefit learning, and to strive for national grade-level academic achievement as an essential part of the total growth of every child
3. To develop within each child good physical and mental health, as a major interest in helping each student establish a positive self-concept and positive social attitudes and practices, thereby allowing each student to adapt readily to his or her own group, society, and culture
4. To implement a curriculum sensitive to the fact that the majority of students are Native Americans whose language, cultural practices, and value systems are indispensable elements of their personal development, and to have the curricu-

lum reflect programs that will strengthen students' opportunities for growth and development in their culture

5. To provide for the special needs of all children, accelerated or remedial, so that instruction will reflect a broad general education, geared to help each child gain the most from his or her abilities, regardless of racial or ethnic background, language proficiency, or any handicapping condition

6. To implement hands-on, cooperative learning opportunities and direct students' participation in their own education, so that they can be successful

7. To promote the concept that the entire community has a stake in the education of all students, that any educational program must be a cooperative program, and that parents must have a unique interest in the educational program and will always be welcome at our schools

8. To develop strong networks for communication and staff development, which will facilitate the staff's unity of purpose, enhance the working environment, and promote honest input into and ownership of the program

9. To promote national standards in our educational system, by meeting accreditation requirements as an integral part of the school's educational goals

The project's statement of purpose, after acknowledging the gap between actual and desired levels of literacy, cites attempts to solve the problem with various standardized instruments and goes on to say, "The goal of education is not scoring well on standardized tests; it is literacy." With the principal's strong encouragement, supportive guidelines from the state, and skillful use of federal funds for training and development, the teachers in the primary school drew on a long tradition of instruction, called the *language experience approach,* to create a new curriculum and an environment suitable for offering it. They developed statements of principle like the following:

> Learning does not come from one source, nor is it best learned from behind a desk, hands folded, feet flat on the floor, and eyes front. Before children enter school, they learned language actively, by interacting with their environment. They used language purposefully to get things done. As educators, we must go back to the roots of learning, to use language to get things done. We must merge our traditional sense of schooling with the real world. What we do in school must not insult our children's past but must build upon their past and encourage future learning.
>
> The classroom should be compatible with the child's natural environment, a place where there is constant language production, beginning with the personal and the expressive, moving outward to explore and expand the boundaries of the environment.
>
> We should teach students not only how to read but also how to love to read.
>
> We should emphasize writing. Writing helps students to think; it provides an organization for their thoughts, and it helps them to find out what they know. Children know much; we should help them discover this fact.
>
> We should look for ways in which we can continue to integrate science and social studies into the language arts and not separate learning into little compartments which cannot overlap.
>
> We can use the children's natural abilities to talk about their personal experiences as a foundation for

moving outward into the more abstract processes of reading and writing.

The classroom tasks and activities must be structured in a meaningful and interrelated manner. The classroom environment must be exciting and, perhaps, not always predictable. Much as in the real world, children must be given opportunities for exploring their environment—measuring, sampling, and using the language as a means of ordering what they see and hear.

When students teach other students, they all benefit. There is direct improvement in self-concept, attitude toward school, and learning. We should take our direction from the teacher in the one-room schoolhouse and let students teach each other.

As educators, we must realize that mistakes are to be accepted as opportunities for learning.

Children need to see adults read and write, and they need to see that adults can be excited about what they communicate.

These and many other statements were backed up by a thorough review of the research on learning and literacy. The principal and his teachers developed a philosophy, an empirical base to support it, and a process for keeping it alive with constant discussion, debate, and experimentation. To see what it looked like, let's return to Alan Davis's field notes:

> The building in which the primary school is housed is old and distinctly lacking in structural features like carpeting or movable walls that contemporary schools use to create a warm informality. Inside the old brick exterior, one walks on cracked linoleum floors down long, plastered hallways with self-contained class-

rooms leading off on either side. But the austerity of the building itself is more than offset by its decor. The walls of the hallways are covered with student artwork and writing, especially writing, ranging from a few barely legible lines of a kindergartener's journal to a third grader's illustrated story. Brightly colored signs welcome the visitor and remind everyone of the importance of writing. The main office opens to the front hall over an open counter, so that anyone passing by can look in or speak to the secretary without having to open a door.

The principal is seldom in the office. He strides along the hallways with a walkie-talkie on his belt, to link him with the office, greeting each child he passes by name, slapping palms, giving "high fives," offering words of encouragement: "Carla! I read your story about the deer. Good job! Give me five!" He drops into a classroom and participates in a lesson about the solar system. He presides over a weekly assembly in which dozens of children receive special recognition for attendance and academic contributions. He is a highly visible presence and a source of energy and direction for teachers and students. He has been principal of this school for eight years. The vision and educational philosophy that have guided the development of the school have emerged collectively, but it is the principal's leadership that has provided the support and continuity to bring about the distinct character of the primary school.

Many of the assumptions that underlie the principal's beliefs about education are reminiscent of John Dewey and the progressive movement. The activities that take place in school should be meaningful in themselves, he says. Worksheets, drills, and other practice exercises are to be avoided except when students fully accept the ends these materials are intended to serve. Children should be actively involved in learning, and the process of learning should be inherently engaging to them. The role of the teachers is not to transmit knowledge directly but to provide a supportive environment and to guide student activity. Curriculum should not be defined through fixed programs of interaction between students and teachers on particular content. Instead, the teachers should determine where particular students are—what their interests are, what they are ready to do next—and select materials and strategies accordingly, given certain established goals. Chief among these goals should be fluency in communication of all forms, but especially in writing.

The development of student writing has been a central goal at the primary school since 1980. The principal and several staff members cite works by Donald Graves and other specialists in the teaching of writing to children in explaining their approach. Writing instruction should begin in kindergarten and should be coincident with instruction in reading, not subsequent or secondary to reading. Children should begin by writing their own oral language, using "invented" phonetic spelling. Reading, writing, listening, and speaking should be integrated into all instruction, not taught as distinct, separate skills. Basal reading texts should not be relied upon.

Instead, students should select their own books to read, and they should read what they and other students have written. Student writing should be respected as meaningful communication, not as practice exercises. The mechanics of writing should be valued as important to clarifying and supporting the message but should always be subordinate to the message itself.

Visits to various classrooms at the primary school leave no doubt that the philosophy of active learning and the focus on communication, especially writing, have had an unmistakable impact on instruction. In a kindergarten class, children are discussing personal experiences that will become topics for journal writing. It is late in March, and their teacher explains that most of these students are now able to encode their words phonetically, with enough consistency to be able to read them back later. The children sit on the floor in groups of three and take turns telling anecdotes. They know that later each will tell the class something that someone else said, an expectation designed to encourage careful listening.

The storytelling is animated, but voices are low.

"We were driving to town in our truck," one five-year-old girl is telling the two boys in her group. "There was a dead bull beside the road. One of its horns was broken off. We don't know what happened to it."

Other stories are told in turn, usually involving a trip to town. Then the full group of twenty-four listens as each child summarizes something told by a member of his or her small group. The written products of previous activities such as this one are everywhere: posted on the walls of the class, in the hall outside, in individual student folders. Some cannot be made out by an unfamiliar reader. But they more typically consist of three to five sentences, written mostly in consonants: "My nam is Ruth I love my mmy I love my ddy r dog hd 6 pps."

In a second-grade class, children are sitting in clusters around tables while the teacher moves from child to child. This is part of a "writing workshop," a sequence of activities culminating in a revised final draft on individually selected topics. Today, students have about an hour to write initial drafts. Of the twenty-two students in the class, about eight appear to be writing or thinking about their writing at any given time. Some of the others talk quietly, some walk to the bookshelf, some look around the room. One reads aloud what he has written, for my benefit: "Me and my father and my brother went out and shot a deer

with bo-and-air-o. My father clend it. Then my
mother cooked deer met and we at it for supr. It was
rely good."

There is a leisurely and relaxed atmosphere in
the class. From time to time, students who have been
walking around sit down and begin to write, while
others stop writing and converse with another child.
The teacher, a young, informally dressed man with a
beard and longish brown hair, walks about the class,
talking with students who are writing or who come to
him with questions. He ignores the students who are
talking with each other or moving about the room.
Efficient use of time is not a priority in this class;
student enjoyment and valuing of writing is.

The twenty-six students in a third-grade classroom are clustered about five tables. Nearly every
available space is covered with student work: paint-
ings of people, eight-foot-long landscape murals on
butcher paper, displays of large rocks, and more. The
teacher, a bearded man in his early thirties, is leading
a lesson on the circulatory system. The children have
written first-person narratives about the blood and are
taking turns reading them aloud.

"I am the blood," reads a child. "I run through
the body. I go everywhere."

At the board, the teacher draws a human figure
and a heart.

"Where does the blood go from here?" he asks.

"Everywhere!" answer several children at once.

"What are some of the 'everywheres' it goes to?"

Hands rise, but the teacher does not call on
individuals. Instead, children begin calling out
answers with animation.

"It goes to the lungs! The arms! The legs! The
feet!"

"What are the lungs like?" the teacher asks.

"Balloons!"

Now the teacher tells the children that he wants

them to form teams, to make life-size illustrations of the circulatory system. At each table, one child lies down on a sheet of butcher paper while the others trace the outline of his or her body. The children quickly designate a model in each group and begin to draw.

The principal of the primary school, Bob Zigmund, is a Polish-American who came to the reservation as a practice teacher from an eastern college and wound up marrying an Indian and settling down here. He's a restless, intense man, always on the prowl, and he reveals a broad grasp of the research that supports what he is doing. I ask him what is wrong with ordinary reading instruction.

"Well, for starters," he says, "kids don't do much reading in ordinary reading instruction. Research shows they spend about 70 percent of their time doing seatwork on skill sheets and in workbooks. Most of the rest of the time is spent reading isolated words and sentences. Only about two to five minutes of every day really involve engaged reading. So ordinary reading instruction doesn't get the job done."

"Didn't I see some basal readers in a couple of classrooms?" I ask.

"Where?" he demands, as if he were going to rush to the classrooms and yank the books out immediately. Then he smiles.

"Well," he says, "we still have some around, I guess. But I don't encourage them, and I don't think they're used. Research shows that basals put far too much emphasis on isolated aspects of language and so-called subskills that don't really exist except in the minds of textbook designers. They're badly written, the sequencing of skills is absolutely arbitrary, the questions they ask aren't about the material kids read, they don't involve kids' higher-order thinking skills, they don't relate at all to my kids' experience, they cost too much, and they don't work. Other than that, I suppose they're all right.

"Look," he continues, "if you want kids to read and write and think, the evidence is overwhelming: aim at their higher mental processes, not their lower ones. Let them initiate their learning activities for their own purposes. Put them in a language environment where all the aspects of language are used, the way they are in real life. Make them read and write and think and talk to each other all the time. Give them good coaching and corrective feedback right when they need it, and surround them with adults who read and write and think and talk to each other all the time. There's no big mystery about this. That's what works."

On the wall behind him is a statement of what he says are research-based principles that everyone in the school should be observing:

> Children want to be good.
> Children like to play.
> Children like to be silly.
> Children want to be respected for what they know.
> Children want to grow up.
> Children want to be noticed for their accomplishments.
> Children want answers to their questions.
> Children want someone to listen to them.
> Children want to teach others what they know.
> Children want to do things by themselves.
> Children are aware of differences among themselves.
> Children want to talk about their families.
> Children like to be entertained.
> Children like to touch, taste, feel, and be active.

Underneath each principle is a paragraph explaining the implications for the child and for the teacher. Bob Zigmund has things like this all over the place.

He takes me quickly through the curriculum that he and his teachers have developed, and he shows how every activity breeds literacy, fluency, and thoughtfulness. The writing curriculum emphasizes that writing is a process of making meaning, in which the teacher guides the student to discover his or her own ideas and language; this process develops from continuous interaction among writing, imagining, and thinking. Students have to write daily on topics of personal interest. They have to brainstorm together, edit others' papers, revise what they write, publish their writing, and enter it in contests.

The curriculum for reading and literature focuses on the need for children to create meaning as they read. Instruction guides students in recalling, interpreting, and critically understanding what they read. The teacher must model an interest in reading and revealing the thought processes used in evaluating and interpreting works of literature. Students must select their own books and read every day. They must be read to by others and share their reading with others. They have to predict, inquire into, and solve problems by reading, and they have to evaluate what they read.

The curriculum for speech and drama offers students opportunities to expand their previous experiences with imitation, role playing, pantomiming, and conversation. It is integrated into all areas and includes storytelling and speaking over the intercom to the entire school.

The curriculum also uses integrated thematic units, the teaching of which involves teachers and students in exploring, creating, and growing more interested in and knowledgeable about particular subjects. Thematic teaching is intended to instill the idea that schools are places to learn interesting things.

The social studies curriculum emphasizes the child's active role as an inquirer into the social environment. Thinking, observing, listening, reading, interpreting, applying information, analyzing, synthesizing, and evaluating are deemed as important as specific knowledge and skills. Students have to investigate the family, the community, and society at large. They have to become familiar with their culture, kinship affiliations, and history, as well as with larger historical events and other cultures.

The mathematics program, with an emphasis on creating, understanding, and manipulating patterns, concepts, and numbers, uses examples from sports (scorekeeping, record keeping, statistics, win-loss records, player information, and predictions) to bring math more fully into students' experience. The focus is on active involvement of math in real-life situations. Every student in the school has been assigned a number. Whenever he or she interacts with another student (or group of students), mathematical problems suggest themselves. How do the numbers add up? Do the individual numbers share any roots? Can they be divided into one another? Are they whole numbers?

The science curriculum uses children's intuition, imagination, language, and critical thinking to help them learn scientific methods and concepts. Investigation and thinking skills are the heart of the science curriculum, but literature, art, drama, music, mathematics, social studies, physical activity, and attitudes are also used to approach the study of science.

Music and art permeate the curriculum. The emphasis in music is on exploring sound and relating music to the other arts. The focus in art is on shaping experience through a visual medium and on relating art to thinking. Observing, analyzing, synthesizing, evaluating, interpreting, comparing, and imagining are considered fundamental to painting, drawing, and working with clay or other media.

Again and again, the child's experience is stressed as the starting point, with emphasis on making connections, using the mind fully, avoiding step-by-step learning, and using reading and writing and mathematics, not for their own sake but in the process of learning what children need to learn. The teachers developed the curriculum through workshops, summer institutes, and committees. Zigmund has established committees on writing, art, science, math, social studies, drama and speech, parents, counseling, social events, budget, and textbooks. One of the teachers, Patty Muller, has inspired and coordinated schoolwide curriculum development.

Zigmund has also squeezed every conceivable penny out of the many federal programs available to reservation schools and to public schools with high concentrations of children receiving welfare. The teachers write grant proposals and travel to conferences around the state. Zigmund takes advantage of every kind of technical assistance that the state offers. His substantive expertise lies in teaching writing and getting kids to share and publish their work; Patty Muller and a half-dozen other teachers supply the rest of the substantive knowledge, but the school clearly reflects Zigmund's vision. It moves on his energy and enthusiasm and cleverness at finding money. The dynamic teachers are people he attracted and hired. The school's reputation was built and is protected by him. His stamp is on everything.

But Bob Zigmund has been helped mightily by state policy. State guidelines for reading and writing support not only writing across the curriculum but also reading as an activity to be valued for its own sake, rather than as a set of skills to be acquired. The state university's school of education is a hotbed of whole-language instruction. It produces teachers who are excited about a curriculum like Bob's and know how to make it work. Surrounded by a district more traditional and conservative than he is, Zigmund has been able to justify his departure from the norm by appealing to the spirit, if not always the letter, of the state's guidelines and curriculum experts' recommendations.

And he needs to justify his program: teachers in the reservation's other schools are skeptical. Alan Davis's observations are salient:

> To explain the persisting differences between the primary and the intermediate schools, it is as revealing to examine the role of a shared social and intellectual culture within each school as it is to examine the policies that influence them. These cultures involve a set of beliefs and expectations about education and the roles of educators.
>
> At the outset, the two schools are very much aware of each other, but very rarely do individuals from one visit the other. The impressions of the intermediate teachers regarding the primary school are largely negative. One teacher visited her nephew's third-grade class last year.
>
> "He had no basal reader! Just library books! No wonder he can't read," she said.
>
> A sixth-grade teacher concurred.
>
> "The approach they use at the primary school is probably good preparation for the high-ability kids. But for the low-ability kids, it lacks structure. They come here without having learned the rules of English. They may understand math concepts, but they haven't learned their computation facts."
>
> The fourth-grade teachers differ broadly in

their views of the primary program. One, a woman who has taught in the intermediate school for several years, is highly critical.

"I've noticed a real lowering of achievement since the primary adopted its approach, especially in the coherence of writing. The students like to write, that's true. They'll write tons. But there is no structure to it, no organization. Their writing isn't precise or complete. It's anything that comes to mind, regardless."

Another fourth-grade teacher, who works with low-achieving students in language arts, had a similar view.

"I support the approach at the primary school," she said. "But I don't see much progress. I'm working on the students' writing, trying to get them to write complete sentences. They don't seem to teach them that."

An exception was the one fourth-grade teacher who considers herself philosophically aligned with the primary school. A young mother in her second year of teaching, she was trained under a nationally known professor of reading, who supported the use of literature and trade books over basal texts, a focus on reading as the interpretation of meaning rather than as a set of skills, and an emphasis on the integration of reading and writing throughout the curriculum. She discussed these ideas with the principal of the intermediate school and found that he supported her in her effort to implement them in her classroom. However, she found little support from the other teachers in the school, and she turned to associations with the primary school teachers for support. These associations have become a central group identification for her. She names particular teachers outside the primary school who "share the philosophy." The suggestion is one of membership in an élite group. In the view of this teacher, who teaches the highest-achieving students, the preparation of entering fourth graders has been excellent.

"The kids coming in from the primary this year were really well prepared," she said. "Their oral reading is weak, but their comprehension is very good. Their math skills were much better than previously. Several came in knowing how to multiply, and some can even divide."

If the majority of intermediate school teachers are critical of what they perceive as a lack of disciplined attention to basic skills at the primary school, the majority of primary school teachers share an equally strong conviction that their approach is both better and widely misunderstood. The development of a shared approach to curriculum and instruction that is viewed with suspicion by many outside the school has created a strong group identification on the part of most primary teachers.

Instruction is a regular topic of conversation among teachers at the primary school. Some of the communication is planned. Faculty meetings are discussion sessions focused on instruction. While we visited the school, discussion centered on issues of ability grouping and retention. The session was voluntary but widely attended and sparked with impassioned debate. A teacher on special assignment as a curriculum specialist facilitates these sessions and provides staff with background readings. Teachers also hold their own periodic writing workshops, and several articles about the school, written by teachers and by the principal, have been published in journals. In addition, staff members have organized a consortium of reservation educators interested in whole-language instruction, which meets Thursday evenings.

As the distinctive reputation of the school has spread, the philosophy of its teachers has become more homogeneous. Several teachers, recently hired from out of state, had heard about the school in graduate school. They applied to teach in the school because they were excited about the opportunity to implement its humanistic instructional approach and because the prospect of teaching Native American children appealed to their liberal idealism. The principal is allowed a direct hand in staff selection. When vacancies occur, he can generally select from a pool of applicants who understand the instructional philosophy of the school and are excited about implementing it.

As a group, in the sociological sense, the faculty of the primary school displays two classic characteristics of a cause or movement: a hierarchy within the group, reflecting, in part, belief and loyalty to the cause; and a tendency to stereotype alternative approaches and reject out of hand all practices associated with them. Uses of basal readers and other textbooks, lecture, practice exercises, and multiple-choice tests are rejected practices—practices that many primary teachers believe result in student alienation and passivity and should be shunned as a matter of principle.

Several Native American teachers and a few whites in the school remain unconverted and continue to use basal readers and worksheets. Other staff members described these teachers as resisting change or slow to acquire good practices, and were not encouraged to visit their classes.

Questions about skill acquisition and monitoring individual progress sometimes triggered defensive responses. For example, questions to a kindergarten teacher regarding phonics instruction were revealing:

"How do children in this class learn the sound the letter *T* makes?"

"You wait until a child wants to write a word that includes that sound. Then you take that opportunity to teach that child the sound associated with the letter."

"Wouldn't you ever teach the whole class a lesson about a consonant sound?"

"What do you want me to do? Give them piles and piles of worksheets?"

I asked a first-grade teacher what information he keeps to monitor student progress.

"Oh, I used to keep all sorts of records in the last school I taught in," he answered. "But we don't do that here."

In fact, some teachers did administer informal reading inventories and maintain records, but many perceived that sort of formal monitoring to be at odds with the spirit of the school.

Because the teachers of the primary school have a strong exclusive group identification, united by a shared belief system, they don't influence the intermediate school or learn from it any more than Catholics learn new religious practices from their Baptist neighbors. Primary school teachers tend to dismiss the instruction at the intermediate school as more of the "same old textbook, drill, and practice." Intermediate school teachers bristle at what they perceive as smugness on the part of primary teachers. Virtually no teacher from either school has visited classes in the other building.

Nine months after our initial visit, things are changing fast on the reservation. At the school board's request, Alan Davis is working with the other schools in Bob Zigmund's district to help make them more like the primary school. Alan has found other whole-language schools on the reservation that claim to be even farther ahead than Zigmund's.

The tribal council has declared that schools all across the reservation must improve dramatically. It has just sponsored a year-long discussion of education, involving hundreds of people from the tribe and the various state and federal education agencies that serve it. Now the discussion is culminating in a summit meeting at the tribal headquarters. Group after group makes its recommendations. Speakers move in and out of the native language. Tribal leaders who seem wooden when they speak English are dramatically transformed into charismatic orators when they move into their own tongue, even though they have spoken English most of their lives. Medicine men periodically give their extended, rhythmic blessings. Grandmothers with impassive faces and spectacular jewelry fan themselves in the crowded hall.

Many of the recommendations are traditional. As in Daviston, progress here means creating schools like the ones that white people have in their suburbs. The news has not reached many people here that even those suburban schools are under pressure to change. Many of the recommendations call for stronger central control and new bureaucracies, to ensure that things get done uniformly: the tribe should create a nonpartisan governing board, a special bilingual-bicultural department, a new financing authority, and reservation-wide goals and standards for students and teachers alike.

But, as one participant puts it, some of the recommendations promise "a new dawn." There is widespread agreement that the traditional curriculum is not appropriate. It does not foster Indian values, does not support the culture, and has been watered down too much. Education must rest on the tribe's philosophy, not on the white world's. A young woman presents models of education based on corn and on all that corn means to the tribe mythically, spiritually, and economically. She speaks of a curriculum woven like a basket. She says the tribe needs a curriculum that includes the four directions: the east, where the sun rises and where sound beliefs and values begin; the south, where the sun shines on our industry and our practical concerns; the west, where, in the evening, we attend to our social relationships, our family and community members; and the north, whence we derive our respect for nature.

"We believe in the full life," she says, "the whole life, the integrated life. That is what our children should believe in, too."

On the evening before the end of the summit, a medicine man asks to have the last word. He is dignified-looking in his baggy sportscoat and open-necked shirt. Instead of a tie, he wears a magnificent beaded necklace. Moving in and out of his native language, he tells us that he is one of only thirteen medicine men left. He deplores this situation and regrets that his people know so little about their language and culture. He says that he has been in both worlds. He knows how the majority culture thinks. First he was an electrical engineer, far away from the reservation, and then he was a lawyer. After that, he was a policeman on the reservation and a lawyer who interacted frequently with other, Anglo lawyers.

"I know how to think and learn in the other way," he said, "but then one day my grandfather asked me to follow him and take his place as a medicine man. There I was, where I wanted to be, doing what I wanted to do, a success in both worlds. I laughed."

But his grandfather prevailed, he tells us. And he studied for twelve years.

"This was the hardest study I have ever done," he says— harder than law school, harder than electrical engineering, harder than police work. "Every word, every rhythm has to be perfect. The chants must be perfect every time. And you have to learn it all by memory. But you can't learn the words and the rhythms and get them perfect unless you know the legends. They don't make sense without the stories.

"Too many of you don't know the stories," he continues. "You can't know certain things without them. I've done the chants for many years now. And I've seen results. Results you can't understand or explain with Western medicine. Hearing comes back. Sight is restored. We may know something that other people don't know. The chants get results. I can't explain it to you. But the most important thing is that you have to know the stories, the legends, in order for the words and the rhythms to make sense, in order for you to know your language and your culture."

As both illustration and chastisement, he launches into a long, apparently obscure legend, stopping periodically to ask questions and rebuke the audience for not knowing the answers. The point of the story seems to be that the legends say in their own way what secular science says in its own way, but the two are not equivalent. To know something in one context is not the same as knowing it in another.

His story goes on and on, sometimes in English and sometimes in his native language. People listen respectfully but not raptly. Just when you think you know where he's going, he goes somewhere else. He never returns to his points about context and learning and education. His story seems to be its own point. It is about twins, one crippled, the other blind. The blind one carries the crippled one, who in turn guides their progress as they travel from world to world on a quest for signs to reveal the meaning of their lives and end their wandering.

This medicine man is chastising his people for losing touch with what he believed was a higher literacy: an inheritance of stories and legends that give meaning to ordinary language and daily life. The twins in the legend are on an endless quest for signs. In conjuring them up, the medicine man reminds us that literacy's oldest, deepest roots are anchored in spiritual quests for significance. Literacy's most profound function is to help connect the individual with larger and larger circles of reference, which ultimately come to constitute the meaning of his or her life.

Our goals in modern schooling are far more modest. Perhaps that is one of our problems. Having a very limited, secular, utilitarian view of literacy—as a means to employment, for instance—we have invented a kind of teaching that cuts literacy off at the roots, diminishing both its appeal and its capacity to empower. By focusing on literacy as a practical, technical matter, we have reduced it. After years and years of mechanical training in what is called reading, students in literature classes are uninterested in the stories and legends of their own cultures; they sense no connection between reading and the things they care most deeply about. After years and years of mechanical training in what is called writing, they emerge from school unwilling to write, doubtful that they have anything to write about.

Something about the way we teach literacy is betraying the very spirit of literacy: the power to make meaning. We saw that power working at the reservation's primary school. The trick is simply to put children in charge of their own literacy, in charge of writing and telling and reading their own stories for their own purposes. Let them feel the power of it firsthand. Guide them through the broadening of their circles, the intersections of their circles with other people's circles, people old and young, modern and ancient. Let them weave themselves into the tapestry of their culture, and show them now and then that they have done so. Make them reflect sometimes on how what they have said and written matches or conflicts with what others have said and written, in their own culture and in others. Show them that, all on their own, they have entered into a great conversation.

The teachers at the primary school are using the whole-language approach to literacy because they think it closely matches the learning habits and tendencies of Indian children. They also think it is better for all young people, bilingual and bicultural or not, because it reunites reading and writing (which have drifted apart in our schooling, for no apparent reason) and attaches both to the purposeful making of meaning. They have integrated various kinds of critical and creative thinking into the whole-language curriculum and prefer to teach such thinking specifically. They believe that thoughtfulness is inevitably a by-product of a richly textured and dynamic active-learning environment anchored in writing and reading. They have been encouraged by some (not all) elements of the new state policy and by various flexibly interpreted federal policies affecting Indian and bilingual students. They are proving that an entire school can reorganize and transform itself in ways that bring about a much higher level of literacy for a much larger proportion of students. We do not know what will happen as these students progress through the later grades, but we have reason to be hopeful.

CHAPTER FOUR

An Urban District:
One Foot on the Gas,
The Other on the Brakes

It's 6:30 A.M., and I am crammed into a horseshoe-shaped restaurant booth with three assistant superintendents and the director of planning and research for the North Urban Public Schools (NUPS). Next to me is Paul Baca, the assistant superintendent for high schools, a nattily dressed, gregarious man credited with turning around one of the worst high schools in this urban district of 56,000 students. He is the highest-ranking Hispanic in the district and is rumored to be in line for the superintendency, if the embattled superintendent steps down or is fired.

Next to Paul Baca is Natalie Wilson, assistant superintendent for elementary schools. A prim white woman, who came to this district three years ago with the current superintendent, she looks at Paul while he makes pleasant small talk, but she seems to be somewhere else and never smiles. Next to her, playing with his coffee spoon, is John Orwell, a somewhat longish-haired, good-looking white man in his late thirties, who came to this district only a few years ago, with a reputation as an innovator and creative force. He is assistant superintendent for middle schools. On my right is Bill Washington, a taciturn black man in his mid fifties, who has been with the district all his working life. He speaks softly and slowly, as if wanting to choose his words carefully and not be over-heard. He is director of planning and research and has set this meeting up for me, so that I can tell these people about my request to do some research in the district.

As we wait for the superintendent, John Peck, to join us, it is clear that no one wants to talk about anything substantive. When Peck arrives and squeezes himself into the booth, there is a measurable increase in tension. Baca abruptly stops talking and does not make eye contact with Peck. I can't tell if the others are ill at ease because of Baca's and Peck's strained relationship or because they are also not on good terms with one another or with the superintendent. Maybe they know something the superintendent doesn't know.

Peck is a large, heavy-set white man in his late forties. He has a boyish face and a myopic squint that gives him a perpetually puzzled expression. He speaks softly and articulately, although he sounds tired. His battles with the school board have been in the papers all week, and everyone has been wondering if or when the ax will fall. He came to this district three years ago, on a four-to-three vote of the board, and has never won over the board members who voted against him in the first place. The black and Hispanic minority communities have both been critical of him from the beginning, arguing that only a minority superintendent can lead the once proud but now troubled district out of its doldrums.

The NUPS student body is about 36 percent white, 25 percent black, 35 percent Hispanic, and 4 percent Asian and Native American. A couple of decades ago, it was mostly white. The district draws on a very highly educated citizenry. Its black population has one of the highest mean levels of educational attainment in the country, and its relatively young Anglo population ranks among the top five most highly educated. Even in a recession, the community seems affluent. It has no slums, no barrios, no ghettos. Back in the 1960s, its public school system was believed to be one of the better urban districts in the country. In the early 1970s, the courts found the school board guilty of *de jure* segregation and ordered busing for racial balance. Anglo families started moving out of the district, and the school board began what became years and years of bitter fighting: member against member, antibusing majority against prointegration minority, and board against the court. No one knows what the achievement differences between ethnic groups were when the struggle against desegregation began, but today they are huge. By and large, black high school students' average rank on nationally standardized tests is in the 30th percentile; Hispanic students' average is in the 33rd percentile; and Anglo students' average is in the 66th percentile. On some tests, the black/white gap is more than 40 points. Two-thirds of the Hispanic students drop out; of those who stay until graduation, 60 percent are in the bottom half of their classes. About half the blacks drop out before graduation.

The statistics describing its educational and economic resources suggest that NUPS should have a much better school system than it has. The business community is dismayed and frustrated. No one can figure out how the system fell so far, or why the much-publicized efforts to improve it have had so little effect. After three stormy years, Superintendent Peck has brought about no dramatic changes, although he has begun to publish test scores by ethnic group, to establish some baselines against which to measure future progress.

As I describe my hopes for the research project, everyone listens attentively. Paul Baca is the first to ask a question.

"When you do this research, what's in it for us? How can you help us?"

I explain that I expect to provide the participating principals and teachers with some insights into the barriers that often hinder instruction in thinking and problem solving. I also offer to do some inservice training and share with them whatever strategies, ideas, and programs we find anywhere else in the country that seem effective in developing greater thoughtfulness.

"How are you going to cover all of the schools?" Baca asks.

I say that I'm going to study and directly help only a few grades and a few schools, not the entire district. I see immediately that this was the wrong thing to say. They look at one another and shake their heads.

Baca frowns.

"It won't work," he says. "You can't help some schools but not others. Noses will get all out of joint. Someone's going to say 'Why does he help your school but not mine?' "

Everyone nods in agreement.

We work out a deal whereby any research data that may help particular teachers or schools will be made available to all teachers and schools. At 7:30, we unstuff ourselves from the booth, and I realize that no one has ordered anything to eat.

Urban school districts are huge organizations about which it is very hard to generalize safely. Almost any type of program you can think of is probably going on somewhere in the district, if only as a pilot project intended to convey the impression that the district is up-to-date. Even the worst school districts in America have a few outstanding teachers and schools. The question is, how do you make these exceptions the rule? How do you create districts with uniformly excellent schools and uniformly high standards and make them uniformly appealing to a highly pluralistic student body?

We have come to NUPS because it is like most other large urban districts. It is under great pressure from the community to improve its services dramatically. Its leaders talk about "bottom-up" changes, brought about by individual teachers and schools as they see the need and opportunity for such changes. At the same time, however, NUPS is a highly centralized and hierarchical organization. Its leaders may be trying to encourage natural, bottom-up innovation, but they have created a policy environment in which such change is unlikely to challenge the status quo. The "storyline" for North Urban Public Schools does not feature classrooms; it features policymakers, administrators, and bureaucrats of various kinds who are creating, through their discourse and interactions, a corporate culture, a climate that is at best neutral and at worst hostile to thoughtfulness of any kind.

Many large urban school districts would be on the *Fortune* 500 list of major corporations if they were in the private sector. Even NUPS, tiny in comparison to New York's or Chicago's school districts, operates on a $300 million budget and maintains its own pension fund, in excess of $400 million. Consider it a $700 million operation, then, but one governed by ordinary citizens who are chosen in elections for which only 8 percent of the eligible voters typically turn out, and who have never before in their lives had responsibility for such a colossal sum of money. Managing the logistics of an organization this size can eat up endless amounts of time and energy, if you let it. There is always something wrong with the air conditioning somewhere, or with the heat somewhere else; asbestos may be poisoning children, or the buses may be unsafe.

"That's what we spend most of our time on," one school board member tells me. She is a thoughtful woman, a former teacher, who felt that the board needed a more liberal voice and was surprised to have won a seat. But meetings are consumed by logistics and by infrastructure and management issues, not by educational issues, she finds. There are schedules to deal with, buses and busing problems ("Did you know that we have to pick up and deliver some of our students *at their doors*?"), safety and insurance problems ("Do you know what's happening to insurance rates for schools?"), pension-fund investments ("There is no accountability for how we invest—did you know that?").

"We have procurement, personnel, and custodial services," she says, "all of which have huge budgets and can throw up roadblocks to anything you want to do, and all of which are run by people who don't know anything about business. We have labor-union contracts, lawsuits, and bond issues to worry about, not to mention the judge, the deseg guidelines, and all of the studies and paperwork we have to do to constantly prove that we're in compliance [with court-ordered desegregation guidelines]."

The sheer load of noneducational issues that have to be addressed is made more burdensome by poor management and data collection.

"We don't really know whether what is in the budget is really there or not," another board member says. "Every year we allocate $300,000 for legal expenses, and every year we spend $800,000. Money that goes into one account gets used in another. Salary money gets used for bus leases or supplies, and supply money gets used for salaries. I don't even know the right questions to ask when I see the budget, because I don't know what it really means."

The district's computerized information system is partly to blame. The personnel accounting system is on one computer system, and the payroll is on another, incompatible one. Budget printouts can tell you the total number of jobs in the district, but they cannot tell you how many are vacant and how many have been recently filled. Some of the district's hardware is new, but there is no appropriate software to go with it; most of its hardware and software is antiquated, but an upgrade would cost millions.

Some people wonder if such systemic issues have completely overwhelmed and smothered educational issues, and whether even the systemic issues have been managed effectively. Perhaps NUPS would inspire greater confidence if it were better managed. Certainly, a sense of pride in its management would create a different working environment and deeper respect for its policies among employees.

When Tony Petrosky and I talk with Paul Baca a few days after the breakfast meeting, he expresses disdain for his life as a professional administrator at the central office.

"I'd rather be back in a school," he says. "I'd go back in a minute. Here, it's a life of quiet suffocation. People get into their own things and lose sight of what it's all about. No one takes any risks. If I could, I'd make a rule that no one could be a central administrator for more than three years. Then they have to go back and teach. And no one should make more money just because they're down here [in the central office]. That's backwards. Teachers should get the most money, not administrators."

We are sitting with him in his tidy office, next to the superintendent's. Last night, Superintendent Peck told the school board that he is going to step down, ending weeks of speculation about his fate. Baca seems ebullient, but he does not want to talk much about his rival's demise.

"I'll tell you this," he says in response to a question about how to deal with a school board as factious and intrusive as this one appears to be. "I wouldn't try to deal with them as a group. You have to go to them one at a time and find out what each one really cares about. Then you find a way to get something from each one's agenda into your overall program. That's the only way. One at a time. Listening carefully. It can be done."

Peck, he implies, kept going to the school board with his own agenda, not theirs. Peck was too much of an educator and not enough of a politician.

John Orwell's approach is closer to Peck's.

"The biggest problem facing this district," he tells us on the same day we interview Baca, "is a lack of philosophical consensus."

If Orwell had his way, he would push for consensus throughout the community.

"The biggest schism we've got is between those who favor centrally determined objectives that should be imposed on all teachers and those, like myself, who think the district needs consensus on some broad goals that each school can then turn into specific objectives and programs, as they see fit," he says. "This school board is writing objectives. That's not their job. But they don't trust teachers. So they're going to write objectives and then test the hell out of kids, to make sure the objectives are being taught. All the research and all my experience when I was a superintendent tell me that this is a dangerous and wasteful way to go."

Orwell was superintendent of a small suburban district before coming here to take charge of the middle schools. He believes in going to the community to get its views, bringing in the best researchers in the country to advise on the best practices, developing consensus, and then empowering teachers and principals to work out the details. One of the first things he did upon coming to this district was to organize a number of community discussions about schooling, but the school board paid little attention to the results.

Paul Baca, long a battler for Hispanic rights and recognition in an Anglo community, doesn't seem to believe that consensus is achievable with this school board, or even with this community. The trick is to find ways of moving ahead in the absence of consensus.

"You take people one at a time," he tells us, "giving with one hand and taking with another. Everything you take away from them you replace with something better."

He is far less interested than Orwell is in talking about the substance of school improvement; he is far more interested in talking about power relationships and political tactics.

Although they disagree strongly about political strategy in a divided community, Baca and Orwell are united in the belief that people in individual schools should have more power to make educational and workplace decisions. In this commitment to site-based management, however, they are out of sync with the majority of the school board's members. Ignoring the results of Orwell's community meetings about the future direction of the schools, board members are busy creating detailed learning objectives and a tight accountability system of tests to drive instruction in every grade. Despite intense criticism from teachers, the accountability approach is defended by many in the community, including the black president of the school board, who believes that "research has shown that this approach addresses the needs of black children and reduces the achievement gap between blacks and whites." He is not specific about the nature of this research, saying only that this was established in New York City.

Natalie Wilson tells us that she keeps herself largely out of these debates.

"I'm just in charge of the day-to-day issues of elementary schools, not curriculum and instruction. Most of my time is spent with issues of personnel evaluation, scheduling, and those kinds of things."

She takes a very practical approach to her job.

"The public is interested in basic skills," she says. "So we emphasize basic skills. Higher-order skills have to compete with basic skills. Higher-order skills are hard to test. If we don't have tests for them, we won't be likely to teach them. I'd personally like to see more thinking instruction and problem solving going on, but it will have to be valued more than it is now for that to happen."

Wilson tries to put the schisms among senior administrators and board members in a positive light.

"We all agree on our commitment to kids," she says. "Our disagreements center largely on perceptions of professionalism. Do you assume that staff is competent? If you do, then you allow discretion and use training and site-based management to improve quality. You let change percolate from the bottom up. If you don't trust staff, you try to set up fail-safe systems. Personally, I think a supportive philosophy works better than the 'gotcha' environment we have now, but I don't run the district. I just try to do my job."

If the mistrust is as widespread as these senior administrators tell us, I wonder how far any kind of thinking program could go in this district.

Shortly after his resignation, Superintendent Peck and I take a ride in his sports car.

"How do you focus a district like this?" I ask him.

"Well, you really can't," he says. "It's a hopeless proposition. When people try to run something like this from the top, they strangle the system in paper, bureaucracy, and meetings. About all you can do is provide vision and step aside and let people carry it out."

"What was your vision?"

He squints into the sun as he pulls out to pass a slow-moving vehicle.

"I guess it's an 'outcomes' vision," he says, "a curricular vision. I wanted to see lots more going on than basic skills, and of course I wanted to get rid of the achievement gap. But I had to start where the district was. We had to deal with the basic skills and had to develop the competency test first, so we could earn the right to do other, better things."

He passes some more cars.

"You know, we *had* to publish those test scores of ethnic groups, in order to know where we were starting from," he goes on. "That was incredibly hard to do. You don't know how hard I had to fight for that. The problem with the current system is that it focuses on processes, not results. We don't know or can't agree about results, so we mandate all kinds of processes: teach this or that, spend X number of hours doing this or that, follow this or that process, and document it all the way along. We regulate so much of the *doing*, but that doesn't seem to alter the results very much, so we regulate it more and more, always assuming that *teaching* and following various procedures are the same things as *learning*—which they're not. I guess what I've tried to do is get people to think about results instead of processes all the time."

We drive along quietly for a while.

"When we get to the results side of things, though," Peck says, "we seem stuck on test scores as the best measures of results, which they are not. So we've teamed up two bad proxies for achievement—processes and test scores—and they drive each other, while the real action happens elsewhere, and for other reasons. Process regulations, which have no bearing on achievement, are pushed to drive up test scores, which have no relation to learning, either. And, to top the irony, we don't even know that there is much of a relationship between the processes and the test results! It's like most of what we can do is out on the margins, not where the action is."

Peck seems relaxed and happy that he's not superintendent anymore. I ask him about his relationship with the school board: "When did it go sour?"

"The second night I was here," he says.

The board president, who had voted against hiring him, called him up at home to tell him what he was supposed to do about various administrative problems.

"I thanked her for her advice," he says, smiling, "and said I'd talk things over with the staff and we'd make some decisions. She blew up. She said she wasn't giving advice. She was telling me what had to be done. I told her I'd look into it. She yelled at me— *screamed* at me over the phone. So I hung up on her. I guess that's when things started to go sour."

He chuckles and pulls out to pass yet another car.

It strikes me after a while that NUPS is like a person traumatized by a great tragedy. The district seems to have turned in on itself, going over and over the tragedy, reliving it again and again, so obsessed that it has only very recently been able to put the tragedy behind it and begin to move toward a normal life. The tragedy in this case was that the district's leaders were found guilty of operating a segregated school system. They argued that segregation had happened accidentally, through the choices that people had made about where they wanted to live. But the court ruled that the segregation was a direct consequence of the school board's policies on such things as zoning, staff assignments, and pupil assignments.

For the next decade, people who ran for the school board did so on one issue: whether they were for or against busing. Board meetings focused almost entirely on the desegregation plans worked out by various judges and national experts, the problems people were having implementing them, and the progress of the board's latest effort to overturn the decision or some aspect of it. Nothing happened fast enough for activists in the minority communities, but everything was happening too fast for opponents of the desegregation effort. Desegregation became the principal—almost the only—educational policy concern of the community and the district, pushing concerns about curriculum and teaching to the margins, or quashing them entirely unless they had a racial angle. The school board developed the habit of being reactive and the tradition of being fractious. It became incapable of either exerting or accepting leadership.

With this sad history and its consequences in mind, Rona Wilensky and I start out to visit the schools where we have been told we can see thoughtfulness in action. We drive to an intermediate school (grades 4, 5, and 6) in an area of the city that is largely black and relatively poor: 80 percent of the students are minorities from what an administrator has referred to as "the lower quartile, both economically and academically." Nevertheless, Natalie Wilson has said that we will find some good instruction here in thinking, problem solving, and creativity. As we wait in the office to meet with the principal, Mr. Dione, I notice a prominent sign at the desk:

Office Responsibilities

1. Follow adult directions the first time given.
2. Keep hands and feet and objects to yourself.
3. Wait quietly at the counter until office personnel can help you.
4. Chairs are for *adults*!

Mr. Dione, a pleasant-looking white-haired, blue-eyed man dressed in a dapper pinstripe suit, comes out to greet us warmly. As we sit down in his small office, I notice a large, computer-generated sign over his desk: WE CAN AND WE WILL ACHIEVE. To the right of his desk is a collection of ceramic clowns; otherwise, his office contains very little. Dione has been in the system for thirty-three years. He came to this school two years ago and may retire at the end of the year, although he is not certain.

He tells us about the "High Achievement" classroom we are to visit, which he describes as "heterogeneous": it involves nine highly gifted students, bused in from around the city, and forty-one "regular" kids who represent, he believes, the full range of achievement. He tells us that now, in only the second year of the program, he is seeing an effect on the kids, whose interest in school has clearly risen. He believes that the latest test scores may well indicate an increase in achievement, but he's not sure.

I ask him what he would do if the test scores did not show increased achievement, and he says he would give the program more time and more room.

"The teachers aren't particularly well trained in this yet," he says. "I think they need more time, more inservice, and so on, to get good at this. I would give them more time before I would draw conclusions from the test."

The district uses the Iowa Test of Basic Skills, a nationally normed, standardized test, along with its own objectives-based test.

He tells us that he thinks the High Achievement classroom has had a spillover effect on the rest of the school. Other teachers have come to see what is happening.

"Some teachers, of course, are tied up in the system's lock-step reading curriculum," he says, "but others have started to ask questions about the High Achievement classroom and have gone and looked at it, and I think they are taking ideas back to their classrooms."

As we talk, I get the impression that Mr. Dione is relatively free of concern about the central office. When I ask him about this, he confirms it.

"No matter what goes on up there, with a school board, or a superintendent, or whatever," he says, shaking his head, "we'll keep things going down here. I think I speak for all the other principals, too. No matter what they do up there, we'll keep the schools running. We'll keep this dang district going, no matter what."

Mr. Dione is clearly as excited about the Assertive Discipline Program implemented at the school as he is about the High Achievement classroom. He can't resist telling us about it. Apparently, this school has had a reputation for years as a place where there are many fights and where few students are interested in education. Last year, a teacher who had heard about the Assertive Discipline Program in another district came to him and wondered if Mr. Dione would be interested in trying it in this school. He put the suggestion to the staff, and there was some interest. Someone came out and did an inservice training on the concept, and Dione believes that it has totally changed the atmosphere of the school. Indeed, as we walk around, we see signs everywhere, indicating students' responsibilities in every conceivable circumstance.

"I've got some teachers who've been here for nine and thirteen years," Dione tells us, "and they say this is the biggest change they've ever seen. I had a teacher who was going to be leaving. But she decided, after we began this program and she saw the results, that she would stay."

Apparently, establishing the Assertive Discipline Program involved getting the entire staff to state for the students, in writing, what their responsibilities are, to hold them to those responsibilities, and to enforce the program diligently. There was no particular magic to it; it was just a matter of getting all the teachers to agree to these steps, and the program seems to have improved the situation. There have been very few fights, by comparison to what there used to be. Students move quietly through the halls, Mr. Dione says (indeed, the school is very quiet), and everyone believes that an atmosphere conducive to learning has finally been established. (See Hill, 1990, for a broader perspective on assertive discipline.)

When we ask Mr. Dione what policy-related matters make it difficult for him to maintain learning as the center of his school's agenda and to improve achievement, he says immediately that his greatest frustration is his inability to hire and fire his own teachers.

"No other job I can think of in this country is so frustrating as this one, where you're the boss, but you're not able to hire or fire your employees," he says. "Fifteen out of my twenty-seven teachers here are on probation for various reasons. But if I really wanted to turn the school around, I would need to be able to get my own people."

Mr. Dione takes us up to the High Achievement classroom, where we meet Marion Walden and Beamy Bruster. It's hard to tell, with all the coming and going, but it appears that about fifteen to twenty students are minorities, and the remaining thirty or so are Anglos.

Ms. Walden greets us and begins to chat with us as children

move around, talking and working in various groups. She has frosted hair, dramatically swept to one side, and long, dangly black earrings.

"You know, I really don't see myself as a traditional teacher," she says. "I'm really more of a facilitator. I do very little direct teaching."

A student interrupts to ask her where to find more construction paper. A girl has made cat's whiskers out of straws and glued them under her nose; she wants to know if they look okay.

"I learn so much from the kids," Ms. Walden goes on. "So many teachers see it the other way around, that they've got all the knowledge. But I sure don't see it that way."

As if to illustrate a point, she extends her hand to the groups of students doing different projects. Some of them are building a balsa-wood structure that will have to be subjected to a weight test in the "Odyssey of the Mind" contest, coming up this weekend. Four boys seem deeply engaged in a discussion about the merits of a new idea that one of them has sketched on a piece of paper. Some students are making costumes, others are rehearsing for various skits, and many are coming and going so regularly that it is hard to tell who belongs here and who does not. In the next room, we are told, some students are practicing brainstorming; across the hall, others are studying Renaissance painting.

Ms. Walden constantly speaks of her students as being "gifted." The principal has not told us that this is a gifted-and-talented program; maybe he figured we knew. I'm a little disappointed because I'm looking for programs for heterogeneous groups.

After a few minutes, Walden wanders off with some students, and so I sit down with Beamy Bruster, who seems more down-to-earth. Ms. Bruster is a heavyset, "drill sergeant" kind of teacher, one you would not expect to find in this kind of setting. She is wearing brown polyester pants and a green shirt, not tucked in.

"This is so scary for me!" she says.

"What do you mean?" I ask.

"Well," she says, "I've been a sixth-grade teacher for years, and I'm the kind of teacher that likes things organized—now it's time for social studies, now it's time for science, and so on. That's how I've always taught, so this business of having no regular lessons and so little order really worries me. I worry about whether or not we're factually oriented enough."

A couple of kids come up and ask her for some materials that they need. She sends them off with a key and turns back to me.

"But then I look at their projects, and I realize that they're learning all kinds of factual things in order to do these projects. And I do believe that we should start with kids' interests. It seems to make a big difference. So I know they're learning, and I like being a resource person, rather than always being a 'this is it' kind of teacher. But it's hard. I worry about it a lot."

I ask her about reading and about how, when kids are constantly doing projects, she can tell whether they're reading much.

"It's obvious, from the projects, whether kids have read a book," she responds.

And it seems to her that they're reading all the time. They've started a "great books" program here, and she enjoys it and thinks that the kids are good readers by and large, even when they come in.

"You have to let them discover. You know, I've really learned a lot from this. The more they discover, the more power they feel, and the more self-confident they get. And the more power they feel, and the more self-confident they get, the more they learn."

As my discussions with these teachers and students proceed, this group of kids appears less and less heterogeneous. The two teachers tell me that all fifty children have been drawn from the top .05 percent of the students; these teachers are not dealing with any young people who are poorly prepared or at high risk for failure.

Ms. Walden gives me a chronicle of her history in the district. She was very surprised that someone "as low on the totem pole" as herself was given this job. The district says that High Achievement teachers are "experienced master teachers" who have received "intensive training," but she was just a substitute teacher, with a personality that another principal (not Mr. Dione) thought would be suitable to the more chaotic High Achievement classroom environment. Ms. Walden was given five days of inservice training and says she reads everything she can get her hands on. In addition, Donald

Davis, the school's official teacher of gifted children, has been very helpful to her.

I ask her if only so-called gifted kids can do the kinds of things that she is doing with these kids—things that involve the students far more in decisions about their work, that involve analysis and problem solving and much more active learning than most students experience. She says she imagines that all kids can do these things.

"But I don't think all teachers can," she adds. "That's the problem. Not the kids, but teachers. Most teachers can't operate this way."

As I talk to the kids, I don't see that they have much in common at all. The range of differences seems as broad as it is in any other classroom. These students do, however, seem to like doing school-type work more than other kids do, and they seem more competitive than most. This is like noticing that the match between what the football coach wants to do and what his players want to do—play football—is particularly close. Gifted and talented kids represent that small group of students who are intellectually engaged and competitive, just as athletes represent that small group of students who are athletically engaged and competitive. What distinguishes these kids from others is their interest in the *game of schooling*, a game defined in intellectual terms. These kids will at least get a shot at thinking and problem solving, because it is assumed that they like that sort of thing. It is not assumed that most kids like intellectual work, and so most kids are given something else to do, something that turns out to be boring because it does not tap what interests them.

Rona Wilensky and I eat burritos with Donald Davis, Ms. Walden, Ms. Bruster, and an art teacher from a private school who works with them once a week. Rona and I get the general impression that they work well as a team. Nevertheless, they say that the "spillover" into regular classes, which the principal has talked about, is not occurring. They feel that teachers in the rest of the school are not very happy about what they are doing. Ms. Bruster says that other teachers believe the High Achievement classroom has "robbed the school of all its good intellect and left them with the dregs."

Mr. Davis tells us that what the High Achievement classroom is doing is "on the cutting edge of school reform. Look at what the program features," he says, reading from a brochure: " 'High-level thinking; interrelationships between and among bodies of knowledge, using content areas that offer appropriate challenge; integration of intellectual, social, and emotional domains; self-directed learning; and independent study assignments.' Isn't that what school reform and restructuring are supposed to be about?"

But he says that other teachers do not visit his or the High Achievement classes. Not many of them have asked for information about how to do what these teachers are doing, nor does the principal encourage visits. More than any of the other teachers, Davis believes that what is happening in "gifted" education could happen throughout the school, and he is intensely interested in seeing some such diffusion of active learning take place.

At the moment, though, "neither the incentives nor the leadership you'd need exist in this school."

As we listen to these teachers, we realize that, while they would welcome other teachers who came to them, it does not occur to them to make any special effort to go out to the other teachers and spread the word more actively about what they are doing. And, when you think about it, it seems that the ideology and packaging of "gifted" programs are at odds with any notion that all children could benefit from the kinds of experiences offered in the High Achievement classroom. The most knowledgeable people in the field, like Donald Davis, understand that what they are doing can benefit all children. On the next level down, however, are people who believe, for their own reasons, in giftedness—something that, by definition, only a few children can have. They have come to believe that the techniques developed to deal with these gifts are unique. Ironically, school districts have put themselves in a bind by advertising their "gifted" classrooms as places where (to quote the High Achievement brochure) "an integrated curriculum approach is used . . . and higher-level thinking skills are emphasized throughout the curriculum." If Mr. Davis and Ms. Walden are right—that all students can benefit from this kind of instruction—and if it is extended to all students, what will be so special about the "gifted" programs? Keeping such programs special turns out to be particularly important in urban districts that are trying to hold on to middle-class white families. Could it be, Rona and I wonder, that the district's policies about gifted-and-talented programs work to limit the number of such programs and to inhibit the spread of their curriculum and instruction to mainstream classes?

After seeing the High Achievement classroom, I go to visit the district's gifted-and-talented (G&T) coordinator, Pat Ashton. She is a middle-aged woman whose dark hair is pulled tightly into a bun. She seems either very tired or depressed. We sit in a darkening office, in a remote district outpost where coordinators, librarians, curriculum specialists, and staff developers are housed.

"We've gotten too far away from academics in this district," she tells me. "There's way too much emphasis on basic skills and facts and stuff that's easy to teach and test. It's unbelievable what's happened over the last ten to fifteen years."

"How did this happen?" I ask.

"I don't know," she says. "Kids don't like academics, I guess. And a lot of teachers don't, either. I put my daughter into a G&T program because she was so bored by the ordinary classroom, and I got tired of all the put-downs of intellect in her school."

Once her daughter was in G&T, Pat took an interest in the field and gravitated toward it professionally.

"It's a frustrating area, though," she says sadly. "High burn-out rate, lots of hassles."

"For instance?"

"Well, you're always battling with someone—regular teachers, policymakers, pushy parents. Regular teachers view G&T as a frill course, or some kind of inequity. Some see it as a put-down of their own ability to meet the needs of their kids. They don't see how you could do any better than they do. Policymakers don't understand what it's all about. They think it's elitist. They either hate it or love it because it's elitist. And bureaucrats hate it because they hate to make *exceptions*; exceptions always screw up the system. We're always screwing up schedules, see? Bus schedules, building schedules, class schedules, counselors' schedules. Those are all supposed to come first. We were supposed to participate in the Shakespeare Festival last fall. But we had to back out because we couldn't get buses to take the kids over to the mall. I had a bunch of kids in the "mathletics" competition. The bus supervisor said he couldn't give me buses at the time I needed them. I drove the kids over myself—which is against district rules, you know. If I had had an accident, I wouldn't be covered by district insurance. It's 'Catch-22.' You're allowed to get the kids places, but you're not allowed to get the kids places."

She says all of this without emotion, in a monotone. This is just how things are.

"And try to get kids out of classes when testing is going on— and it's going on all the time," she continues. "And if you give up and stay in the building, you have to pay the custodian $28 an hour to sit and wait for your meeting to end. So they get you one way or another. You're a captive of the building, really; a captive of the schedules. So a lot of things you might think of to do with bright kids—things in the community, things in different environments or places—forget it!"

These kinds of problems turn out to militate against integrating students into activities like the "Odyssey of the Mind," too. Minority students live in one part of town, Anglos in the other. Rules about when and where school buses can run make it impossible for integrated teams to practice, unless a teacher is willing to violate school policy by driving the students to their far-flung homes.

I ask Pat Ashton about the program's policy decisions and get another earful. She has just had a meeting with administrators this morning, about adopting the Philosophy for Children program, a high-quality course of readings and discussions that has been adopted in over five thousand classrooms around the world.

"You should have been there," she says. "It was classic. The assistant superintendents, the subject area coordinators, a couple of curriculum people, and me. We've been studying this for months. First question: 'Won't we get sued by some fundamentalists for this kind of thing?' Next question—from Natalie Wilson: 'How does this fit into our basal-reader program?' Of course, all of the curriculum people wanted the program in their area or not at all. Where do you put a philosophy course? We don't have a place for it. It's not on the map. Then somebody says we shouldn't affiliate with the university on this—that's one of the requirements of the program, that you have to coordinate with a philosopher in a university. 'Isn't that elitist?' somebody says. This is what I mean about put-downs, see. These people think philosophers are bad people or something. They don't see what they might have to do with education."

"So what finally happened?" I ask.

"They tabled it. They voted to study all the other possible thinking-skills programs commercially available and then decide."

Saying this, she finally allows herself the slightest smile.

Fletcher Middle School is a large, 1950s-style school nestled in a very comfortable, affluent neighborhood. It has the reputation and characteristics and even the look of a suburban school, but its population is about 55 percent minority and includes a good number of bilingual students. Its student body falls into two classes: students from wealthy homes in the area, and students from very poor homes who are bused in. I am greeted by Dr. Holmes, the principal, who turns me over quickly to the assistant principal. She tells me that Rona and I are to spend the day with an eighth-grade team, and she takes me to the room of Ms. Francis, a mathematics teacher, who greets me nonchalantly. She wears no makeup and is dressed in something close to a house dress, with shoes that are close to slippers. She has just taken the "Math Counts" team to a first-place win in the metropolitan area and to seventh place in the state. This period is her "Math Counts" period, a sort of enrichment-study hall period devoted to special kinds of activities for students. She explains that the kids have been letting off steam since returning from the competition, and she's been letting them do other things; they have earned their stripes.

She plays a videotape called *The Man Who Loved Numbers*, about a mathematician named Ramanujan. I find the tape interesting, but of the sixteen students there, it appears that only half a dozen or so agree with me. Many of the others talk quietly to each other or do various other kinds of work. The classroom is spare in its decoration, with the exception of posters featuring animals that seem sympathetic to the perspective of students. I realize that I see these in schools all over the country—pictures of shar-peis or basset hounds, with statements like "Hang on, Baby, Friday's coming," and so on.

As the videotape goes on, kids come into and leave the room, and Ms. Francis works with an individual student or two at her desk. When the tape is over, there is some mumbling but no structured discussion at all. Ms. Francis passes out a diagram on graph paper and says, "What do you think that is?" Then she quietly walks among the students as, one by one, they take guesses. Again, it is not very structured; but, sooner or later, several kids figure out that it is a way of showing the Pythagorean theorem. Ms. Francis mentions casually that there are 370 ways to illustrate the Pythagorean theorem, and then tells the students to take the drawing home and think about it.

Class ends, and we go off with Ms. Francis to the teachers' lounge, where we're joined by Anne Hopkins, the social studies teacher on the team. She has just been working on a newspaper, written and produced by students, for the fifth and sixth graders, who will be coming next week for their orientation. (The sixth grade will be joining the seventh and eighth next year, to complete the middle school.)

"They're going to get it translated into Spanish," she says.

Rona asks if students will do the translation. The teacher seems surprised by this idea and says there simply isn't time to have students do the translation.

We talk a little about the transition from a junior high school to a middle school, and the teachers seem to be satisfied with how it has gone. They like teams, and they think the parents' conferences are enhanced when parents can talk to several teachers at once. These teachers have had only a three-day inservice training, however, to prepare them for the middle school. There are inservices coming up on how to do interdisciplinary units and on whole-language instruction. Meanwhile, it appears that the teachers have had to figure things out for themselves.

They say they have not been able to do much in the way of interdisciplinary teaching, simply because they are so intent on preparing their own subjects and because schedules make it very difficult to coordinate. Now and then, a science-and-math "thing" can be done, or one in English and social studies, but the teachers have never attempted a four-person theme approach to anything, and they find it unlikely that they ever will. They know that the middle school is supposed to be oriented toward the developmental needs of children and to be less academic than a junior high, and they know that high school teachers prefer the old academic orientation.

They themselves seem more like junior high teachers than middle school teachers—more interested in their subjects and in preparing students for the academic trials ahead of them. Certainly, Ms. Francis sees herself as a mathematics teacher, and a good one, not as a child-development specialist. She feels that she has to teach algebra, and because algebra does not blend in with other subjects, she finds it hard to be interdisciplinary. Timing is also an important constraint on being interdisciplinary.

Ms. Hopkins thinks that the district's competency objectives in American history constrain her efforts to be interdisciplinary and to develop the kinds of thematic units she might like to do. As she speaks, it's not clear to whom or what she is referring when she talks about the district curriculum. She seems to be talking about some vague somebody, somewhere downtown—somebody who has imposed these objectives in the past and will now be changing the curriculum, so that next year it will not cover the entire span of American history. Why this person may have changed it, how it may have been changed—none of this seems clear.

As we talk with the teachers about tracking (or ability grouping) in the school, something that middle schools are philosophically disinclined to do, they all mention the social pressure among black children not to succeed. Ms. Francis says that many times she has seen talented black students leave her mathematics courses—not because they couldn't do the work, but because they were losing their friends, and they needed to be with their friends and be popular. Everyone shares a similar story.

Ms. Francis says that she operates on a mastery system and believes that students should have multiple opportunities to get it right. Students may not know something on the day you schedule the test, but they may be able to come back later and understand.

She lets anyone into her algebra class who wants to be there. Kids who have not been recommended have still been successful. She says she has lots of faith that kids can learn, and they know she won't give up on them. They know she will provide them with help if they are willing to do the work. The ones who don't make it are ones who are not willing to work. She teaches the class in a way that doesn't assume prealgebra skills, in order to admit those who haven't been prepped in seventh grade. She also works with and stays in touch with parents, so that they know what's going on.

Ms. Francis organizes her classes into a high-ability group and other, heterogeneous groups. She won't have a low-ability group. The algebra group and the prealgebra group can't be together, because they are learning different things, but she doesn't separate the slow ones from the prealgebra group. If she did, they wouldn't see other students doing their homework, and there would be no peers to help them.

According to Ms. Francis, it is a waste of time to focus on basic skills. Students should be allowed to use calculators when they are taking standardized tests. The focus on basic skills detracts from the thinking aspects of math. All in all, there should be less arithmetic. Unfortunately, there are no good books written for that type of math, and the teacher who wants to do it has to create all the materials herself. That puts too great a burden on the teacher.

We are joined by Dianne Bruner, the English teacher, and Mitch Brant, the science teacher. There is some discussion of class size, which will be going up to thirty or thirty-five students next year. The teachers feel that, although the district has lowered pupil-to-teacher ratios in the elementary schools, the ratios have been raised in the middle schools. As I visit the classes, however, I seldom see more than twenty to twenty-four kids in a room, and so I wonder if this fear of huge classrooms is really justified.

We talk a bit about what the teachers mean by the term *high* as applied to general classes. The social studies teacher says that a "high" American history class would use a better book. The one she's using now has only three pages on the Civil War. She needs a better one to teach a "high" class. To earn an A in her class, it is not sufficient just to do the regular assignments; you must also do extra-credit projects. These projects call for more thinking skills. In the past, there were lots of students doing the projects, but this year there is only one, a girl embroidering a map. This teacher's attitude seems to be that the way classes go depends on the luck of the draw; she does not see her responsibility as interesting students in special projects. One special assignment this year was to consider the question "What if Lincoln hadn't died?" and the effect he might have had on Reconstruction. When I ask why all the students weren't asked to do this, the teacher looked as if it had never occurred to her to ask them. She thought for a minute and said, "I want them to do the basic assignments first."

The science teacher suggests that *high* means extra credit, more complicated laboratory work, and different texts that provoke more thought. He already uses a standardized test to select students for what he considers his "high" science class. He also says that he grades "high" students differently, by a different standard. He feels that the transition to being a middle school has diminished the emphasis on academics. Teachers are expected to cover a tremendous amount of material, because of the district's minimum-competency exam, as well as meeting lots of other needs. This teacher finds himself hurrying through the book, so that he can familiarize students with the vocabulary they will need for the exam. Since the exam asks for factual recall, he feels that he has to drill students on that, and that slower students will not get the basics by being taught higher-level skills.

For Ms. Francis, what *high* means is very obvious. It refers to algebra students and others whose math is clearly beyond the usual level for middle school.

As we talk, we learn that the English teacher has been taking a course in critical thinking and questioning, and that she is excited about it. A couple of other teachers in the room have also been taking it and are equally excited. One shows me a book she is reading on the "junior great books." This critical-thinking initiative seems to have been started by teachers and encouraged by John Orwell; it is based on the instrumental enrichment approach of Reuven Feuerstein. One man at this school has apparently had a good deal of training in it, and other teachers have seen the results. Thus, by word of mouth, this approach is spreading in this school. There is no official policy, but people clearly feel that John Orwell is supportive.

Ms. Bruner, the English teacher, is just coming back to work after having raised her children. She doesn't know what she should expect her students to know, and she doesn't know how to find out. When she left teaching, there had been lay readers, who helped grade compositions. Now there are none, and their absence affects what she does. As an eighth-grade teacher, she feels obliged to correct every mistake her students make, but that takes time, and she can't assign as many papers as she would like to. She would prefer to provide opportunities for students just to write about their thoughts. She thinks they would benefit more, but she can't reconcile this idea with her belief that she should correct every mistake, and she thinks the parents will be upset if she does not.

I go to her English class and watch her work with twenty-one students. She has them read segments of a story. At frequent intervals, she asks them what's going on, what the character might be thinking, what the character's motives might be, what might happen, and so on. The format is basically recitation, although she is trying to do some questioning along the lines of what she has been learning in the course on critical thinking and inquiry.

"Can you rephrase that?" she asks some students when they give answers or read passages. "How would you compare his attitude here to his attitude at the beginning of the story? Have you ever seen an example of someone doing this in your life?"

She has said in the teachers' lounge that she's trying hard not to answer her own questions. But I can see that she still has that tendency and is still nervous about waiting very long for a response. Nevertheless, she conducts a capable, one-at-a-time class discussion about the text, and I am persuaded that any student who paid attention—and I would say that fifteen of them probably did—would have deeper comprehension of the story as a consequence of the way she has made them think about it. She still has not mastered the art of getting kids to talk with one another or going beyond one-at-a-time questions or letting students pursue a particular idea. Because the discourse frame is primarily recitation and everything has to go through her, she cannot expand the discussion as much as she would like to. At the end of the class, she passes out composition assignments, to the accompaniment of some moans and groans. One kids says, "Do we have to do this?" She says, "Yes." He says, "But we had a good discussion," as if that should be sufficient.

I go to Ms. Hopkins's social studies class, where many of the students are the same ones I have just seen in the English class. Ms. Hopkins begins class with a discussion of immigration to the United States. It is based on their homework assignment and on readings in their textbook. Suddenly a kid says, "That's just like Japan," and the teacher is somewhat startled, unprepared for a discussion of the relationship between immigration at the end of the nineteenth century and immigration today. Nevertheless, a discussion about Japan begins to flower as various students speak up on what they know about Japan; perhaps they also saw the series on Japan that I watched on television the other night. But they seem quite knowledgeable, and very soon they are talking about Japanese education.

Ms. Hopkins clearly has an opportunity for an interesting discussion about parallels between the past and the present, as well as about education, if she wants to depart from the lesson plan for a moment, because there is a lot of animation in the room, and most of the kids seem to have heard something about education in Japan. I see her struggling with this temptation, sensing the possibilities, but she quickly decides that she cannot let the discussion go in this direction. She kills it with some "know it all" generalizations that quell the students' energy and dampen their enthusiasm. The teacher begins to move on, but the discussion about Japan has stirred the kids up, and when she mentions a show about immigration that was on television last week, it only gets them going again. This time, however, several also remember a recently broadcast interview with Charles Manson.

"We're not talking about Charles Manson," she says. "Haven't gotten there yet." The implication is that she wants to talk about the past before she talks about the present.

She then introduces a filmstrip called *Visions from America*. It is a very saccharine, almost jingoistic production about poor immigrants who come to this land, have a hard time at Ellis Island, have hard times finding work, but are happy together. Papa works, Mama works, the children sell bread. Papa gets a plan. He saves money and starts his own store, then sends his children to school; and now the store is in the hands of the narrator, and the general feeling is that everything has gone according to the American Dream. As the narrator looks back on this wonderful experience, it seems to him that his family's poverty, not to mention the discrimination and the injustice they faced, were good for them because it made them work harder. There is no discussion of this filmstrip. I suspect that a good many eighth graders see it as somewhat unrealistic, but I'll never know.

Ms. Hopkins turns now to a political cartoon in the textbook. It shows rich people keeping immigrants out of the country, but behind the rich people are the shadows of their own immigrant forebears, all of them poor and carrying little sacks and bags, as if no wealthy person has ever come to this country. She does get a good discussion going about the meaning of the cartoon, despite her desire for specific answers to her questions. (*"That's* what I was looking for!" she often says.)

Meanwhile, Rona Wilensky is observing Ms. Francis again as she works with prealgebra students of mixed ability. Here are Rona's notes:

> The room is pretty stark. The chairs face forward. The walls are mostly empty. The board has some information on the week's program.
>
> *Get out your homework, pass it up. You'll need a ruler. Help yourself.*
>
> *Look at what I'm handing out. You'll have five minutes to study it and write down your observations on a separate sheet or on the back. You must write it down:*
>
> *Observe relationships.*
> *Explore it.*
> *Use your ruler.*
> *I will ask everybody.*
> *Look at areas of figures.*
> *What kinds of figures?*
> *Count squares.*
> *Be precise.*
> *Think of other ways to measure than with a ruler.*
> *Compare things. Which sides are longer? What's the same?*
> *You're a detective, you can do it.*
> *Keep looking.*
> *If you don't look, you can't find it.*
> *You may use a calculator, of course.*

*I don't care about grades. Do you? Yes? Well, then, it counts.
We're going to share.*

After about ten minutes, she begins the discussion.
She always calls on individual students; she does not
respond to hand-waving. By the end of the class, she
has called on almost everyone to make an observation
or go over familiar ground. She asks questions and
waits for answers. She reformulates questions and
waits. When necessary, she goes back to some earlier,
easier step and asks another question and waits. When
she tells the class something, it is based on what a
student has said. She accepts all answers. She pushes
for precision. She stays in front of the room. If someone disagrees, she goes back and works it out. Only at
the end of the period did I sense the need to get on
with it. She doesn't allow students to leap ahead of the
class and shout out the ultimate answer, which is the
formula of the Pythagorean theorem. She tells the student trying to show off, "I want everyone to have a
chance." At the end of the class, she praises them for
a job well done.

Not all the students were engaged. Not all listened as carefully as they might have to each other.
But she was unrelenting in her method of asking questions and waiting for answers. She made students talk
about what they knew and made them make their
answers precise.

She did not use the chalkboard but, instead, an
overhead projector with an erasable screen. This allowed her to face the students all the time.

This was not a class of the best and the bright-
est. But she made all of them work and pushed all of
them to discover the relationships for themselves. It is
clear that they have had little experience manipulating and playing with shapes and figures. They have
no intuitive sense of space and objects, and so her
work is that much harder.

Her manner isn't warm and engaging. At first,
she seems bored and plain. But she is perhaps the best
teacher I have seen so far and by far the best teacher
I observed in her school.

I return to the teachers' lounge, where a discussion is going
on about the difference between the English class that I observed
and one that Rona observed, which did not go nearly so well, since
the students were "smarter" and could not be focused on the text.
Ms. Bruner is angry about how the so-called smarter kids, who "are
supposed to be able to do all this thinking stuff better than other
kids," get so wild and creative and opinionated that their discussions are not any fun.

"No one ever listens to anyone else," she says. "They just
keep saying the same thing over and over, and it drives me crazy."

I end the day by going to observe Mr. Marshall, the teacher
of thinking. He is a black man with wire-rim glasses, a bit of a
paunch, and a very casual, relaxed, intelligent approach to kids.
Unlike the other teachers, he introduces Rona and me, asks us to
say a word or two, and gives the students an opportunity to ask us
some questions. The students want to know where we got our degrees and if we know any famous athletes. Mr. Marshall then proceeds to tell them about his trip to New Orleans, where he has been
observing thinking programs.

At first, this seems like a wonderful idea, but he turns it into
a lecture and recitation (about rivers and levees and so on) that is
rather disjointed and unstructured, although it is punctuated with
thinking-type questions: "Why do you suppose they would bury
people above the ground? Why would they name something Canal
Street?" Around the room are signs: IMPULSIVENESS STOPS EFFECTIVE
THINKING. MY THINKING DETERMINES THE QUALITY OF MY EDUCA-
TION. The "Success Path" is also posted; it is a twelve-part list of
things that lead to success.

Mr. Marshall does reinforce thinking, and when students get
confused, he asks them to stop for a moment, think about what they
want to say, and try again; but this is not a particularly inspiring
class. Several of the students pay no attention at all and are even
rude when he calls on them. These are Hispanic guys who mumble

to each other in Spanish and whose manner, dress, and every gesture dramatize their rebellion.

Rona and I come away from Fletcher Middle School thinking about how profound the changes are that people are trying to make in schools, and how superficial the attempts are to train people, whether teachers or administrators, to deal with these changes. Consider the philosophical underpinnings of the middle school, its dependence on a thorough knowledge of developmental theory. Now consider that the teachers have had only five days of inservice training on what a middle school is, with very little follow-up. You begin to see why there is a widespread feeling in this school district of having tried all kinds of things that haven't worked. The real question we ponder as we leave is whether anything has ever really been tried very thoroughly.

The academic model that made the junior high school popular among the affluent parents clearly remains the model that the school wants to pursue, regardless of the middle school–oriented philosophy. It is also obvious that many teachers, who speak articulately about the need to challenge the children of the poor, find it very difficult to actually do so. They seem not to believe that these children will ever really catch up or be able to perform as well as the middle-class and affluent children do.

I also cannot help noticing how important it is to teachers to have a "high" class; it is a measure of success and status in the school. Regardless of what the literature says, and regardless of policies to the contrary, I suspect that, among teachers, the need for a hierarchy of students is as inevitable as the need for a hierarchy of teachers. Like other groups of people in large, bureaucratic organizations, they create such hierarchies, whether we want them to or not. Teachers apparently estimate their own quality and esteem according to how they view the quality and esteem of their students. If they cannot distinguish themselves from one another in terms of real capital (as people in the private sector can), they will distinguish themselves in terms of what symbolic capital they can find.

A year later, I have an opportunity to return to Fletcher. Things are not going well. As it does every year, the district has shuffled principals around. In some districts, this is called "the dance of the lemons," an annual ritual intended to ensure that good and bad principals are equitably distributed and shared by all. Urban school boards generally do not like principals to be in one place for more than four or five years. They say that this policy maximizes principals' talents and keeps them from getting into a rut or burning out. One assignment is apparently perceived to be about the same as another, which tells you something about the job. Principals are not consulted about the shuffling. It is as likely that a bad principal will be moved out, to the staff's delight, as it is that a great principal will be transferred, to the staff's dismay. Cynics say the policy is designed to prevent any principal from building a power base with teachers and parents that might threaten central control of a school.

In any case, Fletcher's principal has been replaced by a black woman, who was previously the principal of a largely minority middle school in a less affluent part of town. The assistant principals have been replaced by a white woman and a Hispanic man from two other middle schools that are reputed to be doing good work with minority students.

I go to meet with them one morning, having heard already that they've been ambushed by a coalition of teachers and parents. Apparently the teachers, including the social studies teacher whom Rona and I met last year, have gone to parents in the neighborhood with worries that the new principal is going to "lower standards" at Fletcher and *really* turn it into a middle school. They did this during the summer, before they had even met the new principal and her staff.

When I arrive, I see a big new sign in the hall opposite the principal's office: HIGH EXPECTATIONS, HIGH CONTENT, AND HIGH SUPPORT. This is the agenda of the new principal, Sarah Knight. The "three highs" have been encouraged by the Edna McConnell Clark Foundation, in New York, which has been awarding large grants to improve the quality of education offered to young people at risk in urban middle schools. Several NUPS middle schools applied for grants in the spring and had to go through a proposal-development process that involved the entire staff and forced them to think creatively about their programs.

Research shows that expectations for poor and minority

children are often lower than they are for other children. Our interviews and observations in this district a year ago certainly confirmed this finding. We were told that poor students had all kinds of problems that made them poor students: short attention spans, poorly developed social skills, fatherless families, bookless homes, depressing neighborhoods, bad role models, cultural dispositions favoring concreteness, low self-esteem, hostility toward the majority culture, physical and psychological abuse, emotional problems stemming from prejudice and racism, to name a few. These concerns were used to justify a focus on low content: basic skills, drill, memorization, seatwork, "dumbed down" materials, and instruction that was at times embarrassingly patronizing and undemanding. Low expectations lead to impoverished content and bad teaching, both of which lead to low performance, which is then used to justify the low expectations and content. This is the cycle that the Clark Foundation is intent on breaking.

Although none of the NUPS schools received grants, Sarah Knight remains impressed with last spring's proposal process and how it brought people together. She is enthusiastic about going through it with her new staff and using the "three highs" as a way of further solidifying the district's commitment to the middle school philosophy. But it is this interest in the "three highs" that landed her in trouble before she even arrived at the school.

I go into the outer office. Ms. Knight has the social studies teacher and one other teacher in her own office. The door is closed, but I can hear their raised voices. After twenty minutes, the teachers leave in something of a huff, and Ms. Knight comes out to greet me. She is an attractive and very intelligent-looking woman who communicates great warmth and a sense of humor, even when she has just had an uncomfortable meeting and is under stress. She rounds up her two assistant principals, and we go to an empty classroom, where they all throw themselves into chairs and heave great sighs. One of the assistants, Mary Lansing, is shaking her head and gritting her teeth. She is clearly angry and frazzled. The other, Ed Sandoval, puts his head in his hands. Knight looks at them and smiles ironically.

"We're having a tough day," she says.

"Tough day?" Ms. Lansing moans. "We're having a tough year!"

I ask them to tell me their story. It seems that last night they met with their accountability committee, a group of parents and other citizens from the neighborhood. Accountability committees, established by the state legislature as part of school reform, are supposed to hold their schools accountable to their communities' norms and expectations. In this case, the norms and expectations are opposed to the middle school philosophy and to much that it stands for.

"The parents said that they want tracking to continue," Ms. Knight says. "They want 'high' algebra classes, 'high' geometry classes, and the semantics classes to go on as always: no watering down with kids who 'don't belong there.' "

"It was unbelievable," Ms. Lansing says. "They'd been prepped. They knew everything we were going to say, and they already had an answer for it."

"Some teachers live in the neighborhood," Mr. Sandoval says, "and they held a meeting in one of their houses two nights ago with some of the key parents. They scared the hell out of them."

"We would say, 'The research says this,' and someone would stand up and say, 'The research says *that!* ' " Ms. Lansing says. "Where did parents get hold of this research?"

"They wanted us to drop the bilingual program," Ms. Knight says. "In fact, they wanted us to drop the whole middle school model."

Suddenly, there is a violent eruption in the hall outside, as classes change. A girl is shrieking at someone: "You have no *right* to treat me like that! You have no *right* to push me around. I've *had* it with you!" The air is suddenly charged with menace, and the three administrators rush into the hall to calm things down. After a couple of minutes they return, shaking their heads.

"What an age. Always ready to pop."

They make light of it; people who work with early adolescents get used to outbursts. But I'm still shaken by the tone in the girl's voice, the primitiveness of her anger and hurt. What is it like to deal with this so often that you get used to it? What would it be like if your children remained early adolescents year after year, forever?

We return to the subject of the accountability committee's meeting. The greatest fear of the middle-class parents is that the junior high school, in the course of becoming a middle school and accommodating children bused in from poor neighborhoods, will lower its standards and render middle-class students uncompetitive when they get to high school. The parents do not trust the school district.

"They told me that they knew I had been sent here to destroy the last good school in the system," Ms. Knight says. "And they weren't going to let me. They said they knew I was sent here to get rid of the teachers who had made Fletcher a great school. I assume that meant the teachers who had met with them the night before."

"Teachers were there, too, you know," Ms. Lansing says. "One of them stood up and said she knew there were a few 'bad' teachers in the school who were only giving 100 percent, instead of the 200 percent that she and the rest were giving. She said she and the others didn't have a spare minute left in their day for more change. Nothing new could be done without losing something that shouldn't be lost."

"What did you tell them?" I ask Ms. Knight.

"I tried to just listen and take notes. I've told them all that I want to know what's happening here before I start new things. I want to be a listener. But Charleen [the new assistant superintendent for middle schools, who had just replaced John Orwell] told me I'd better say something, or they'd eat me for lunch. So I told them I thought we were not meeting the needs of all the children in the school. I told them we needed to get rid of dull, boring remedial classes, and we could do this in ways that wouldn't water anything down. I told them we need to challenge all students more. And I told them that the NUPS was committed to middle schools and had been moving toward middle schools for eight years. So then, you know what this parent said?"

She laughs just thinking about it.

"Nobody's ever asked me a question like this. He says, 'What's your role, Ms. Knight? To speak for the board of education, or to speak for us parents?' I was dumbfounded. I told him the board pays my salary, *and* I want to speak for parents. Wrong answer. Not good enough."

"What they really want," Ms. Lansing says, "is to withdraw from the NUPS. They want to be a 'school of choice,' like President Bush talks about, they said. They want this to be *their* school, not the district's."

"One of our parents, near the end of the meeting—and he's probably the most influential one there—said if we did not back away from this middle school thing, he was going to take his girls out and send them to private school," says Ms. Knight. She shakes her head sadly. "White flight," she says. "Here we go again."

I visit Lyndon Baines Johnson High School, an "alternative learning center" for students who have dropped or been thrown out of regular schools. I'm met by the principal, Harold Jackson, a heavyset, pleasant-faced black man with a warm handshake and clear eyes. After a while, I notice that he has a prosthetic left arm, with a hook at the end.

We go into his office, a very homey place, and he asks me to sit down at a round table.

"I don't know about you," he says, "but I've spent so much of my life working around a kitchen table that I put one in my office to work around."

He laughs. There are many books in the office and various signs (HONOR YOURSELF WITHIN) on the wall, pictures of him and his family, names of students—it's a friendly office.

As long as the door is open, students wander in and out. While we're talking, for instance, a girl walks in.

"I'm here," she says.

And he says, "Fine, go to your blue class."

She walks off, and he turns to me.

"Now, she hasn't been here for days," he says. "I don't know where she's been. But, you see, she had to come in and just tell me she was here. She's telling me something."

Shortly afterward, a boy walks in and asks the principal to sign something. After the boy leaves, Mr. Jackson says, "Now, did you notice he's an Oglala Lakota? You notice how he walked into my office? It was difficult for him. You have to be attentive to nuance. You really have to be able to read what they are telling you. That's why we have the first of our three mottoes: 'Learning must go on at all times.' "

I ask him about the second motto.

"It's 'Respect. Respect for yourself, and respect for others.' The third major rule is 'No fighting, no drugs.' "

Mr. Jackson, who has been teaching for twenty-seven years, believes that good teachers are catalysts and facilitators. Their job is to be good listeners, to figure out what a particular kid needs at a particular time and the particular way to give it to him. He thinks administrators make it very hard for teachers to be creative or innovative. If he had his way, he would turn teachers and students loose—on the city, for instance.

"The city's a classroom," he says. "That's where they can really learn."

"Is transportation a hassle?"

"It can be. But you can get around that."

In the early days, kids were brought to school by taxi and by special buses at special times, and it was difficult. He gets around all that by just issuing bus passes and telling them to get here when they can. And this does seem to be how it is: during the morning, kids wander in who have apparently just gotten up or who have been gone for a couple of days.

"Administrators have to show creativity," Mr. Jackson says, "not just ask for it from teachers. Administrators have to show what needs to be done. They have to make mistakes, too. They can't try to be perfect. But if you want teachers to be a certain way, then you ought to be that way, too."

I ask him whether you can teach an administrator to be that way, or whether they're born that way.

"You can teach 'em," he says. "I could teach them. I'm good. I know how to do it. Of course, they have to love kids. If they don't love kids, there's not much you can teach them. Lovin' kids and being honest with them and with yourself—that's what it takes."

He takes me down to Mr. Wilson's classroom. Mr. Wilson is a tall, loose-limbed black man in a sweatsuit who teaches social studies. There are eight kids in the class, and they are doing assignments that are written on the board: "Read page 155 to 161, write summary, make up twelve questions with answers."

Mr. Wilson goes out to make a phone call, and I ask the kids what they like about this school. They tell me that it's much better than the schools they came from.

"Why?" I ask.

"Well, in the other schools, you didn't get no help," a kid says. "Here, if you ask for it, you get help."

Another kid says, "You can sit anywhere you want. They're not on your case all the time. Teachers here, they'll drive you home, they'll play ball with you, they help you if you're in trouble."

Most of them claim that they learn more here, too.

When he returns, Mr. Wilson describes how the school works.

"You have to see everything as a lesson. You have to take whatever opportunity you get in a given day with any kid. You don't do much lecturing because you gotta see where each kid is. It's more like tutoring ninety-two kids than anything else, and being a parent to them, as well. There's so many things each of these kids faces. So many problems they have, not just one. And then, this is a [grade] 7-through-12 school. We've got, in any classroom, kids across the whole range of classes. So what you're dealing with is kids with a whole bunch of problems—and on any given day, you don't know which one's the big one—all mixed together with kids who are at different stages of development, different ages, different levels of knowledge. And most of them need a hell of a lot more attention than other kids do.

"You need to understand where each kid is," he continues, "and deal with where he is right now. Like, a kid'll wander in, like that kid just did, and I haven't seen him for a couple of days. Okay, he's late. I'll get around to talking to him about being late. But right now, I want him to get to work, so I'm not going to hassle him with that. Later on, when the time's right, I'll talk to him about being late, and I'll tell him, he goes to some job, and they're not going to let him keep it if he shows up late. He's just going to have to learn that. But right now, the vibes I get is he needs to sit down, and he needs to start workin', and I don't need to hassle him with this punctuality thing.

"Everything's a lesson," he goes on. "You gotta be on your toes and look for all these opportunities. A kid's talkin' dirty, you say, 'Hey, let's bring your mother in here, a bunch of your mothers, all of you guys, and you talk dirty around your mothers.' And then they'll say, 'Well, I don't wanna talk dirty around my mother.' And you say, 'Why not?' And then you say, 'So if you don't want to talk dirty around your mother, how come you'll talk dirty around these young women?' Everything's a lesson. Maybe today you can't give 'em a math lesson. But maybe there's a more important lesson.

"You gotta think about the alternative. If a kid is here today, then he's not home breakin' into my house, you know what I mean? He's not out on the street. So maybe I don't get him to learn a math lesson today, but I kept him out of *your* house. And maybe he got some strokes here that he didn't get someplace else. Or he learned something about being a man. These are the little things you're lookin' for all the time. And if you pay attention to them, then you also see the places where you can get some learning in, too."

Just then a punk kid comes in. His head is shaved except for a red swatch in the front, which falls down over his eyes. He's wearing a cut-up black T-shirt, jeans, a black coat, and assorted punk jewelry.

"Hey, how'd it go?" Mr. Wilson says.

"Cool," the kid says. "It was neat."

"Well, I want you to write that up for me. Hear?"

"Yeah, yeah, I'll write it up."

Mr. Wilson tells me the kid's been gone for a couple of weeks, to an antinuclear demonstration in Nevada. To get credit for the "global reach passage," he will write his experience up and present it to Wilson. The passages, which represent the curriculum here, are introspection, practical skills, career experience, odyssey, global reach, vision, and logical inquiry. Every student at the Johnson alternative learning center has to work through those passages to get a diploma. The passages stress problem solving, reasoning abilities, creative thinking, and use of chance.

Students have to prove to a passage committee of teachers and peers that they can deal with interpersonal awareness and growth; that they've acquired a skill that they once depended on others for; that they've developed a marketable skill that could lead to sustained employment; that they've been on an intellectual, spiritual, or physical quest; that they've done an independent project, of almost any nature, that demonstrates some form of creation; that they've been involved in a social-research analysis project (that's the global reach passage); and that they can demonstrate and apply principles of logical inquiry. If they can do that through journals, classwork, portfolios, and being grilled by a passage committee, then they get a diploma. There is no grading or testing, but there is a lot of tutoring and support.

Students are also asked to keep journals about what goes on in their lives. They meet in their "family groups" at the beginning of each day and discuss issues. Mr. Wilson believes in capitalizing on every opportunity to have a discussion and trying to make the discussion a learning discussion for everybody, whether it's about foreign affairs or Madonna.

The atmosphere here is certainly more relaxed than in the usual school. A radio is playing in the classroom. Kids wander in and out with cans of pop, eating candy and chewing gum. They obviously have a good deal of the latitude that they were denied in ordinary schools.

I go to another classroom and watch two English teachers try to work on writing with half a dozen recalcitrant young men. They all hate to write, and so the two English teachers are trying to get them to think in terms of symbols and how to order them to tell a story. They try to get the boys to lie down on the floor and imagine that they are cave men, but most of the boys won't do it. The teachers do at least get them to close their eyes and start thinking about what a cave man might want to draw on the wall.

Several of these guys look like they are probably pretty good at graffiti, but they can't quite get into this cave-man-drawing-on-the-wall thing. For some time, a certain amount of resistance is mounted by the boys against one of the teachers, while the other slowly circulates around the room, rubbing necks, patting, looking over shoulders, whispering to a student.

"Are you all right today? You look a little tired."

"Yeah, I'm okay," the kid says. "I'm just a little tired."

They manage to get the boys out into the hall and drawing on a large piece of paper. But it's slow, it's irritating; they're resistant. As Mr. Jackson said earlier, the word these kids have heard most in their lives is *no,* and so it is the word they use most. They all say no to almost everything at first.

So this is teaching in the teeth of "no." This is teaching people who say, "I don't want to do anything. I don't want to do this. I can't do this," day in and day out. It is easy to see why all these young men were thrown out of regular classrooms. Nevertheless, very slowly, they start doing just a little bit of what the teachers would like them to do.

A boy joins them. His mother has come to school with him. She sits up against a locker, watching him draw, now and then telling him what he hasn't done right, or yelling at the little child she has brought along.

In the midst of this, Mr. Jackson comes along and says to me, "Hey, come on down to the office. There's a disciplinary thing going on. You might be interested in it."

This morning, he made a P.A. announcement that no hats, scarves, or headbands would be allowed in the school because of an incident that took place two days ago, when a number of gang members were found inside the school and in cars outside. Anything that smacks of gangs will be taken away. The principal has also banned portable tape players because they're always being stolen.

I go to his office, and he explains that the three young men and one young woman seated around the table are on strike, and they have rebelled against his ruling on hats. He has impounded their hats, and they have gone on strike and demanded a "sounding board," which is the school's court of law.

I sit with the students as they outline the reasons for their grievance. One is a scrawny white kid with a heavy-metal T-shirt and long, greasy blond hair. Another, a black kid, has long dreadlocks. The girl seems to have a permanent scowl. She slouches in her chair, arms crossed. The third boy is a seedy-looking blond with a tattoo on his bicep. They argue that the principal's ruling is unfair and unjustified.

"It's an overreaction, man," says the black kid. "It was an isolated incident. We're not in any gangs. Those kids didn't go to this school. He's out of line."

They tell me that hats are part of their "identities."

"He's denying us the right of self-expression," says the kid with the tattoo.

They decide to ask a kid named Tony to represent them at the "sounding board" tomorrow. The principal calls Tony to the office, and he agrees to be their advocate. He's a good-looking, extremely articulate, fast-thinking black kid who is clearly an immediate and instinctive leader. He quickly negotiates for the release of the students' impounded hats, pending the hearing on the issue, and agrees that they should not wear them until the issue is resolved.

The principal tells the students they can have their hats back but asks them to leave the school if they are still on strike and not to return until the court session tomorrow. They take their hats and leave.

Soon one of them, the one in the heavy-metal T-shirt, returns.

"I want you to know, Mr. Jackson, that I believe in the cause. I believe in everything the kids were saying, and I am on strike in my heart. But you know that if I leave this building, my probation officer will have me in court, so I'm staying. But I really believe in the strike."

Mr. Jackson says that he understands. After the kid leaves, he says, "That took a lot of guts." Jackson explains that, to the students, he often seems to be a barbarian. He does this on purpose, he says. It's a way of getting them to think and learn about democracy and authority.

It is often said in urban districts that the students face so many difficulties that academic instruction is pointless. The best you can do is try to give them esteem, food, shelter, even love, if you can—and a diploma, so that at least they have a chance to get a job where they might get further training and education. No one who visits urban schools can deny that many students have difficulties or that many, especially the older ones, are not interested in schooling as we currently conduct it. Maybe they would be interested in some other kind of learning experience; maybe not. Maybe they are wrestling with things far more important at this point in their lives than academics. Certainly, they are more capable of doing interesting academic work than they or their teachers realize.

But for many of them, that issue was decided long ago. They will tolerate school and do what they have to do to squeak through. If they stay at it, they will throw their mortarboards as high as anyone else at graduation. They will be justifiably proud of their accomplishments. But they will be the entry-level laborers that everyone complains about, the ones who do not read or write very well or think critically or creatively about ideas.

It happens that I am in town for the twentieth anniversary of the filing of the suit that led to court-ordered integration of the North Urban Public Schools. I go to a meeting to commemorate the occasion. Many of the people who were instrumental in the case are there, including the family whose name the case bears. It is like a class reunion of sorts. People greet one another with hugs and laughter about how they have aged, changed their hairstyles, put on weight. A historian from one of the local universities reviews the events that led up to the filing. He praises the school board that reigned in the 1960s, many of whose members are present. He notes that in 1964, twenty-five years ago, the board passed its first policy statement declaring the intention to integrate the schools. He sketches the events leading up to the election of the district's first black board member, a humble but absolutely resolute woman, who rises, at his urging, to warm, sustained applause. It was she who, in the midst of the turmoil surrounding the assassination of Dr. Martin Luther King, introduced the resolutions that began implementation of voluntary, comprehensive desegregation. Thus began a period of intense struggle and strife. In the largest board election in the district's history, the majority supporters of integration were replaced by opponents, who immediately rescinded the integration resolutions. Ten days after they did so, the suit was filed. Now, twenty years later, after countless hearings and trials all the way up to the Supreme Court and back, the case is not over, and litigation continues.

The acting superintendent (he replaced John Peck after we visited the district last year) arrived in the late 1960s. He rises now to reflect on what those years were like.

"It was like driving with one foot on the accelerator and the other on the brake," he says. He had been an assistant superintendent at the time. "We always had to have two plans in our pockets, one going one way and the other going the other way. We had some board members and the court telling us to move ahead with all deliberate speed, and we had a majority on the board telling us to put on the brakes. Just as would happen if you drove your car that way, we began to smell something burning."

Buses were bombed. The school board was bombed. Fights broke out in the schools. Teachers threatened boycotts and went on strike. Board members testified against one another in court.

"People ask me what it was like," he says, "and, to be honest, I don't remember much. There was no time to reflect. We went from one crisis to another. I was tired and beat up. I hardly ever saw my family. It's all a blur to me."

He left the district in the early 1970s, to become superintendent of a less contentious district. But in 1988, after retiring, he was brought back as Peck's replacement, to help the district find a longer-term superintendent.

What was it like to leave the district and come back almost twenty years later?

"I feel like Rip Van Winkle," he says. "I came back and went into some meetings, and they were the same meetings I had left two decades ago. It was eerie. When I left, we had 93,000 students, about 75 percent of them Anglos. Today, we have 56,000 students, and only a minority are Anglos. When I left, we were saying that if we integrated this district, achievement would rise. But it hasn't. Poor kids performed in the bottom quartile then, and they perform in the bottom quartile now. When I left, we were trying to get rid of 'racially identifiable' schools. We haven't done it. Our schools are more 'racially identifiable' than ever, and we no longer have enough whites in the city to change the balance, regardless of how much we try to bus them around. The definition of an integrated school when I left was 50 percent Anglo. The court has lowered it to 40 percent, and even that won't work anymore—not in this city, and not in any major city in this country.

"Today I say, 'So what?' So what if most of the kids in the school are poor or black or Hispanic? What are you going to do about it? Then, we were saying that racially identifiable schools were inherently unequal. We were saying, in effect, that a poor kid or a black kid could not learn unless he was sitting next to an Anglo kid. Well, we don't have enough Anglo kids to go around. Are we saying we can't educate those kids, then? Do any of us really believe anymore that we can't provide quality education to poor kids and minority kids unless there are Anglo kids in the classroom?

"I'll tell you what," he says. "If we believe that, we'd better get out of the business. Can kids learn if they're not sitting next to an Anglo? You bet they can. And they'd better, too, or it's all over. That's all I've got to say. They'd better, or it's all over."

The meeting ends with everyone agreeing that it would be nice to end the litigation. The attorney for the plaintiffs these twenty years says he would like it to end, and it should have ended long ago, but he doubts it will end any time soon. He is worried about resegregation of the schools if the court releases the school board. The attorney for the schools says he would like the case to end soon, too, but he doesn't know when that will be.

The superintendent's analogy about the accelerator and the brake is apt. For twenty years, the district has been like a crowded car jerking back and forth along the highway, various people wrestling for the steering wheel, someone's foot always on the gas, someone else's on the brake. The car has not gone very far.

We visited many more schools in this district than I have mentioned. In most of them, a few teachers were challenging young people to use their minds more fully, to think about things more deeply. There were even entire schools—elementary schools, anyway—devoted, like the school on the reservation, to a promising form of whole-language instruction. We found a computer "magnet" program in one high school that may be the most sophisticated in the country, and we visited a Montessori school that was clearly head-and-shoulders above the district's ordinary schools in its effectiveness. I could tell you about these outstanding teachers, programs, and schools, but that would obscure the huge, overriding point I want to make about this district and the many districts like it around the country: they do not provide the climate in which a literacy of thoughtfulness for all students is likely to thrive and spread; quite the contrary. Programs conducive to thoughtful, active learning are at the margins. Whole language–oriented schools are fighting upstream against heavy resistance. The Montessori school is under constant attack because it is perceived as too expensive. The computer "magnet" program prevails because it has strong support and legitimation from outside the school system.

We spoke with teachers and administrators in the high school that everyone said was improving the fastest, and we looked at a newly completed attitude survey of all 160 staff members. They said they were a caring, high-quality group of professionals. They said they had a good college-prep program, good counseling, and a good principal. They said they were good at "enforcing the rules." But they worried that they were spending too much time on the kids who don't care, and too little on the ones who do. They said the curriculum is not relevant to many young people, is too fragmented, and should not be controlled centrally. They said not enough parents care. Communication among themselves and between them and the community is poor.

The primary barriers they perceived to real improvement were "district politics" and "centralized decision making." They saw few incentives or opportunities to do anything new or different. The three most often repeated refrains were "We're powerless," "Central administration controls us," and "It's society's fault, not ours." The staff was split down the middle on the goals of schooling: half said they knew what they were, half said they didn't. The majority questioned whether the school was really organized the right way to get the job done. One-quarter of them said conflict was dealt with openly, one-quarter said it definitely was not, and half weren't sure. Only one-third said openness and straightforward communication were rewarded. In this school, in this district, in this community, there is one foot on the gas, one on the brake.

CHAPTER FIVE

The Politics
of Literacy

The North Urban Public Schools are struggling because the community and a long succession of school leaders have been unable to deal constructively with racial fear and mistrust. Some administrators told us that the district had been successful because it had "kept the lid on" racial tensions for two decades. Success in urban school districts is often defined as the avoidance of large-scale violence. It is easy to imagine the kind of working environment such an attitude creates. Think of what it would be like to work in a company whose managers define success as the absence of an angry mob of customers sacking the store and assaulting the employees. Maybe the reason so few urban districts have produced inspiring visions of the future is that they have such dark visions about what might have happened if they had relaxed their guard.

The Courts and Policy

What we can call *judicial policy* is at the center of the NUPS dilemma, in a number of ways. To begin with, of course, the district was found guilty of having created a segregated school system, *as a matter of policy*. When one incumbent school board would create a policy in favor of integrating the schools, another would rescind the policy. Judicial intervention in the district was an effort to

change the district's policy and make it commensurate with national policy respecting civil rights and constitutional guarantees.
The court retains its jurisdiction over the matter because it is not
yet convinced that the school board will support a policy guaran-
teeing that there will be no "racially identifiable" schools in the
district. Moreover, the court recognizes that the state has passed a
law expressly forbidding busing for the purpose of achieving racial
balance. If the court withdraws from the case, school board
members will be obliged to obey state policy, which requires them
to dismantle the integration plan so laboriously established and
protected by the court for two decades. Here, federal policy is in
direct conflict with state and district policy.

The circuit judges who have overseen the desegregation case
have made it clear that they are not educational policymakers. Nevertheless, the case has profoundedly affected education in the district. Equity policy has influenced what people have talked about,
as well as what they have been afraid to talk about. It has determined which students sit next to whom in class, with whom they
go to school, and whether they go to public or private schools.
Teachers and administrators have spent entire careers working under court order. Fighting the court has cost the district untold millions of dollars, which could have been spent doing something else.
Equity rules and regulations have proliferated, and a bureaucracy
has emerged to see that they are known and enforced.

In certain respects, this is just to say that equity policy has
influenced educational institutions, just as it has influenced all
other American public and private institutions over the last half-
century. Some institutions and people have responded more creatively and constructively than others, but all have had to adjust.
What is more to the point here is how a change in national policy
on equality of opportunity has affected the chances that a literacy
of thoughtfulness will spread through certain kinds of school systems as fast as the need for it was spreading in the world around
the schools.

Equity policy affects the discourse, the conversation, in the
school district (a point we will return to later), and it has an impact
on the policies that shape curricula, instruction, and assessment.
These are the policies that teachers see affecting their classroom

behavior most directly, and all teachers have been powerfully influenced by a concept that lies at the heart of equity policy and many a desegregation effort: *compensatory education.* As the term implies, compensatory education is designed to make up for things that some children—particularly poor minority children—do not have, but which the curriculum and structure of schooling assume are common to all students. In the 1960s and the 1970s, the list of these social and educational deficiencies was very long. According to a considerable body of research, poor students were thought to lack the drive and motivation of middle-class students. They were not believed to be "learning-oriented." They were believed to be less able to use standard English to represent and express ideas and feelings; they had been found to speak a restricted kind of language, with less detail than middle-class students' language and fewer complex constructions. Thus, to the extent that language sophistication is a precondition for conceptualizing, they were believed to be poor conceptualizers and problem solvers. All of these research findings influenced the kinds of programs that people developed to deal with inner-city poor and minority children, often in response to court orders (see, for example, Gordon and Wilkerson, 1966).

Research has also suggested that poor children are more comfortable with concrete frames of reference than with abstraction. They are apparently better at concrete, short tasks than abstract, long ones. They are said to depend more on real-life experience than on symbolic experience in developing ideas, more on street talk than on standard English. They do not appear to be patient listeners in the ways needed for success in school. They are not good at delaying gratification. They see little reason to pursue knowledge for its own sake. They have low self-esteem. Many of them are angry and do not trust mainstream people. These research findings also led directly to a spate of programs and materials designed to compensate for such deficiencies.

Three points about the assumptions undergirding compensatory education are especially important. First, the research overwhelmingly concentrates on the weaknesses of poor children; very little research has been done on their strengths. Second, these weaknesses are deficiencies in terms of the traditional organization and content of schooling. Very little thought has been given to the idea of changing schooling to accommodate new kinds of students; all the effort has gone to changing the students so that they will fit into the schools. In essence, what compensatory education tries to do is make poor children into middle-class children in their experiences, attitudes, values, and performance. Third, the underlying assumptions about poor students' motivation, language, and conceptual development have militated against offering them a literacy of thoughtfulness and have favored a low-level, atomized, concrete, basic-skills curriculum. The language of that curriculum has been so simplified that it is both boring and artificial. It has been stripped of richness and context and made fundamentally meaningless, which is to say unabsorbable by normal people, except through memorization, whose effects last only for a few hours or days.

Although the courts certainly did not invent this curriculum, they have played a powerful role in reinforcing it and locking it into place. In the case of NUPS, compensatory education is specifically endorsed by the court as part of its remedy. Moreover, since compensatory education calls for frequent testing, and since its success can be gauged only by standardized tests, the court's monitoring of the district has institutionalized an assessment technology that goes hand in hand with the basic-skills curriculum for poor minority children. The more poor and minority children a district has had, the more this curriculum has spread. Although it began as a curriculum for a few students, in many urban districts it became the curriculum for the majority. Whole schools qualified for federal funds for disadvantaged students and adopted the compensatory assumptions, curriculum, and teaching technology that went along with the money.

The policy of compensating for the weaknesses of *students* with respect to *schools,* rather than for the weaknesses of *schools* with respect to *students,* is backed by research and has often been supported by court orders. It has had a powerful dampening influence on the environment for literacy in the North Urban Public Schools. But it need not have had this effect, because it has also stimulated some innovations that still hold promise. Compensatory education brought a number of extra staff, aides, volunteers, and specialists into the schools. It encouraged experiments in team teaching, heterogeneous grouping, and nongraded programs where students work at their own pace, regardless of grade level. Transitional classes for transient students sprang up, as did individualized learning that engaged students more actively and concretely in their education. Teachers experimented with merging two or three class periods, in order to get one long, more intense class period, and schools experimented with ways to lower the teacher-to-pupil ratio and create longer-term ties between teachers and their students.

All of these innovations took place in various ways in the North Urban Public Schools over twenty years. Unfortunately, they took place on the margins—one or two teachers here, one or two there, a school in one part of town for a couple of years, a school in another part of town for another couple of years, until key personnel left or were transferred. We visited an elementary school principal who had begun a whole-language program for disadvantaged students (like the one we visited on the reservation). She was so impressed with the results that she adopted the program for the entire school, but she told us that this had meant a fight all the way against the district and its basic-skills curriculum and testing program. She had to spend an enormous amount of her time running interference and dodging attacks from the central administration.

Thus it appears that some aspects of the compensatory philosophy have led to innovations conducive to a literacy of thoughtfulness, while others have discouraged such literacy. The latter aspects sprang from research about the language development of poor children: their preference for the concrete over the abstract, and their apparent deficiencies in concept formation and problem solving. This research could be interpreted as supporting a rich symbolic medium for poor children, as well as extra experience with thinking, making meaning, and solving problems; ironically, however, its practical application turned out to support just the opposite. Most disadvantaged children were presented with impoverished language environments and virtually no opportunities to think, write, discuss, make meaning, or solve problems. Somehow, the belief that poor children could not understand the elaborated and abstract language of traditional schooling led to the creation of reading programs and materials that denied them any exposure to such language, *for their own good.* The technology of mass education was already good at breaking knowledge and skills into thousands of little standardized, decontextualized pieces, which could be taught and tested one at a time. In this setting, noble beliefs and good intentions seem to have been miscarried. Poor children, arriving at school truly in need of enrichment, received in enrichment programs a poverty of language experience, made even more profound by the fact that their own language experience and resources were totally discounted. There are good reasons for believing that such early experience, dominated by so-called compensatory language, sets students up for failure in the middle grades, the point where real-world language, which is more complex and abstract, becomes the lingua franca of academic work. Having always been sheltered from it, poor students suddenly find themselves left in the dark. Compensatory reading and basic-skills programs have proved more powerful and central to the curriculum than have the more liberating innovations also spawned by the compensatory philosophy and its research base. Thus, the possibility that compensatory education can stimulate a literacy of thoughtfulness has been expressed so far only on the margins, not at the core of the system. The courts, ironically, in their efforts to help these students, have reinforced a curriculum and a medium of instruction that only keeps them behind.

Fairness and Policy

After talking with a number of people around the district, we saw that the dominant idea of fairness in the NUPS is the notion that everyone deserves an opportunity to meet the same standard. It is like setting a high-jump bar at five feet and giving everyone an equal chance to clear it. If some do not, you can still say that they had the same opportunity as everyone else, and so the contest was fair. Standardized tests operate in this way. Everyone is given the same questions, in the same circumstances, and with the same amount of time to answer. The curriculum for kindergarten through grade 8 is standardized to ensure that all students are exposed to the same objectives. Resources are allocated in this way, too. Every school receives a standard amount of money per full-time student of a particular kind. In the same way, minority students are allocated across schools, and each school has a standard percentage of them. The state constitution under which the NUPS operates says that education must be "uniform." The teachers' contract specifies numerous ways in which all teachers must be treated the same. State and local bureaucrats see to it that key procedures are uniformly applied and followed. Objectivity is scrupulously pursued throughout the district, to ensure against bias of any kind.

This model of fairness has been useful in spotting, monitoring, and sometimes ameliorating the differential treatment and performance of minorities, but it has some drawbacks. When this model is applied to learning, the principal problem is that we know from the start that a considerable number of people will not be able to make the high jump. Human talents and motivation being as diverse as they are, some people will just never be able to get over the bar, no matter how hard they try. They're too short, they do not have enough spring in their legs, they cannot see any point in doing this, they are afraid—there are countless reasons. To these people, the contest is clearly unfair. What is the point of an equal opportunity to do something that you cannot or do not want to do?

This model of fairness also tends toward certain kinds of corruption. If we want to see success, we tend not to set the bar very high to begin with. When students still fail to clear it, we either lower it more or put them into a different game entirely, a remedial game in which subskills tend to become goals in themselves, unrelated to the original goal of getting over the bar. The subtlest form of corruption that this model breeds is belief in the illusion that decisions are being made objectively (meaning scientifically or mathematically) and are therefore fairer than they would otherwise be.

In these circumstances, what would the NUPS have to lose if it experimented more aggressively with new metaphors of fairness? Mortimer Adler, in an informal conversation at the Aspen Institute of Humanistic Studies in June 1989, suggested two different metaphors: fairness as each individual being filled to capacity, and fairness as each individual absorbing all that he or she can absorb. Each has different implications for how schooling might be conducted.

"The first metaphor is of people as containers," Adler said. He was speaking with a group of community leaders interested in helping the North Urban Public Schools. "With respect to any particular piece of knowledge or particular skill, I might have a pint capacity, for any number of reasons, while you might have a quart capacity, and someone else has a gallon. Maybe we're talking about calculus or some subcomponent of calculus, or maybe it's throwing a football, or whatever. We have different capacities because we're different people, with different endowments and interests at some particular time in our lives. Now, in this model, what is fair is that all of us should be filled to capacity. If I've only got a pint-sized capacity for calculus, it should be filled to the brim, but so should the fellow with the gallon capacity be filled to the brim. We both get as much calculus as we can take. It's not fair to say that only gallon-sized people should take calculus, and it's not fair to expect me, with my pint-sized capacity, to know what the gallon fellow knows. What's fair is *fullness*. We all should be full. And we should be full of the best, full of cream. It shouldn't be cream for some of us, and skim milk for others."

Does this model support the practice of tracking in schools— "dumbing down" books for the slow readers, and placing students in vocational programs because they are not "college material"?

"No," Adler said. "That's a different matter altogether. What this model suggests is that all students should receive the *same* curriculum, not a different one, but it should be tailored to their situations. Each of us should take calculus up to our capacity, if we believe that calculus is necessary for the good life."

Moreover, capacity is an individual matter; for each individual, it is specific to particular skills and subskills. No group of thirty students could possibly share one profile of capacities enough to justify giving them the same course of instruction. In his school-reform tract, Adler wrote, "The best education for the best is the best education for all" (Adler, 1982).

What would schools be like if they adopted this model of fairness? First of all, we would have to know people's capacities for all kinds of things much more accurately than we do now. Diagnosis of individual strengths and weaknesses would be much more sophisticated than it is today.

"That's a problem," Adler said at Aspen. "You'd want to be sure that you had gauged a student's capacities correctly. You don't want them underestimating their abilities. We don't really know right now how to gauge capacities accurately. But, of course, we don't know what their high-jumping capacities are, either, in the first model. And we never really find out. Maybe the students who make it over the bar could have made it over a much higher one. We'll never know."

The difference is that in the first model it is every student against the bar and against every other student; in the second, it is every student against his or her own capacity. The power of the fullness approach to fairness is that it forces us to pay much more attention to each student's capacities and judgments about whether he or she is full.

Adler's second metaphor for fairness imagines "that each student is a sponge of a certain size, when it comes to a particular skill or set of skills. Then fairness means immersing your students in a sufficient amount of liquid to ensure that each [sponge] fills itself up automatically."

Whereas the container metaphor depends on knowing each child's capacity and ensuring that a teacher fills it, the sponge metaphor places responsibility for fullness on the student; the educator's job is to make sure that there are enough learning opportunities for all sponges to absorb as much as they can naturally. The student is a more active learner in the second model, and the teacher is more of a broker between student and a rich learning medium. Fairness means providing a learning medium so rich and appropriate that all sponges naturally fill themselves up.

Like the container metaphor, this one also assumes a good deal of knowledge about students' interests and capacities, knowledge that we currently do not gather. The sponge metaphor, moreover, requires us to know how to create environments where students of all kinds and backgrounds will tend inevitably to be natural, active learners. Like other models of fairness, this one undoubtedly has its typical corruptions, too. Teachers can assume too easily that learning is "natural" and not put enough effort into teaching students how to learn. They can pride themselves on having done enough if they merely provide the medium but do not help students learn how to take greatest advantage of it.

The Montessori school that we visited in the North Urban Public School District struck me as coming closest to the sponge metaphor. The Montessori classroom is rich with learning opportunities, and children are allowed to follow their interests and actively engage the environment; teachers see to it that each student is absorbed in learning, and they reinforce learning strategically throughout the day. This Montessori school faces difficult dilemmas, however, because it is in a district where the "equal opportunity" model of fairness predominates. Accordingly, the Montessori school's administrators are constantly battling central administrators over the fact that their costs exceed the average cost per school. Montessori administrators have been told that this discrepancy is unfair to the other schools, and they have been kept from seeking grant money to document their success and pursue even more adventurous learning opportunities.

With this model of fairness, we say we have been fair if we can prove that all students have had the same opportunity to meet a certain standard. In the model based on the container metaphor, we say we have been fair if we can prove that each student is filled to capacity. In the model based on the sponge metaphor, we say we have been fair if we can prove that we have provided a medium rich and deep enough for all students to actively and naturally absorb whatever they need. Each model requires a different kind of knowledge about students and learning environments, as well as different kinds of testing and accountability.

Each model of fairness also says something different about who is responsible for students' learning or failure to learn. The first model focuses on one standard; if a student does not attain it, the failure is presumed to be his or her fault. The second model focuses on capacity; if a student is not full, the educator is presumed to be at fault for not knowing enough about the student's capacity and how to tailor the subject to it. The third model focuses on environments for learning; if a student does not learn, it is presumably the educators' fault for not providing a rich or inviting enough medium. None of the models of fairness is free of the possible corruptions that could make it seem unfair. Therefore, it may make some sense to use all three models in evaluating the fairness of an educational system in the most robust way.

Here, however, we face a fundamental choice fraught with political and economic dangers: the choice between *treating differ-*

ent people the same and *treating different people differently.* The high-jump, "equal opportunity" model of fairness—the prevailing model in American schooling today—is based on the notion that different people should be treated the same and subjected to the same standards. No one questions the importance of that principle in the spheres of law and politics. In education, however, the standards—translated into school courses, objectives, hours of instruction, and degrees—tend to be those that so-called successful people have created, and to which they ascribe their success. (Whether meeting those standards has anything to do with success is another matter; what seems to count is the belief that they do.) This is not the same as treating everyone equally under the law.

From a social perspective, treating different people the same is legally required, politically wise, and even economically efficient, but it is not educationally sound. It doesn't square with the realities of learning. From an educational perspective, treating different people differently is sound practice, but it is politically and economically difficult, not to mention illegal under some court-ordered desegregation guidelines. Our history with respect to treating different people differently is too sordid to justify much trust that we know how to do it fairly, either in the social world or in our schools.

What we see in large urban districts like the NUPS is a mishmash of efforts to treat different people either the same or differently, according to varying schools of thought about what is fair. On the one hand, administrators try to treat everyone the same in school assignments, per-pupil cost allocations, and exposure to the same curricula, tests, and promotion and graduation requirements. On the other hand, administrators have bowed to certain group differences by creating special programs for poor students, gifted students, handicapped students, and so on. Teachers subject entire classrooms to the same curriculum, at the same pace, with the same tests, but good teachers also know full well that their students have widely differing capacities and interests, and such teachers struggle to attend to these differences. The *institution* of schooling is committed to one notion of fairness, instrumentalized throughout; the *practice* of helping students learn requires commitment to other notions of fairness, politically and economically at odds with the institution's notions (see MacIntyre, 1981, pp. 174–189, for a helpful discussion of practices). The institution is answerable to the realities of the law, as the law embodies principles of fairness; practitioners—teachers—are answerable to the realities of human learning.

Public schooling, precisely because it *is* a public responsibility, will always involve a conflict between the laws of the land (which create the institution) and the laws of learning (which are the core of the practice that the institution houses). The conflict may be clear or unclear, healthy or unhealthy, productive or unproductive. In many school districts, it is unclear, unhealthy, and unproductive. By focusing on children's legal rights to a "thorough and uniform" education, districts have overstressed the importance of the institutional aspects of schooling. They have created such enormous amounts of bureaucracy, paperwork, and testing to ensure uniformity that they have directly (through mandates, rules, and regulations) and indirectly (through the ensuing climate) circumscribed and distorted the very practice that they have been trying to promote. Central to a healthy tension between institution and practice is leaders' realization that the tension is there to begin with, cannot ultimately be resolved, and constantly needs to be understood and negotiated.

Differing values and differing notions of fairness can coexist in a healthy relationship, so long as they are openly acknowledged and subject to continuing inquiry. The fact of the matter is that learning is a highly individualistic phenomenon that cannot be fully standardized, cannot be made uniform. The harder we try to make learning uniform, the less learning takes place; but the more we try to individualize learning, the less fair and practical our efforts seem. Perhaps the best way to deal with this situation educationally is to take the direction that Tinder (1980, p. 70) suggests: "The very meaning of equality is best put in terms of community. To enjoy equality is not just to occupy the same social and economic level as everyone else, although that may be part of it. It is to be addressed and listened to in matters of the greatest moment. I am not accorded dignity by someone who feeds me but does not care what I think. Even animals may be given food and shelter; the decisive signs of respect are serious listening and speaking. The dignity of a person consists in the right fully to participate in the search for truth."

Tinder defines community as inquiry itself: "Only cooperation in the most serious human concerns—and this means above all in the exploration of being—calls forth a community," he writes (p. 31). "Our one serious responsibility is that of understanding the truth as fully as possible and in that way becoming ourselves. We form a community only by being united in the acceptance of that responsibility." He does not insist that there can only be community, *once we have found the truth;* he says that community "lies in sharing the truth, and if this is so it must be inherent in the very process of *searching* for the truth" (my emphasis).

Neither fairness nor community, then, need be defined in terms of social unity and uniformity; the terms can be jointly defined in relation to a particular sort of inquiry, a search for the truth, in which everyone participates with equal respect. The solution to the dilemma posed by the existence of different notions of fairness, and by the tension between institutions' and practitioners' roles and values, is not to try to resolve things one way or the other; it is to become more truly a community of learners, to inquire into the most serious human concerns, and, in doing so, to create, for whatever fleeting moments we can, a community. That is what great teachers do; that is what great principals and superintendents do; that is what a literacy of thoughtfulness is all about. As an expression of democratic community, an unfettered literacy is both the end toward which education strives and the means by which it moves there.

The Governor and Policy

Executive educational policy includes what the governor says and does and what the people who report to the governor do and say with respect to education. Governors are elected by all the people in the state. They command media attention and can powerfully influence what people in the state talk about. They can propose budgets, veto legislation, and run state agencies, including the department of education, and they can do these things in ways that either support or discourage reform efforts. They can also establish highly visible blue-ribbon task forces, publish their own reports, give awards, run grant programs, commission special studies, mobilize the business community, marshal resources, and do a number of formal and informal, substantive and symbolic things that encourage others to move in the same direction. When a governor gets a bee in his bonnet about something, knows how to use the office effectively, and can stay in office long enough, he or she can bring about lasting change. Anyone who watched Bill Riley and his wife stump around South Carolina for school reform—or Bob Graham in Florida or Bill Clinton in Arkansas—can testify to the power of a governor to call attention to issues and make things happen.

As the North Urban Public Schools fight their battles and struggles to move ahead, I spend some time with the new governor, who is trying to decide what he wants to do in education. Like most other governors, he has visited the Far East and is concerned about his state's role in the international economy. Economic development is one of his highest priorities. Again and again since he was elected, he has linked the state's economic future to the quality of its educational system.

I join the governor and a team of aides he has assembled to help him work up short- and long-term plans for his educational initiatives. We sit casually around a table in his office in the state capitol, eating sandwiches for dinner. Outside, ominous clouds have brought on a premature darkness, and we see lightning advancing upon the city from the west. Everyone else in the capitol has gone home. The governor has had a tiring day. He has called the legislature back into session to deal with a transportation bill, and negotiations on the bill have been tough. He's a Democrat, and the legislature is predominantly Republican. His popularity is high, but some key legislators are refusing to go along with his proposals.

"We'll get there," he says with a sigh, referring to the negotiations, "but it's like pulling teeth. Anyway, we're here to talk about education, not roads. And I want you to notice that I have four people on my staff devoted to education. I don't have any devoted to roads. None for prisons, either. Four people is four times as much as I have for any other subject. That's how important this is."

The governor is a man of medium height and stocky build, whose face is hard to read. He talks slowly, measuring his words. He's not a great public speaker, but he has been in government for many years, and he knows how to get his points across powerfully in small groups. While he is talking, you can't imagine anyone interrupting him. Even when he pauses, you know he hasn't finished thinking yet.

His aides have put together some ideas about the kind of educational vision he should articulate and the kinds of initiatives he should push that may lead to significant changes in education. The governor does not appear to have read the briefing papers ahead of time. He scans them quickly as his chief of staff makes a few preliminary remarks about the agenda.

"Let me tell you what I think my vision is," the governor says when the chief of staff has finished. "I've been thinking a lot about this. Let me see if I can say it."

He pulls a small tape recorder out of his pocket and sets it on the table in front of him. Then he leans back in his chair and begins to talk, slowly, looking at the ceiling and out the window and, now and then, at one of us.

"There are four or five things that I think are important," he says. "Let me start with the most practical point of view, the most politically urgent aspect of this thing: the economic angle. We've got to raise skill levels in kids a whole lot. The most immediate challenge is to get our kids near the top, internationally, especially in science and math. It's a productivity thing. Our kids just aren't competitive, which means our workers won't be competitive. We've got to really turn that around. We need much higher expectations for everyone. And we've got to push the top up. Our best kids have to get even better. And all kids are going to have to learn how to think and how to solve problems and how to be creative. Like somebody said, we've got to outsmart the rest of the world. I believe that."

He chews on his sandwich for a few moments, thinking.

"But not all our kids are going to need that high-level science and math," he continues. "The majority won't need it. There won't be high-tech jobs for everyone, and you don't push everyone toward that abstract stuff. Just the ones who like it and have talent in it. You do a better job of motivating them, and you give them lots of success experiences. And you get out of their way. You don't hold them back by making them stay with everyone else. If they're ready for more, you give them more, regardless of what grade they're in or how old they are. We can't afford this lockstep stuff. We have to turn talented kids loose.

"So that's number one, I'd say, in terms of immediacy and the politics of this thing. You have to take care of the economic and productivity issues, and that means asking lots more of the system and really raising expectations and pushing the top up."

The lightning is much closer now, and it has started to rain. The clouds look like tornado clouds. We're all just sitting there in the safety of the governor's office, taking notes and listening while he thinks out loud.

"Number two is something I put even higher value on than the economic imperative," he says. "If the first one is the most immediate, this is the most fun. It has to do with the human thirst for knowledge, the joy of learning and things like curiosity. Our schools should cultivate that thirst, that joy, that curiosity."

Now he starts to get animated and looks at us as he talks.

"I mean, there's *so much* to know out there. The world is so *interesting!* The words that come to mind are *exploration, adventure, diversity, stretching the envelope.* Kids should be asking 'What is there to know? What talents do I have to develop?' I mean, I'm learning all the time. I *love* learning! It's one of the great pleasures of life. How can kids get bored? It's not human nature to be bored or uninterested in knowing things. If a school doesn't cultivate that love of learning and that desire to express what you know and to grow, what is it doing?"

His excitement about the adventure of learning reminds him of a time when he was in Indonesia, living with peasants. He tells us about how the illiterate peasants in this village delighted in learning the simplest things from one another. Each night, they would take turns describing objects and experiences. The point of the conversation was to see things as others saw them, to learn even

about familiar things and experiences, because there was such pleasure in doing so.

"Number three means the most to me," the governor goes on,
after his story about Indonesia. "I think it's the most important
outcome of all. We need a system of education that transmits and
enhances values. Things like caring, trustworthiness, accountability. Things that build character. Kids need to know that cooperation
is as important as individual competitiveness. We need to celebrate
diversity and teach tolerance. An education system isn't the only
place where values should be transmitted, but it is certainly one
place, and a key place."

Now the storm is directly over the capitol, and lightning
seems to be striking all around us. The governor has to stop talking
periodically, until the thunder subsides. He continues to describe
his vision.

"Fourth, I'd say that all kids need an appreciation of history,
of that which has gone before. They need to know what happened,
and what was good and bad, better and worse, about it. And fifth,
they need civics—the tools of living with order and justice. They
need to know about democratic institutions, and how they work,
and what they as citizens have to do to keep this one working."

He turns back to his sandwich, but we can tell that he has
not finished talking.

"Now, those are things I care about," he begins again.
"You've got to deal with the economic thing, you've got to make
learning a lifelong adventure, you've got to transmit values and
develop character, you've got to teach an appreciation of what has
gone before, and you've got to develop the tools of citizenship."

He gets up and starts walking around the office.

"Now, how much of that could I say?"

"All of it," one of his aides replies. "It's a great vision. Just
lay it out the way you just did."

The governor is doubtful. He shakes his head.

"I don't know," he says. "I don't know if I can say it all,
politically. The economic thing, yes. That's okay. But look at what
we're talking about here. We've got to get everyone shooting *much*
higher than they ever have. I mean, we're not talking about little
changes here, we're talking about *major* changes in the system. So

what's that going to mean? We've got to define that higher performance, especially in science and math, then communications.
That's a big job. Then we're saying we've got to do away with the
lockstep business in education—everyone going at the same pace.
We're saying whoever can do it, let's turn 'em loose. How do you
do that? What are we talking about here? That's a huge change, and
I haven't any idea how you do it. Do you?"

No one volunteers an answer.

"Then we have to deal with the fact that most people won't
have high-tech jobs. They're going to have service jobs that won't
be all that challenging. Those people are going to need other ways
to use their intelligence and creativity, because they won't need
them on the job. How do you explain that? How do you deal with
that piece?"

Again, no ready ideas.

"We're going to have to blow away the employment practices
of public schools, too," the governor continues. "Tenure's got to
go. For teachers, and for administrators, too. People just won't put
up with it much longer, and you're not going to change the system
unless you can hire and fire like everyone else."

For several years, the legislature has been considering bills to
abolish tenure, but they have been turned back by the teachers'
lobby. So far, it's been a Republican issue, but if the Democratic
governor is going to support the abolishment of tenure, the next bill
could well pass.

The governor continues to pace. He talks with increasing
irritation about educators and people who head educational organizations. I have heard a story from one of his aides, who no longer
works for him, about the time, shortly after he was elected, when
representatives from all the state's major educational organizations
came to his office to tell him what his priorities for education
should be. After they left, the governor said simply, "I don't ever
want to see those guys again."

Tonight, as he is carrying on about educators, he comes up
to me and says, "I have a good ear for authenticity. You know what
I mean? You develop that in politics. You can hear when people are
authentic and when they're not. Most of the educators I've listened
to don't have it."

I nod in understanding, if not in total agreement. I am beginning to see the depth of his disenchantment with the system and its
advocates.

He sits down and stretches. People talk a bit about what he
has said and about how such a message can best be conveyed. They
agree that it is strong medicine, but they don't think it's politically
dangerous. The governor has a 75 percent popularity rating. He can
say anything he wants to say, especially since he feels so strongly
about this issue. After a while, he enters back into the conversation,
to clarify his vision and get some practical next steps laid out.

"We've got to get other people into the schools, and get kids
out of the schools into the community," he says. "Kids need exposure to lots of models. Lots more people should be going in and out
of schools—I mean, just to have role models from the community
come into the classroom and talk about their most embarrassing
moments, or their most joyous moments, or their hopes or fears. It
makes a difference. It gives kids people to identify with. It motivates
them. It gets those values in there. What we're trying to figure out
is how to open the system up to outside forces."

He starts to get animated again.

"What we need to do is get people to see that education is
a community thing, not just a school thing. I was back in my
hometown last week, and I saw the potential to open things up all
over the place. For instance, there was this weed-spraying going on
over by the high school. What is weed-spraying about? Well, part
of it is chemistry. You want to teach kids chemistry? Get them to
study what's going on with pesticides. Take them down to the cam-
era shop, and take them inside. What's going on there? Chemistry.
Take them to the sewage-disposal plant—chemistry. Chemistry
isn't just what's going on in the classroom. It's all over the community. This town is so small, they haven't always been able to have
a chemistry teacher at the high school. And it's a farming community, so a lot of kids don't take chemistry. But chemistry has been
going on all around it, and you could get those kids interested in
chemistry if you just showed them that it's all around them. That's
what I mean about education being a community thing.

"Or take another example," he continues, leaning across the
table and using his hands to emphasize this point. "Johnny says

he's going to drop out of school. Johnny's classmates and teachers surround him and say, 'We're not going to let you drop out. If you drop out, we've failed, not you. You've got to stay because we're all in this thing together.' How often does that happen? What would happen if people did that? How do we get them to do that?

"Or how about this," he says. "Every kid should be guaranteed an educational godparent—some adult in the community, who will be there for mentoring, or whatever. Can we make that happen?"

People discuss ways of making that happen. The governor has obviously already thought about this, because pretty soon he says, "Look. I've got 50,000 people working for me. Right?"

He looks at his chief of staff, who nods in agreement.

"Can I tell them they all have to become educational godparents? Is that something we can do?"

He gets up again and paces back and forth.

"See, people, what I keep thinking about is, what can I make happen right out of this office? As a staff, I want you to learn what's in this control room. I mean, think about this as a giant control room, with all these levers around us. What are the levers? Okay, we have higher education. That's a state apparatus. Biggest employer in the state, too. That's a lever. I have the vocational education board. That's a lever. The community college system. Another lever. The prison system. Is there some way we can use that? Some angle? We've got the national guard. You see those guys driving up and down the freeway every weekend in those army trucks? You know why they're doing that? Because they don't have any other goddamn thing to do! So they just drive around. That's another lever in this control room. Is there some way we can use it? See what I mean? Drug and alcohol programs. My job-training office."

He goes to a flip chart and begins to draw.

"Look at it this way," he says. "This is the community. Now, how many things that we control go into this community? Job training."

He draws an arrow.

"Welfare."

Another arrow.

"Community college."

Another arrow.

"Health."

Another arrow.

"You get the idea. So, now, how do we use all these things, so they carry the same message? So people keep running into the same messages when they go here, or here, or here? How do we get these things working together? That's what I'd like to know. But that's what we've got to do."

The Legislature and Policy

While the governor was working on his strategy for restructuring the educational system, the legislature passed a school-reform law and the state board of education issued new goals for educational excellence.

The language of legislative and board policy is everywhere the same. It is a language of administration and law, an instrumental language of getting things done. It speaks of goals and objectives, maximization, implementation, standardization, validity, accountability, planning, rules, regulations, measurement, and consistency. It employs words like "shall" and "deems" and such expressions as "no later than" and "in such form that." The language suggests a particular way of thinking, a particular view of the world. It is a world in which people and things can be controlled and measured, in which you can predict events, in which you know the relations of cause and effect, in which you can hold things uniform, if you want to, and can apply standards to the social world, as you might apply mathematical principles to the physical world. This is an extremely important way of thinking and talking about the world, but it is not the only way. We do not talk to our children or our loved ones or our friends in this way; we do not talk about art in this way, or about history or literature. We do not discover or learn in this way. The language of law, institutions, and bureaucracies (and its embedded rationality) is different from the other languages of everyday life (see Habermas, 1984). The language of legislative educational policy is different from the language of learning, a fact we will come back to later in this chapter.

That said (and always kept in mind), what does the legislation establish that might have an impact on the North Urban Public Schools? It calls for an analysis of how to maximize the use of technology for enhancing educational opportunity. It is not clear exactly what this means, which is both good and bad: good, because the vagueness leaves plenty of room for the analyzers to define their territory; bad, because one simply cannot be sure what the legislators had in mind. Maybe this point has to do with broadcasting educational programs to remote parts of the state and has no real application to the school district.

The law also calls for an analysis of the system, to see whether it "addresses the diverse learning needs of various student populations." This is a good idea, although it would seem that a great many people in the state have long since concluded that the system is a failure in this regard, and they do not need another study to prove it.

The law calls for "financial and other incentives to school districts to achieve educational excellence," reflecting an effort to sweeten regulatory policy with incentives policy. Many critics of educational reform say that schools are overregulated already; what they need is motivation and rewards, not more regulations. Unfortunately, what this legislation calls for is incentives for raising test scores on "nationally accepted measures of student achievement." Given the amount of "teaching to the test" that already goes on in the district, an incentive to tailor teaching to even more standardized tests is unlikely to help; it most certainly will not lead to more critical and creative thinking or problem solving, since nationally standardized tests do not assess these more complicated skills. Moreover, I can't help wondering about the wisdom of rewarding schools for raising their graduation rates. Could that be an incentive to award diplomas, regardless of students' readiness?

A possible answer to this question is suggested elsewhere in the law. The law calls for improved attendance "through the provision of engaging learning opportunities." This is a considerable move (slight as it seems) away from typical dropout and attendance policies, which assume that students should be in school because they should be in school. This law is saying that school *must be engaging*. Now that the law has been passed, I wonder whether students can sue a school on the grounds that it did not engage them.

Equally positive is the use of the term "learning environment," which I have not seen in any previous policy statements, here or in any other state. The law calls for learning environments based on high expectations, challenge, and a "staff that is responsive to the individual needs of students." Can one get an injunction, I wonder, against classrooms that clearly are not environments for learning?

The section of the law that addresses local goals and objectives is heavy on regulation and measurement. It calls for each district to come up with its own way of measuring achievement, but it also calls, paradoxically, for regulations to ensure that whatever measurements a district comes up with are capable of being compared. In other words, the districts can do whatever they want, as long as they all do more or less the same thing. Thus is district linked to district, state norm to national norm. If the links are wrongheaded, what is linked is also wrongheaded; the wrong measure for one is the wrong measure for all.

School-reform legislation is like this. Good ideas are mixed with bad ideas, old ideas lie next to new ideas, a desire for diversity and local experimentation is contradicted by a desire for uniformity and standardization. Trust is mixed with mistrust, regulation with incentives. Goals and objectives abound, but the overriding vision—the context that could give them meaning—is absent. Why this goal, and not some other? Where will we be if we go in this direction, and not in some other? Some ideas are too clear; some are too vague. Some sentiments are liberal and educationally progressive; some are conservative and educationally reactionary. You can see the "horse trading" and compromises that had to be made as the bill worked its way through hearings and readings and committee meetings and cloakroom negotiations, toward its eventual wording as law.

In obedience to the law, the state board set its goals. The state graduation rate, which has been constant at around 75 percent for two decades, will somehow improve by 2 percent per year over the next six years. The graduation gap between minorities and Anglos will somehow go away. Educational achievement will somehow rise every year for six years. Schools will define yet again the proficiencies they are aiming to inculcate year by year. Somehow over the next six years, ethnic groups will achieve a parity they have not achieved in two centuries. These are the goals. No one we talked with believed seriously that they could be met. Everyone had been working toward such goals throughout their professional careers, and no one had seen much progress. But maybe this time it would be different.

Rule Makers, Program Makers, Bureaucrats, and Policy

Besides these duly constituted policymakers, other people powerfully affect policy through their official roles as interpreters and appliers of policy. These are the rule makers—state department of education officials, for instance, or central administrators, who write regulations that are supposed to follow logically from the policies, and who develop programs that are supposed to carry out the intentions of policymakers. I say "supposed to" because acts of interpretation are involved here, and the regulations and programs developed by rule makers and implementers are often controversial in how they embody the spirit or follow the letter of a policy. Rules, regulations, and programs—the derivatives of policy—often touch people's lives more directly than the policies that spawned them. We are all aware of beautiful and noble policies that have been translated into nonsensical rules, regulations, and programs (there's many a slip 'twixt the cup and the lip).

Policymakers, rule makers, and program makers create the raw ingredients for the policy environments in which teachers understand and carry out their jobs. These policy environments are part of larger symbolic environments—corporate cultures, if you will—that establish norms of behavior, motivational climates, and value systems. Administrators can sweeten or sour the environments according to their management and leadership philosophies and styles. Professional norms and ideas are also part of the mix: professional groups may have lobbied for certain policies to begin with, and subject matter experts may well play decisive roles in applying policy to practice.

In the North Urban Public Schools, we found that direct

links between specific policies and specific instructional behaviors were hard to find or sustain. Policy *environments* certainly affect teachers and administrators, although not always in the ways we might predict. Policy certainly encourages some kinds of school and classroom discourse while discouraging other kinds. It rationalizes the educational system—that is, it defines what is reasonable, creating structures of consciousness that guide the ways in which people tend to define problems, talk, and actually think about what they are doing.

As we observed educators doing various things, we asked them why they did them that way, and we listened for answers related to policy. Many teachers said they taught what they did because it would be on the state or district test. Many said they taught what they taught because it reflected the curricula they were "supposed to" teach. Many others lectured and conducted recitations: "That's all there is time to do." But in every school we visited, there were other teachers who paid no attention to mandated tests or curricula and who had their students working thoughtfully, regardless of time constraints. Across the district, some schools were very rulebound, while others seemed comparatively free of constraints. We have to conclude that particular policies do not inevitably constrain all teachers, administrators, and schools. In our opinion, new and insecure teachers and administrators were most likely to say that they were constrained by particular policies, rules, or regulations. A number of teachers and administrators also blamed policy for behavior that seemed to us more related to professional training and experience. More influential than specific policies or professional habits, however, was a general schoolwide or districtwide attitude about the binding force of rules and regulations, as well as about the degree to which teachers could be trusted to interpret and apply the rules according to their own professional judgments about students and learning situations. That attitude is a function of policy itself—how it sounds, and what values it promotes—and of the ways in which leaders choose to interpret and apply policy.

The language of policy is mostly what sociologists call *instrumental rationality*. It is a language of getting things done, a language of things and processes and institutions. It embeds a presupposition that we live in an objective world, which can be mastered through goal-directed interventions. It is the language of science, law, economics, and administration. But practitioners, who depend on policy-guided institutions for their practice, speak a different language (Habermas, 1984; MacIntyre, 1981; Jackson, 1986). The language of learning is intersubjective, person to person, not objective. It has to do with people reaching understanding, which is fundamentally different from getting things done. To be successful, the practice of teaching requires moral, practical, expressive, and esthetic modes of rationality. You have to be able to talk about what may be right or wrong, well formed or distorted, elegant or ugly; you have to be able to express feelings and biases and let the person you are learning with express them, too. That's how learning happens. But these ways of thinking, conversing, negotiating meaning, and collaborating in the search for and creation of knowledge and understanding require legitimation and space where they can be practiced. To the extent that instrumental rationality crowds out or replaces a language of learning, a literacy of thoughtfulness (for adults, as well as for students) has no institutional legitimacy, no way to sustain and reproduce itself, even when people in the institution say they want a literacy of thoughtfulness. So long as they are thinking about it instrumentally and not actually practicing it, they are unlikely to achieve it.

Tension between institution and practice is inevitable, but in the North Urban Public Schools, it is an unhealthy tension. Conversation sounds vague and bureaucratic, and intentions are unclear. People seem unable to get to the bottom of anything. Jargon substitutes for authentic communication, and talk seems systematically distorted and evasive. In the absence of leaders sensitive to the need to preserve and expand space for a language of learning, policy language can shore up such an unhealthy climate.

Educational policy has an institutional force and is expressed in instrumental terms. It influences what people do—not so much because it tells them what to do as because it establishes norms of rationality and communication, ways of thinking about things, and a vocabulary with which to describe and structure institutional experience. It structures (and sometimes overdetermines) the discourse it engenders. Leadership requires at least an intuitive grasp of this situation.

When we left the North Urban Public Schools, we went on to find leaders who have created the space for a critique and a dialogue through which people can become aware of the structures of thought implicit in their language. These leaders have created opportunities for people to explore, in an unthreatening way, the presuppositions embedded in their own and others' language, through formal and informal conversations oriented toward reaching understanding, not compliance. These leaders understand that what needs "restructuring" is not just inside schools or districts; it's also inside people's heads.

CHAPTER SIX

When Teachers Talk

It's a warm March afternoon. Looking out the school windows, I see people in shirtsleeves walking up the hill slowly, enjoying the first taste of spring. Inside, I am seated in a soft chair, listening to sixteen teachers who are discussing a passage from Plutarch's *Life of Pericles.* The group includes four English teachers, three social studies teachers, two computer teachers, two special education teachers, a physics teacher, a Spanish teacher, a health teacher, and a physical education teacher with a whistle around her neck. The discussion is being led by John Davis, a teacher trainer for the Schenley Teacher Center at Schenley High School in Pittsburgh, Pennsylvania.

The teachers are wrestling with a statement that King Philip makes to his son Alexander (one day to become Alexander the Great). The king is admonishing Alexander for playing his flute. He says, "Aren't you ashamed to play so well? A king should be able to enjoy music, he should not be able to play it."

What can this mean? One teacher suggests that it has to do with menial versus kingly roles.

"He's saying that it's beneath a king to actually work," she says. "That's for others to do. That's the point of being king."

"Well, maybe," another teacher says, "but I think he's saying something about the importance of enjoyment. Kings should know how to enjoy things, appreciate their beauty. And that's more important, more kingly, than actually doing things. Maybe you can't enjoy music when you're playing it. You have to be really listening to it, getting into its form. The person who's playing it is using some of his mind to play it. The king can use his whole mind to really appreciate it."

"Is there anything in the text that can support that point of view?" John Davis asks.

The teacher reads for a bit but does not come up with anything. Another teacher volunteers an interpretation.

"What about this?" she asks. "Maybe it has to do with Plutarch's earlier point, that with most things we don't feel a desire to imitate the maker, but with virtue, we do."

"How do you mean?" someone asks.

"Well, maybe music is like virtue. The king is really calling Alexander's attention to virtue, not music. He's saying that a king should want to imitate the maker of the music . . . "

"Then that means he should play it," the Spanish teacher says, "but he is saying *not* to play it."

The other teacher is uncertain of herself. She gets flustered.

"Yeah, you're right. It doesn't seem to make sense. But it's something like that. Maybe the maker of the music is different from the player of the music. I don't know. I just don't know why he would tell this story here unless it was connected to the part about virtue . . . "

She looks at John for support, but he is impassive and says nothing.

"Look at the part about the sculptor," an English teacher says. "He says, 'No person looking at the great statue of Jupiter by the famous sculptor Phidias ever desired to become another Phidias. For it doesn't follow that if a work pleases us by its beauty, the person who made it deserves our admiration.' But he says that virtue and nobility aren't like that. They do make us want to imitate the people who are virtuous and noble."

"I don't agree with him about that part," a social studies teacher says. "Lot of times when I've seen something beautiful, I've wished I could have made it. Haven't you?"

The group goes on. The teachers talk about the class system in Greece. They talk about father-son relationships. Somehow they start talking about Spaniards and Japanese people. John keeps

bringing them back to the text or asking them for supporting reasons for their opinions.

The teachers are learning how to participate in and conduct
a discussion. Some are clearly uncomfortable with the process. They
are self-conscious and tentative. It is hard for them to venture opinions among their peers. Teachers are used to working alone behind
closed doors.

As they struggle with the meanings of various passages, I'm
struck by the difference between this discussion and so much of
what I have observed in classrooms around the country. Here,
meaning is hard to fix; lots of interpretations seem reasonable. People talk for an hour about a short passage and still have disagreements and loose ends to pursue. In classrooms, it is assumed that
passages and stories have only one meaning, and that thirty-five
students get it with one reading and almost no discussion. This
contrast comes up in the debriefing session that follows the
discussion.

John asks the teachers how the discussion felt, and what they
have learned from it. One teacher says, "It shows how we're all so
different." Another says, "It was hard for me not to take what Joe
said personally." Tony Petrosky, who is observing with me, tries to
get them to compare this experience to their classroom experience,
their feelings to their students' feelings.

"I noticed that you had no consensus about the meaning of
several passages, and no consensus about the meaning of the whole
piece," he says. "How do you square that with what you English
teachers do when you ask for the main idea of a passage or a work?"

The English teachers aren't sure what he is driving at. He
tries again.

"You've just had an experience trying to find out what a
short passage means, and you've found lots of meanings and lots of
different interpretations about what is going on. If that's true for
you and for this passage, why isn't it true for your students and the
stuff they're reading?"

"Because," one of the English teachers says, "in the material
they read, there *really is* only one main idea."

Transfer of what these teachers learned to their classrooms
has some way to go, but the idea is that if teachers do not learn and

practice the principles of discussion, they will never be able to help their students do it. And it has been decreed from the top, here at the Schenley Teacher Center, that there will be more discussion in the classroom.

"What we're trying to do is enable students to take more responsibility for their own learning," John tells us after the teachers leave. "They're going to have to be more active in responding to what they are studying. These discussions teach them how to deepen their understanding of material, how to listen, how to respect the opinions of others, how to question, how to think critically."

That's why we're here: to look at the critical-thinking program in an urban district that has made a major commitment to a much higher level of literacy for the full range of its students.

"What we want the teachers to learn," John goes on, "is that they can share the responsibility for learning with their students. They don't always have to be up there in front, making things happen. They can sit in the circle, like I just did, and observe their kids in the process of learning. It's a different role for them and for the kids."

The district is using the St. John's model of classroom discussion (see Comber, Maisttellis, and Zeiderman, 1985). It is much like the "great books" approach and the one used by Mortimer Adler and the Paideia Group, except that it focuses on short excerpts from classical texts (for example, Aristotle, Plato, Kierkegaard) rather than on whole works. The selections are not tied to the curriculum or to the expertise of individual teachers; in fact, teachers are trained to lead discussions of unfamiliar material, so that they will learn how to rely on discussion, not authority, to conduct their classes.

I ask John how typical the teachers we just watched are, and what the effects of the discussion training have been so far.

"Well, these teachers were pretty green," he says. "The group hasn't solidified yet. Their listening skills are not great. There's still a lot of ricocheting going on—you know, one person ricochets off another, and then another ricochets off him, and they don't stay focused. So they'll need another eight to ten seminars before they jell. But just to get them into the notion that they are part of an intellectual community is a major goal here, too. A lot of these teachers have never talked about ideas the way they did today. Not when they were in school, not in their education courses, not in their schools. It's a whole new thing. And it excites them, once they get over the initial risk of it all. Our studies show that they talk to each other more after they have been in these seminars. That's the primary outcome so far. There hasn't been a lot of transfer to the classroom yet, but they are talking with each other more about ideas, and that's a big change.''

"Are they likely to transfer this to the classroom if the discussions aren't connected to what they're teaching?" I ask.

"We'll see," John says. "They should, eventually, but that is a bone of contention around here. We know we can't train them in pure discussion if we keep them within their subject area. So we have to start out this way. Once it becomes a habit for them and for their students, it should carry over. Time will tell."

We get out of our comfortable chairs and begin to tour the facility. The level of comfort of these chairs is in fact one of the most noticeable differences between this school and any other we have visited. The room was designed for adults. Schenley also seems to be a good place to hold seminars on Plutarch: it is filled with Greek statues, and the school's teams are called the Spartans. But the school wasn't always a place that people associated with intellectual discussion; it was once tough and troubled.

It is in Oakland, close to downtown Pittsburgh and to the universities. Oakland is ethnically mixed—Italian, Greek, Irish, Polish, and black residents—but heavily black, and it is relatively poor in the area that the school draws on. In 1978, the school population was 99 percent black. In 1981, the Pittsburgh desegregation plan integrated most schools, including Schenley, but the school was slated to be closed. At the urging of the superintendent, Richard Wallace, and with a Ford Foundation grant and the hard work of two hundred volunteer teachers, the school was revamped and reopened as a teacher-development center and magnet school. About half the students now come from the Oakland neighborhood, and the other half come from all over Pittsburgh. Gang and safety problems are gone, and school pride is high. Of the approximately one thousand students, two-thirds are black, and two-thirds are eligible for free or reduced-cost lunches. About one-quarter of the professional staff of ninety-five are black, including the principal.

Schenley offers three high school diplomas: a general diploma, an academic diploma, and a skills-center (vocational education) diploma. It also offers magnet programs in international studies and high technology and the Center for Advanced Studies, a state-funded program for gifted students. About 60 percent of the students are in an academic program (half of them in the magnets), 10 percent are in the skills center, and the rest are in the general program. The general program is being phased out all over the school district, on the grounds that it is not sufficiently focused or intense. An interdisciplinary committee of teachers and administrators is looking into ways for the vocational and academic curricula to be combined. The biggest hurdle so far seems to be the state regulations that make it difficult to integrate academic and vocational coursework.

As we walk around the school, John Davis fills us in on the teacher-development aspects of Schenley.

"Besides the discussion training, we're also helping teachers learn and practice more about writing," he says. "We're doing training here on how to integrate artistic and esthetic experiences into the content areas, and how to get more critical thinking and discussion into the district's arts program. And we're also working on the Syllabus Examination Project here, which is an effort to develop tests and curriculum that will get all students using higher-order thinking skills across the curriculum."

The long-range goal is to have all secondary teachers go through eight weeks of critical-thinking training. Elementary teachers go through a similar training at the Brookline Center, modeled after Schenley. Fundamental to all the programs is the principle of learning by doing.

The animating notion of the Schenley Teacher Center is that to infuse critical thinking and generate more active learning among students and teachers alike, one has to help teachers redefine the curriculum, instruction, and testing all at once; working in only one area at a time will not get the job done.

The district uses a turnkey approach to training.

"We began with about sixty-five of the center's staff here

taking sixty-six hours of inservice in 1985," Davis says. "Then these people went back to their classes and led discussions while being watched by their colleagues, who gave them more feedback and fine-tuning. They continued to develop their discussion skills for the rest of the year, and then they became our clinicians in 1986. They helped train, observe, and coach another cadre, which included teachers from two high schools and three middle schools. These will then become clinical advisers next year, and so on."

With a grant from the Rockefeller Foundation in New York (we soon learned that Pittsburgh excels in going after and getting grants), the Division of Arts Education began a multiyear collaboration with researchers from Harvard University to develop critical-thinking approaches to artistic experience. The program was based at Schenley and soon became a subject of national interest. It has not only pioneered promising improvement in arts education but also broadened the scope of the critical-thinking program and led to the development of new techniques for assessing complicated performances and productions by students.

The Syllabus Examination Project (SEP) at Schenley involves having teachers review the existing curriculum in Pittsburgh, to see what can be done to move away from an overemphasis on students' recalling facts and toward an emphasis on their analyzing major themes and relationships. The long-range goal is to overhaul the curriculum and, concurrently, create new assessment tools that get at students' skills in analysis, synthesis, evaluation, interpretation, questioning, deep reading, and extended writing.

The syllabus for a new SEP course in U.S. history affords a look at how the project works. Exhibit 6.1 shows the skill objectives and content objectives of the course, as well as a sample essay question. The syllabus also lists fifty-seven key terms that students should know by the end of the course. Two points about the syllabus are important. First, it has a focus; it does not try to cover everything imaginable. Second, it is for all students, not just for college-bound or gifted students or those in advanced classes.

Few school districts in the United States have a facility like the Schenley Teacher Center, where teachers can go for minisabbaticals, try new teaching strategies, get feedback from resident "clinicians," participate in nationally recognized programs, attend group

Exhibit 6.1. Syllabus for U.S. History.

Skill Objectives

The student will be able to:

- Raise questions about events, situations, ideas, pictures, or artifacts
- Infer reasons or causes for and effects of situations or events
- Explain or predict from raw data or limited information
- Interpret and analyze maps, tables, graphs, cartoons, original documents, and other nonnarrative materials
- Compare and contrast events in different parts of the world or different time periods, or different versions or accounts of the same event or situation
- Evaluate outcomes or consequences of events in relation to reasons or causes for the events
- Take a position and defend it, with reference to primary or secondary sources

Content Objectives

The student will be able to:

- Describe the development of the United States, in terms of five main themes: diplomacy, economy, politics, society, and culture
- Recognize the distinctive characteristics of the American colonies and the reasons for separation from the mother country, 1750–1780
- Explain the rationale for establishing the key political institutions and traditions of the United States during the period after the Revolution, 1781–1800
- Describe the tensions in American society due to changing boundaries and interests, 1800–1850
- Examine the causes and results of the Civil War and Reconstruction, 1850–1877
- Identify the economic, social, political, and cultural changes in American society, 1877–1917
- Evaluate the changed relationship between citizens and the government brought about by the Great Depression during the 1930s
- Explain the significance, both to the United States and to the world, of the United States' becoming a world power, 1940–present
- Review the key social changes that have taken place in American life and in government domestic policy since 1945

Sample Essay Question

The following is an example of one type of essay question found on each examination.

You will be given excerpts from statements by Woodrow Wilson and George Norris regarding the U.S. entry into World War I. Read those excerpts, and answer the following question: As part of their arguments, Wilson and Norris suggest different reasons for the U.S. entry into World

Exhibit 6.1. Syllabus for U.S. History, Cont'd.

War I. Which man do you think was more accurate? Write an essay in
which you (1) describe the reasons suggested by each man and tell how
they differ, and (2) explain why the speech you endorse offers a more accurate description of U.S. reasons for entry. Base your explanations on any
knowledge you may have of historical events that you may be able to use
to provide supporting evidence for your position.

clinics, and participate in "externships" with other schools, businesses, or local colleges and universities. No other district has such
a facility devoted fundamentally to critical thinking and backed by
a strong district policy and strong leaders. It has not come cheaply:
the district has put $12.5 million into teacher development over the
last five years. We leave Schenley High School for the time being,
eager to know both how the district has evolved to this point and
whether this investment is paying off.

In 1979, the gap in achievement between minority and Anglo
students in Pittsburgh was substantial: 35 percent more white students than black were achieving at or above grade level in reading,
38 percent more white students than black in language, and 28
percent more white students than black in mathematics. By 1984,
that gap had been cut at least in half in all cases. But, according to
Paul LeMahieu, director of research, testing, and evaluation for the
Pittsburgh Board of Public Education, that may be about as much
as the gap can be reduced. We visit LeMahieu at his office in the
district's labyrinthine central administrative office building.

"You'd expect reforms that are focused on basics and school-
effectiveness research to raise their test scores," he tells us, "especially among poor minority students and those most in need of
increased attention to basic skills. But, to the degree that those reforms don't pay any attention to multicultural environments or any
of the other environmental influences on achievement, there will be
clear limits to what you can accomplish. Some of the achievement
gap is because schools aren't doing their jobs well with respect to
minority students. Much of it is a consequence of social and economic conditions."

LeMahieu is a confident, animated talker, who has obviously said these things often in the last few years.

"Now, maybe the cultural and economic differences are things we need to get rid of in students, and maybe they're not," he continues. "We don't really know that all students have to be a certain way in order to learn. That attitude is disrespectful of the members of a multicultural society, and it gets us off the hook of trying to figure out what each student really needs. So we're trying to think of new ways to shrink the gap farther, both in terms of attending more to higher-order skills and providing a better affective and cultural environment for learning. We may have done all we can do with a basic-skills approach."

LeMahieu attributes the successful narrowing of the black/ white achievement gap to the Monitoring Achievement in Pittsburgh (MAP) program, wherein learning outcomes are clearly defined, instruction focuses on commonly held objectives, and students' progress is assessed four to six times throughout the school year. Pittsburgh currently has MAP tests in mathematics, reading, grammar, composition, critical thinking, and science.

"The MAP tests are designed to give teachers the kind of diagnostic feedback they need to make sure that each student is meeting basic objectives," LeMahieu says. "MAP scores aren't published or used to assess teacher progress in any way. They can't be. There's an irony about diagnostic testing. You can only learn from errors, from wrong answers, so if you're pushing for high test scores because there are high stakes involved, you won't learn from them. So, from our point of view, it's better not to publish those scores. This is really a teacher diagnostic system."

Pittsburgh's MAP program seems to have allayed the community's concern over "the basics," according to LeMahieu; now it is possible to think of the higher literacies. The class discussion project and SEP "represent MAP taken out to the next generation," he says. "We're trying to redefine the curriculum and decide what's really important, and streamline it by at least a third, so that there's some breathing space for higher-order events to occur. That's our new aim."

SEPs have begun in classes in U.S. history and world cultures and are being explored and piloted in English, trigonometry, analytics, and statistics. This year, the project is also beginning to explore social studies, algebra, general science, and earth and space science. Later on, there will be SEPs for American democracy, biology, geometry, chemistry, and physics. This activity represents nothing less than a total overhaul of the secondary school curriculum—refocusing and upgrading it, blending in more discussion and writing, and throwing out the trivial.

We ask LeMahieu what he thinks are the major policy barriers to moving in this direction, and he mentions three. First is the tyranny of the curriculum.

"One of our biggest problems," he says, "is the urge to cover everything. There's no breathing space for reflection or discussion, so the SEP has to reconceive the curriculum around themes and open up some room for discussion."

He is worried, however, that people are lockstepping their way through the new SEPs, just as they lockstepped through the old curriculum, and that the SEP could become as tyrannical as the other curriculum. He doesn't seem to have any explanation for why this occurs, and so he doesn't have any ideas about how to stop it.

The second barrier is teacher training. LeMahieu believes that teachers' behaviors for eliciting discussion need a lot of shaping.

"We've had to bump heads with all this 'direct instruction' training a lot," he says, "because that stuff doesn't really apply for discussion."

Direct-instruction training emphasizes classroom management and ways in which teachers can tightly control students' activities. It focuses on the traditional role of the teacher, instead of the roles that emerge when students take greater responsibility for their learning (Hunter, 1976).

The third barrier is the testing program.

"If you haven't thought about your testing program, it's probably in the way," LeMahieu says. His and the superintendent's philosophy is that if SEP testing becomes increasingly like European written and oral examinations, it will improve higher-order skills, and the other kinds of testing will be able to be downplayed or eliminated.

The district is trying now to build observational instruments, so that discussions can be observed and the quality of discussions can be gauged. For LeMahieu, the best test, at a minimum, gets out of the way, encourages discussion, and doesn't pretend to do everything.

"We've raised the quantity of discourse stupendously in this district," says LeMahieu, "and we're reasonably confident that, because of that, the quality has gone up, too. We take the YMCA approach to discourse: if you throw people in the pool, they swim."

LeMahieu is aware that much of the district's success has depended on massive teacher training at the Schenley Teacher Center, which the district is not going to be able to afford forever and is now scaling down. The plan is to ask each high school to focus on a particular issue, so that in the future each one will become a scaled-down Schenley or Brookline, and teachers will be sent for training to schools that have developed expertise in particular areas.

We leave Paul LeMahieu and go on to meet with Stanley Herman, an associate superintendent. Herman is very natty and looks somewhat like a banker. He greets us warmly, obviously accustomed to welcoming visitors who are favorably disposed to the district.

"What has happened in Pittsburgh is Dick Wallace," Herman says, referring to the superintendent. "He deserves the credit for what we've done so far."

Wallace is often spoken of as the best superintendent in the United States. When word got out that he was a finalist for the chancellorship of the New York City schools, the teachers' union and the community came to him and offered him a lifetime contract.

"Before Dick," Herman says, "the focus was totally on bureaucracy, holding things together. Communication was terrible. There were at least five or six three-ring binders on standard operating procedures. When I was a principal, in order to write to another principal, I would first have to write to my superior at the administration building. He would then okay the letter and then send it to the other principal's superior, who would then initial it and send it along to the principal. That's how it was."

Wallace immediately changed all that. He wanted to open up communication and discussion, in the district and in the community. He asked everyone to take a hard look at what was wrong with the schools. He did a needs assessment. He took the board on a series of retreats, and the board members emerged with a set of priorities. The first one was to improve educational achievement.

"Then Wallace surrounded himself with creative people," Herman goes on. "People like Paul LeMahieu, and people who would not ordinarily work for a school district. They'd work for him, but they probably wouldn't work for anyone else in the country. A lot of them were short-timers, people he'd bring in to focus on one problem. He didn't overload people so they had to do so many things they couldn't do any one of them well. And then he gave them room to work. He told them what to do, and he trusted them to do it. When I first came onto his team, I asked him what he wanted me to do. He said, 'I don't care what you do, as long as it's something different!' Later, he got more specific."

According to Herman, the MAP program was a necessary first step in moving the district to where it wanted to go. People had to get organized around central goals, and the community had to be put at ease about basic skills. Herman points out that the MAP objectives were sent home. Parents were asked for help in the MAP at Home program, which trained six thousand to seven thousand parents in thirty-hour workshops, even using cable television. Principals were evaluated on what they did with MAP data when they talked to their teachers about it. Thus, MAP was a fairly intensive program for the district.

"Our mathematics people now believe that the math MAP has outlived its utility," Herman tells us, "and the kids have the basics down. Some people are saying the same thing about the critical-thinking MAP. It's time to move on. And that's what we're trying to do with the SEP examinations—go beyond the basics, to ensure that our students are really educated."

Getting acceptance from teachers has been a problem, he thinks, but it's been progressing slowly.

"The magic is in reaching a consensus," he says, "It's not in the objectives, it's not in the testing. On some issues, it's taken two years of discussions to get the kind of consensus necessary to make something work, even in a district that has exemplary relations with its teachers. The key is to make it a learning experience for all teachers. If you don't do that, you don't get anywhere.

"Some board members say, 'Why do we have to keep all this staff development going?" he goes on. " 'The teachers have master's degrees, they've been trained. Isn't that enough?' But it's not enough. That continuing development is absolutely key. That's where you get the learning and the ownership. Without the ownership, nothing is going to happen."

Herman expresses great frustration with state officials in charge of special funding. The district has battled year after year over state rules and regulations about how to do things. Pittsburgh school officials believe that they know some better ways to do some things, but state officials have withheld money when those things have been tried. The state once held up $6.5 million and said it would have to send the district's "deviant interpretation" of the regulations to the attorney general and other bureaucrats for a ruling. The money was released when Superintendent Wallace threatened to sue the state.

What challenges lie ahead? According to Herman, the district needs to tie the discussion program into textbooks and supplement the texts because they're so poor.

"We don't have much clout," Herman says. "They're writing textbooks for Texas and California, not us. So we'll have to make our own stuff."

The teachers will have to get comfortable with using the discussion model, as well as with developing assessment models and integrating them into instruction.

"Principals have been difficult to change, as you might expect," he says. "It's going to be a long process. They aren't at all sure they like this notion of collaborative decision making. It's not what they were trained to do or deal with. But we'll get there. Dick [Wallace] is here until he retires, and everybody knows it. They can't wait him out."

We witness the Wallace style at a principals' meeting the next day. He is a dapper-looking man who, like Herman, resembles a banker. He sits in a child's chair in a school library while curriculum staff explain the SEP examination to about forty administrators. The curriculum staff clearly lean on Wallace's silent presence as they explain their programs to a largely implacable group, turning often to make eye contact with him and mentioning his name frequently.

Joanne Ersch, the language-arts curriculum developer, begins by saying that the SEP is the next step for MAP, away from the basics.

"We're trying to revise the entire tenth-grade curriculum," she says. "We've brought in cutting-edge consultants."

The principals listen silently. She laughs nervously. They watch. She explains that SEP curriculum developers are focusing on Shakespeare's *A Midsummer Night's Dream.* Under the new proposal, students will view three to five videos of the play, each offering different interpretations and productions. They will be asked to compare what they see in the various videos and then write about the differences. Thirteen teachers and seven hundred students are currently piloting this approach, she says.

While she explains the plan in detail, she seems increasingly unnerved by the silence of her audience, and she turns toward Wallace in proportion to her apparent nervousness. When she has finished, a tired-looking principal asks, "How does this address the kids' question about why they are reading Shakespeare at all?"

"They should know about Shakespeare because so much of the language they speak, and so many common expressions, can't really be understood if you don't know about Shakespeare," she says. "They have to be told that. They have to be *shown* that, actually. And Shakespeare is part of our culture. If they don't know him, they won't be able to participate in the culture. But how much Shakespeare should they know? We're working on that now."

In any case, she says, the students are doing well on the tests, doing more homework, and giving good feedback. Teachers are keeping logs and debating as they go through this process, and it looks as if students in the pilot program are enjoying Shakespeare.

The principal does not pursue this topic. Maybe he is speaking for himself. He does not seem to like Shakespeare very much.

Joanne Eresh gives way to Ray McClaine, who tells the principals about the U.S. history SEP and various teachers' concerns; for example, that there is not enough time to cover the syllabus. He says that there should be enough time because they've been trying to eliminate a third of the curriculum to open up time for writing and discussion.

"If your teachers tell you that they didn't have enough time," he says, "you tell them to follow the quarterly guidelines, which will give them a third more time than they have."

Another principal says, "My magnet teachers are complaining that this new SEP course is diluting their special course and will be undermining the uniqueness of the magnet school, because everybody will be getting what they're offering, making their program less unique."

McClaine says he thinks that there is plenty of room for the magnet to do things that the core curriculum will not do.

Now a principal says that there were too many failures on this quarter's SEP examination; his students are guinea pigs and are being hurt by this pilot. McClaine says that the teachers may indeed be writing items that are too difficult; this is always a problem in raising standards. On the last test, in one school, a group of teachers decided that a score of 50 percent was passing. The principal nods his head and seems to feel that this is a fairly good standard. McClaine says he saw that twenty-seven kids got "zero"—didn't even try, didn't write anything, didn't even guess on the multiple-choice section. He's clearly disturbed by this.

"We cut the failure rate in half this last test," he says. "We're out front. We don't want to penalize your students. But after all, we're trying to raise standards."

A principal says, "Our kids are having trouble writing social studies essays, because they are writing the way they were taught in English. Why are we confusing kids so? Why don't we teach them one way to write, that they can use no matter what their course?" McClaine isn't sympathic.

Like so many other meetings, this one is superficial. People just present information. Little time is left for asking questions or answering them or dealing with anything complicated.

The woman running the meeting begins to call it to a close and invites Richard Wallace to comment, but he demurs. She makes some logistical and scheduling announcements. Then, just as she is about to adjourn, Wallace, as if on second thought, says, "Well, I do have something to say." He rises from his little chair.

"I just want to say that the MAP was to ensure that we were meeting our obligation to teach these children the basics and the fundamentals, and to give them the tools they need in order to be educated."

He speaks quietly and makes eye contact with individuals as he does so.

"But now the SEP is to make sure that they are *educated* before they leave us."

He lets that sink in.

"I also want to correct something that Joanne and Ray said about the curriculum," he says. "They said that the things in the new curriculum are important to teach. I want to stress that they're not important to teach. They're important to learn."

Again he pauses to let the sentence sink in. Principals who were almost asleep during the earlier presentations are wide awake and attentive now.

"This syllabus-examination effort is going to totally change the curriculum," he goes on quietly. "And I realize that this is going to call for different ways of transmitting knowledge. 'Teacher talk' won't accomplish these goals. Kids aren't going to learn this material by just sitting there. They're going to have to get more involved. We're going to have to get more involved. They're going to have to write more and discuss more and take charge of their own learning."

He reminds the principals that this is going to mean culture shock for them, the teachers, and the students.

"We've had low expectations for minorities in the past," he says. "We demonstrated with MAP that if you raise the standards, they can do it. Now we're moving away from skills, and you're going to see the same thing. If you expect them to do the analysis and the evaluation and these higher-order things, they'll do that too—you'll see."

Although he says this in a quiet way, he conveys great determination. Behind his words is a clear imperative: you *will* see.

When we visit him, Richard Wallace describes himself as "relentless, in my quiet way." He says his success is due to a number of things.

"I've been able to tap foundation money pretty successfully," he says. "It's enabled me to free some good people to work full-time on important pieces of the plan. It's given us time to go about this thoughtfully, instead of helter-skelter.

"Second, I don't have any serious political problems to deal with. Look at New York, for instance. The educational problems in New York will never be solved as long as the political problems remain as they are now.

"Third, I have a great relationship with the Pittsburgh Federation of Teachers."

Wallace lunches monthly with the leader of the teachers' union, and the two of them worked out new teacher contracts early for the last two contract periods. The current one will last until Wallace's retirement and was signed six months ahead of schedule.

"Fourth," he continues, "I have no relation to city government," he says. "I have fiscal and operational autonomy in the schools. I control the custodians, for instance. Because of that, I've inherited a school infrastructure that was in excellent shape: good school buildings, good maintenance."

Wallace is obviously proud of additions that he has made to some schools. The architects' drawings hang in his office, evoking the days when a superintendent's whole career was judged by the amount of building he did.

"Then I'd say that I was lucky to come at a time when the details of the desegregation plan had been worked out," Wallace goes on. "The previous fifteen years had been hard ones. But the toughest part of it was over, and I didn't have to worry about it. I'm not saying racism is over, you understand, or that we don't have black/white issues. We do. I'm seeing some signs of a new wave of racism coming up, and we're jumping on that. And the effects of discrimination aren't over for these kids. This isn't something that just goes away. It's what you live with and keep working on. It's at the center of almost everything we're trying to do here.

"Another thing I'd say is that I run the bureaucracy. It doesn't run me. After eight years, the bureaucracy still doesn't know what to do with me. I make sure that the people in the schools make more money than the people down here. In most cities, the epitome of success is to be in this building, not in the school. I don't want

that. When I have people here, they're here on temporary assignment. A lot of them are being paid for by other monies. When
they've done a particular job, they go."

Another factor that Wallace brings up is his belief that staff
development is the key to any transformation of a school district.
He points out that the massive staff-development effort that the
district went through—$12.5 million in five years, $10 million of it
out of his budget—created a common language and developed a
new spirit, without which reform cannot go anywhere.

"You have to believe that people have unlimited capacity to
learn and grow," he says. "You have to have high expectations. And
you have to keep hammering. They may not think they can do
more, but they can. They always can."

It's the same with students, Wallace believes. One of his heros
is Jerome Bruner, the psychologist who has said time and again that
any child can learn anything (Bruner, 1986). Wallace's background
is in educational psychology.

"Finally, I guess I'd say the needs assessments we did with
the community have been critical. They told us that people don't
want interest in reading to decline as kids get older, the way it does
now. They told us that we had to close that racial achievement gap,
had to get at science and math, had to bring more critical thinking
and questioning into the classroom. So we've had board agreement
about priorities. Whenever I've gone to them and said we needed to
move ahead on one of these priorities, they've given me what I
needed."

"You mean you've never fought with your board in eight
years?" I ask.

Wallace laughs.

"Oh, we've fought about lots of things," he says. "But not
our priorities."

What are Wallace's plans for the next five years? He want to
develop the centers of excellence in each high school, and he wants
to restructure the secondary schools so that they have smaller units
and schools within schools. He wants to see more challenging spe-
cialty programs, and he wants to establish an agenda that addresses
the whole student, not just the student's mind.

"The dropout rate has gone from 35 percent to 22 percent

and then drifted slowly back up toward 27 percent," he says. "There is just so much you can do about a dropout rate with cognitive programs. We've got to give these kids a sense that someone knows them and cares about them."

To that end, he is heading a task force aimed at a five-year program on "personalization." We are not surprised to learn, as we leave his office, that his district will be awarded a $12.5 million grant to move in this direction.

It happens that Richard (Rick) deLone, one of the Aspen symposium participants mentioned in Chapter Two, was also doing some case-study work in Pittsburgh for the Education Commission of the States (ECS) around the same time that Tony Petrosky, Sam Stringfield, and I were doing our interviews and observations. Rick was examining the situation faced by at-risk youth in the district, with a special focus on Schenley High School. His observations, presented here, support Richard Wallace's belief that the district will have to do more to engage the full range of students in high-quality educational experiences:

> Schenley's curriculum offerings are certainly representative of the best that the Pittsburgh system has to offer: stress placed on academics through MAP, quality vocational education, and magnet programs. The school's CAT [California Achievement Test] scores (for white and black students) have risen dramatically over time, which indicates that something good must be happening there. However, it is not at all clear that the academic needs of all students are being met. Some of the staff feel that . . . disproportionate . . . attention and resources are given to magnet-program students, when in fact it is the mainstream students who need them most. Vocational education teachers who teach skill-center classes complained that, in spite of MAP, many of their students were still not academically prepared for the technical courses they must complete. While the teachers felt that they had high-quality, well-equipped programs, and that the work expe-

rience connected with vocational education helped attract and retain students, they also felt that the magnet programs were siphoning off the best students.

Discussions with the magnet-programs coordinator revealed more evidence that all students, especially those most likely to be at risk, may not be benefiting from all Schenley has to offer. He reported that even in the magnet programs, there is tracking: college-bound (international studies and some high-tech students) and vocational (students who are completing a high-tech program in the skills center). The former get more academics; the latter, more skills training. While the magnet programs do not have admissions standards, he reported that some at-risk ninth graders have trouble wih the course material. So far this year, ten ninth graders have dropped. "After all," he said, "this is a scholars' program."

Certain teachers spoke openly of their preference for teaching classes in the magnet programs over mainstream classes, referring to mainstream classes as having students who are "problems" and who lack motivation and basic skills. (It's important to note that classes in magnet programs average twenty-two students, while mainstream classes average thirty-four.)

In our review of Schenley's curricula [Rick deLone was accompanied by Bernardine Watson], it appeared that at-risk students may well be slipping through the cracks academically, especially since so much attention is focused on the special programs. A closer look at the social climate at Schenley indicates that . . . the social needs of these students are [probably] being overlooked as well. Discussions with students and teachers reveal that there is little mingling between the magnet and mainstream students.

At first glance, this kind of social organization appears logical, since it is normal for students to form their friendships among classmates. At Schenley, however, social separation based on curriculum track takes on deeper significance. First of all, more than half of the students in the school's magnet programs are white, and at least three-fourths of the students in the mainstream program are black. As a result, social segregation often becomes racial, even though race may not be the true basis for it.

Second, some teachers report, and with great concern, a sense of anomie among mainstream students. After all, Schenley is a special school for special people. There is lots of attention for the students in the magnet and gifted programs, but little special attention [is] paid to the mainstream student.

We go now to a discussion of Hobbes's *Leviathan*, at Rogers Middle School, a magnet school focusing on the performing arts. Twenty-three students are sitting in a circle. Everyone reads the passages, and then the teacher reads them aloud. They include Hobbes's famous description of man in a state of nature, where every man is every other man's enemy, and life is "solitary, poor, nasty, brutish and short." Several students begin the discussion by agreeing with parts of the text. It's true, one of them says, that the differences between people are, as Hobbes says, not very great. Discussion quickly centers on the line "the weakest man has enough strength to kill the strongest." But is it cheating if someone attacks someone with a weapon? Soon the students are swapping stories about fighting or being beaten up. Girls say things like "That's why I hate boxing and wrestling," and so on. The students wander away from Hobbes, into the concerns of early adolescence.

After a while, one girl goes back to the text and says, "It's true that every man is every man's enemy in a state of nature." For a moment, it looks as if the students are getting back on track. But, once again, a student begins to talk about Mike Tyson and "Refrigerator" Perry and their respective marital problems. On this rhythm goes: they wander off for a while, until someone brings them back to the text. They talk a little about that, and then go off again. Some of this going off on tangents is good. It may lead them to think, in the context of their own lives and times, about the points Hobbes raises. But they would be more likely to make those connections if someone pointed them out explicitly. Someone could say, for instance, "To judge from your comment, it sounds as if you believe Hobbes means . . . ," or "So what this means to you in *your* life is. . . ." But the students in this group have not come that far yet in their discussion skills.

Afterward, we ask the students what they think of these discussions. They tell us that discussion is fun, that it cuts across social lines and has made them friendlier with people. They have been able to express themselves better, they say, and they have learned from seeing multiple points of view.

At a teachers' training session after school, we ask the teachers how the discussion project has gone for them. They tell us that the students have come to like the camaraderie, and that, contrary to some predictions, they enjoy talking about obscure and difficult works.

"They carry the conversations out into the halls," one teacher tells us, "and into the cafeteria. You can hear them arguing about philosophy in the lunch lines."

"I think they are better at thinking on their feet now," a math teacher says.

"Some of them," a librarian adds. "But I wonder what we're really improving. I think that it's their verbal literacy that's being improved, but not their reading literacy. They're saying things like 'I think I heard you say this' and stuff, which is good. They're becoming better active listeners. But I don't see any improvement in their reading habits."

Students are also sometimes asked to write about the discussions and how they feel during silences, and the teachers say they seem to like this kind of writing. An English teacher says that she thinks her students are getting better at backing up what they say and write, and she attributes this improvement to the discussions.

One teacher, however, wonders whether any higher-order thinking is really going on.

"Kids are talking a lot about their experiences, but are they doing any real thinking?" he asks.

John Davis says that researchers are studying the nature of the discussions. They have been analyzing hours and hours of videotaped discussions but have not yet come up with a good way of categorizing comments in terms of the kinds of thinking the comments represent.

The next day, we see two more discussions. One, at Langely High, is of Paul Simon's video "Boy in the Bubble." The students view the video and read the lyrics, which the teacher has typed out for them. The teacher seems nervous and unsure of herself. She constantly peppers reluctant students with questions.

"What's in the bubble?"

No response.

"What do you think the bubble represents?"

No response.

"Do the rocks have any symbolism for anybody?"

"I think it's people watching over us all the time," a girl volunteers shyly. "People watch us."

"What do you mean they watch us?" the teacher asks. But she leaves little time for the girl to elaborate on her idea. "Are you saying it's like we're in a glass, and people are watching us? Like we're in a bubble?"

Whatever training the teacher may have had in discussion, she has obviously forgotten it. She has automatically slipped into a familiar recitation format. This video should be a very good stimulus to discussion, given the amount of time that teenagers spend looking at videos; but the teacher, much to her own frustration and everyone else's, seems unable to let the discussion move. Furthermore, she has an agenda, an interpretation that she seems to be pushing. I get the impression that she sees the "boy in the bubble" as having something to do with protecting babies: she's trying to get these girls to think about how important it is to protect their babies when or if they have any. Personally, I see no connection between this view and the videotape or the lyrics, but that's not something that can be debated by me or anyone else, because the teacher never quite puts it directly on the table.

Although this teacher has participated in the Schenley training, she has a long way to go. Maybe this is her first videotape, and maybe our presence has made her nervous. But there is another lesson here besides the one about how hard it is to learn to conduct good discussions. I realize that I have just been assuming that students would love to talk about a rock video, because they watch them so often; but what this episode tells me is that teenagers are as inexperienced in looking critically at videos as they are in looking critically at texts. They don't know how to look critically at anything. Distancing themselves from an event or an experience, analyzing its parts and their relationships, and elaborating its various meanings for themselves and others—these are not things that many teenagers do naturally, even with events or experiences that mean a great deal to them. An experience's relevance or interest means nothing in itself.

We go next to a discussion of a newspaper article, which criticizes the way the press has made a heroine of a girl who hired somebody to kill her abusive father. This is a unique discussion because the fourteen kids are all in special education, and most have been declared mentally retarded for educational purposes. The teacher reads the whole article to the kids and then asks, "Who is the most wrong? The girl? The father? The newspapers? Or the guy who killed the father?"

One little guy named Charles quickly comes to dominate the whole class. He has a piercing intelligence and a rapier-like wit, and he cannot shut up. The teacher's effort to get other kids into the circle is futile; Charles and another boy, Walter, are basically duking the issues out alone. They even begin to call each other names. Charles says that if Walter picks on him, he'll kill Walter, who in reply asks Charles how he liked being in a trash can the other day. Nevertheless, something very rare is taking place: students in special education are being treated as if they had minds to use and ideas that matter. Although they are sparring verbally, they are not actually fighting, and the conversation interests and engages most of them.

Later, at another teacher inservice at Langely, I ask the teachers how the discussion groups have been going. Again, the teachers are very positive. They feel that the discussions provide an outlet for the students. Kids gain new perspectives on the teacher and on each other. They are more sociable. The teachers agree that the process is slow. Some kids take a long time to come in, and sometimes it is difficult to see any immediate improvement. The teachers see the advantage of having kids who are not good at written work excel in discussion and gain new respect among their peers, and they say they have seen this happen. The teachers also think that the discussions have enabled them to see their colleagues in a different light.

"There just is not enough time in an ordinary day for me to really get to know my friends, the way you can get to know them in one of these discussions," one teacher quotes a student as saying, and she says that it is as true for teachers as it is for students.

An art teacher talks about how discussion builds a sense of community in the classroom. Another teacher talks about how discussion wipes away barriers between whites and blacks and between kids at different skill levels. The teachers talk about the risk that discussions permit people to take, putting their ideas in front of others and thinking aloud in front of others. Students have become somewhat better questioners, some teachers say, even in content; students will say, "Well, we discussed a point like that some weeks ago, and our conclusion then was. . . ." One teacher says he's a better questioner now, too, and another has lengthened the amount of time he feels he needs before he gets a response.

As we watch more discussions and talk to more teachers, it becomes clear that the discussions are a positive force in promoting literate discourse and thoughtfulness among teachers and students. Although the discussions are not integrated into the curriculum, and although incentives to integrate them do not seem very strong, they are still serving an important function by creating the thoughtful environment within which more and more students may well exert pressure to discuss things. Teachers and students alike say that their listening skills have improved, and a number of students talk about the strange experience of having their minds changed by what other students have said.

I drop in on a sixth-grade science class. I am met at the door by the teacher, a tall, ungainly, sad-faced man wearing unironed pants and shirt. He begins the class by saying that he wants to review briefly what the class did yesterday, because so many kids were gone. He puts a transparency up on an overhead projector and explains what a transparency is. Then, in an affectless, deadpan way, he marches through the workbook questions that are on the transparency, about dinosaurs and fossils. He asks the kids to tell a story about how something becomes a fossil. One kid tells a very lively and interesting story about a saber-toothed tiger. The story reveals a good deal about how a tiger could hunt, but no knowledge at all about how a fossil could be formed.

The kids rattle on about violence, about preying on things and being preyed on. (Middle schoolers sometimes seem obsessed with violence.) The teacher goes back to the questions on the transparency. He skips over a question about a bug caught in amber, but a kid catches him.

"How'd that bug get in the amber?"

The teacher puts him off for a bit and then goes back.

"Think about it," he says. "How could it happen?"

The students figure out that it might have been from sap.

"If it's sap, what time of the year do you suppose that insect got caught?" the teacher asks.

They figure it was spring or summer.

The teacher, with his deadpan delivery, goes on to tell a story about a man finding a mammoth in Siberia. The story is confusing. He says that the mammoth was probably killed in an avalanche, but then he says that the mammoth had grass in its mouth, indicating that it must have lived in a tropical climate. Some kids begin to ask questions, but he says, "Not too many questions. We have to move on."

When he checks students' answers to various questions, he says, "How many people have that answer? If you didn't have it, put it in." There's no discussion of wrong answers. His vocabulary is poor, and his diction is terrible. The supposedly brief review of yesterday's lesson consumes the entire period, during which I observe several children doing all their other work from other courses (one girl seems to be doing very detailed personal graffiti about her boyfriend). Several kids get up and sharpen their pencils, but when they return to their desks they don't use them. During the period, I am hit twice by paper thrown toward the wastebasket next to me.

The teacher breeds no confidence at all in his knowledge of science or in his teaching ability, nor does he raise any hope that he will ever be interested in improving himself. He's very "laid back" and likes to take kids on field trips, but he is clearly manipulated by his students.

I observe a third-grade class at an all-black elementary school in what has been described as one of the toughest areas of the city.

A policeman, Officer Sproul (also know as Officer Friendly), is there to talk to the children about drugs. He passes out various worksheets and conducts a recitation in which he answers his own questions.

"Anytime a person that is not sick but takes a drug, that is what?" he asks. "Drug abuse," he answers. "That penicillin is for what? Curing. That's gonna cause a whole lot of what? Trouble."

The children like Officer Friendly a lot and give him a boisterous response. After he leaves, their aged, sickly-looking teacher, a white woman, administers a spelling test. She places great emphasis on following directions and doing things when told to do them.

"Eric," she says, "I've told you not to write your name until I've shown you how. Have I given you directions? Wait for me. Barry . . . I do not see numbers, and I don't see folding yet."

Multiplication exercises are done aloud by the entire class, rhythmically chanting "Three times two equals six, six times four equals twenty-four." When there is multiplication with carrying, the class shouts that out, too: "Put down four, carry the one. Seven times seven equals forty-nine." It's hard to tell whether everybody is chanting. Some students' chanting seems tenuous, but their hesitation goes unnoticed in the general din.

These exercises are followed by the assembling of level-eight readers, while other students do seatwork. The readers are working from a well-illustrated collection of African and Asian folktales. "Aren't you glad you passed out of group seven?" the teacher says. Yes, they are.

On the board, she writes vocabulary words that will figure prominently in the story they are going to read. Then she begins a ritual through which the children go with ease, while I flounder, trying to figure out what in the world this is all about. The children clap out the syllables in a word, and then the teacher says, "I'm looking for a pattern." One child suggests a pattern like "vowel-consonant-vowel." Then the students have to put in accents, consonants, and so on, so that eventually the word on the board looks like something written in Russian script rather in English. I notice that the teacher is working directly from the teachers' guide.

During this exercise, I reflect that a good deal of higher-order thinking may be occurring on the children's part, just because they have to know all this stuff about this particular textbook publisher's approach to teaching reading. All this mumbo-jumbo, making dia-critical marks and learning a mental language about phonics, takes up time that could otherwise be spent in actual reading.

Eventually, the class moves into the reading. The students read a page. The teacher asks some questions from the guide, probes a bit, and moves along.

I move on, too, to a fifth-grade social studies class. The students are studying discovery: famous people who have discovered new lands in the new world. It is a very active class. The students are obviously interested in discoverers. The entire lesson is con-ducted in recitation format: "It was very, very, very, very what? *Far.*" Twice, in a positive way, the teacher encourages students in their efforts to remember all these explorers' names and where they went: "That's all right, we've got plenty of time. We'll review and review and review, and we'll get it all straightened out." Another of her questions is "The saddest thing about Columbus was . . . what?"

One student asks, "If Columbus named Indians 'Indians,' do scientists know if they had any real names of their own?" The teacher says that is a very good question, and that she isn't sure.

Physically, the class is very active, with kids jumping up and down, sometimes getting out of their seats with their hands raised, squirming, squeaking, trying to get the chance to go to the map or the blackboard and point where a certain explorer went. I sense opportunities here to talk about black explorers or other black peo-ple, and about Indians with respect to exploration, but the empha-sis here is on memorization of names and expeditions.

At the end of the week, I visit a huge high school complex on a hill overlooking other hills covered with row houses. It is a school of 1,850 kids. The school is divided into two buildings, to make it a little more manageable. Besides the principal, there seem to be four deans, two intervention specialists, a head counselor, four grade-level advisers, and two liaison counselors for all the students in special programs: a big staff.

The school draws on seven or eight different neighborhoods and, as a consequence, has an identity problem, given that many of the people in the different neighborhoods do not like people from the others. I speak with a teacher reputed to be one of the best in the school. She's a very severe-looking woman. Her hair is pulled tightly back in a bun, her eyes are rather startled, her manner seems highly aggressive and defensive at the same time. She tells me that she began as a curriculum writer in the SEP and has enjoyed it. It is clear, however, that she is far more interested in gifted students and kids who want to be scholars than she is in general students. She sees the SEP as something that provides innovation for main-line teachers; but for the very creative teacher (and she sees herself as one), the SEP is constrictive.

She found that when she did the SEP exam in world cultures, her students were great and she was great, but when she used the guide for scoring essays, lots of students did badly. She says it broke her heart. She is not very interested in the discussions. She says that she is by nature a teacher-centered person. She doesn't like "a lot of B.S." She travels all the time and shares her adventures with her students.

I go to her class and watch her give a slide show on her summer dig in Israel. The presentation is chaotic and virtually incoherent, but the students love it and write down everything she says. They learn about a lot more than the ruins. They learn about Israeli politics and military history and battles, and about anything else she happens to think of as she randomly associates her way through the slides and her experiences. She takes great pride in her knowledge (two master's degrees) and her experience (twenty-two summer trips), and she does not fail to point out that the people with whom she associates have "many, many Ph.D.s."

She introduces every conceivable nuance, detail, thought, anecdote, or association, with no focus or pattern that I can discern. I have absolutely no idea why the children write down some of the things she tells them, but these are "advanced studies" students, and this is what she feels they want. She may be considered a great teacher by some students and parents; she is certainly the most ec-centric teacher I have ever seen. I cannot tell whether she gets her students to think or, if she does, what in the world they think about.

Pittsburgh has set out to do what no other urban school district in the United States has attempted. Richard Wallace has a bold vision of an urban educational system that offers all students the kind of high-quality curriculum and instruction now reserved for a few. Simply to articulate such a policy and move ahead at all is to move far ahead of the majority of urban districts in this country. To have gone even farther than that—by training teachers, developing tests of critical thinking, streamlining, focusing and upgrading the curriculum, and measurably improving students' achievement—is all the more remarkable.

But Richard Wallace is no magician, as he would be the first to admit, and Pittsburgh has a long way to go before his vision becomes reality on a large scale. Except for the discussion sessions (the importance of which I do not want to minimize), we saw little in the classrooms that would differentiate them from classrooms anywhere else, and the discussions, still in the pilot stage, were taking place every other week and were unconnected to the main curriculum. What can be learned from Pittsburgh? To what degree is it a *different* kind of school district from NUPS and the others, and to what degree is it the *same* kind, but working better?

This question offers one way of looking at the school-reform debate of the 1980s. Some reformers have said, in effect, that our basic model of schooling is fine but is just not working very well. If it were an internal combustion engine, they would say that it needs a tuneup or a valve job or a rebuilt carburetor; to them, Pittsburgh would represent a smooth-running, relatively high-performance engine. But other reformers wonder whether the model itself, even cranked up to peak performance, will ever do the job that is needed; for them, what is needed may be, as Glasser (1986) suggests, a jet engine. In that case, Pittsburgh will never get where Richard Wallace wants it to go, unless he is able to keep the old model running well and simultaneously create a brand-new one that can eventually take over.

Certainly, a case can be made that Pittsburgh is distinguishable from NUPS only by the fact that the things that are broken in NUPS are not broken in Pittsburgh. NUPS has not had stable or strong leadership, while Pittsburgh has—in the superintendent, the school board, the central administration, the unions, and the community. NUPS lacks a coherent agenda for improvement, largely because it lacks leadership; Pittsburgh, while far more coherent, is

(to use a word that Tony Petrosky suggests) somewhat schizophren-
ic. NUPS still has not settled its desegregation case, while Pittsburgh settled its case before Wallace arrived. Thus, NUPS has been
under court monitorship, while Pittsburgh has not. NUPS suffers
from chronic mistrust and tension between management and
teachers; Pittsburgh, by comparison, is relatively harmonious.
Partly because of its own troubles and partly because of its community's troubles, NUPS has not received much in the way of community support or resources. The Pittsburgh schools, situated in a
corporate-headquarters city and led by a superintendent who knows
how to work with the business community, have had generous in-
fusions of private money (somewhere between $50 and $63 million
over the last eight years, by my count) and considerable public
support. Because it has had all these blessings, Pittsburgh has been
able to dream, to set its sights on a literacy of thoughtfulness for all
students. Because it has had none of these blessings, NUPS has been
reactive, stuck in the past, and caught in ever-tightening downward
spirals.

Wallace's approach to leadership and management is traditional, not innovative. Working with the community and the board,
he has established goals and priorities. He has assembled a strong
central staff to see that the goals are carried out. The staff has involved teachers, principals, and outside experts while retaining control over all events and decisions. Task forces and advisory groups
have all been centrally managed. Fund raising has also been centrally managed and turned into a fine art.

Wallace is a master communicator. He has clarified communications within the central administration and opened chan-
nels up and down the hierarchy. Some would say that most of the
communication has been downward, but it is clear that at least some
has been upward. Wallace's communication with the public has
been well orchestrated by a sophisticated, centralized communications apparatus. The superintendent is an old-style 1960s techno-
crat, in the Robert McNamara mold: a believer in data-driven
decision making, planning, careful policy development, key stake-
holders' involvement, alignment of goals, systematic implementation, evaluation, and use of feedback to improve the process. MAP,
which was Wallace's brainchild, is a classic objectives-based testing

system implemented in a classic top-down way. This is standard operating procedure; it is what most superintendents have been trained to do over the last thirty years. Wallace is just better at doing it than practically anyone else in the country. He is a virtual genius at it, and he has found conditions for doing it that, if not ideal, are nevertheless as close to ideal as an urban superintendent is ever likely to find.

What we began to wonder, however, as we interviewed school people and observed classes far away from the talented, articulate, persuasive central staff, was whether this traditional school-improvement model was suitable for developing the literacy of thoughtfulness toward which Wallace is ultimately aiming. The distance between the vision of the central staff and the reality in the classrooms gave us pause. Why aren't the classrooms more dynamic? Why, after eight years of critical-thinking training, isn't there more questioning and inquiry and writing going on? Why do lecture and recitation still dominate? Why don't the discussions reshape day-to-day classroom discourse more dramatically? Why have test scores reached a plateau and even started to decline?

One answer may be that there has not been enough time for everything to mature, but other explanations also suggest themselves to anyone who has visited a number of urban school districts. Tony Petrosky, who not only worked with us on this project but has also worked on the development of the critical-thinking tests in Pittsburgh, suggests that the problem is fundamental incompatibility between the mandated, basic skills–oriented implementation approach, on the one hand, represented by MAP and "direct instruction" training, and, on the other hand, the approach required to create and sustain genuinely thoughtful conversations along the lines of the St. John's program. In his notes, Tony made the following observations:

> When the MAP project began, it was modeled after mastery tests on which students must achieve 80 percent mastery to move on to other objectives and tests, and there was considerable resistance from teachers who saw it as both a teacher-accountability problem and an attempt to direct the curriculum by directly

testing the sets of objectives that were to be taught. But teachers developed the tests, mimicking well-known standardized tests, and it came to be identified as a series of teacher-constructed tests, though the project began and proceeded by top-down mandate. The MAP tests are largely multiple-choice. Each item represents one (of ten to thirty) minimum objectives for a subject, by grade level. Each test has multiple forms, and the tests are supposedly diagnostic. The test results sent to teachers, principals, and parents indicate whether or not a child answered each item correctly and whether a particular tested objective has been taught.

Teachers reported that the English composition test and the critical-thinking essay had been institutionalized to the point where students are often given practice on typical exams two or three times a year before the exams. Then the actual exams are administered, and often this constitutes the only writing students will do in English or social studies during the year. Principals are supposed to confer with teachers once the test results are returned, but in fact the principals we interviewed said they find it difficult to manage the time to speak with teachers. The teachers we interviewed felt pressured to teach to the objectives (this was one of the goals of the tests), so much of their time goes into preparing students to take the tests rather than, as a high school English teacher told us, into designing a curriculum based on the students' needs.

There is a strong feeling among teachers, especially those elementary school teachers we interviewed, that the curriculum has become the objectives tested by the MAP tests, although the board administrators we spoke with contested this perception and argued that MAP objectives were minimum objectives, and that the curriculum was laid out in scope-and-sequences and in textbooks.

These mixed perceptions seem to signal a set of

basic inconsistencies having to do with the purposes
and effects of the MAP tests. From the superintendent's perspective, the tests are key tools for the
teachers' monitoring of students' basic skills, and they
should not interfere with the curriculum or be used for
teacher accountability. From the principals' perspective, the MAP scores are a certain means of identifying
those teachers whose students are performing well and
those who are performing poorly in basic skills and,
as one high school principal told us, the "teachers in
need of attention." From the teachers' perspective, at
least from those we spoke with, the MAP tests hold
them accountable for teaching basic skills, and the
tests have created curricula that emphasize those skills.
This appears to be particularly so for those elementary
teachers who are responsible for multiple subject areas
and, therefore, multiple MAP tests. One elementary
school principal, voicing strong support for her
teachers' perceptions, told us, "MAP was supposed to
be one-third of the instructional time. Now it's 90 percent of the time, and the teachers and principals are
evaluated on the MAP results, no matter what anyone
says to the contrary."

When the district officially adopted the Made-
leine Hunter instructional model, at the superintendent's insistence, and positioned it as the key element
in its mandatory staff-development program, it legis-
lated a procedure for teaching—and, more impor-
tantly, for thinking about teaching and learning—
that directly supported the emphasis on basic-skills
instruction. At the same time, it set the ground for one
of its major policy schizophrenias, by creating an official instructional model suitable for lecture and recitation but incompatible with work in discussion and
writing. The Hunter model used in Pittsburgh places
a high premium on direct instruction, and so teachers
are encouraged to think of learning in terms of skill
and content mastery. They are required to follow a

format for instruction that proceeds in a lockstep sequence, from anticipatory set (an activity to set students' expectations) to stating the objective, then to
direct instruction, checking for understanding, guided
practice, and independent practice (homework). This
procedure works, as one teacher pointed out, for direct
instruction in addition or subtraction, but it doesn't
fit the classroom discussion model. It doesn't fit well,
either, with the teaching of writing, unless one takes
the position that learning to write involves the mastery of a series of skills defined by grammar, and learning to write essays or stories involves the gradual
mastery of sentences, then paragraphs, then whole
essays.

Taken along with the district's MAP tests, the
Hunter model brings forward a grim sense of mistrust
in teachers' abilities to teach and monitor their students' work. In the context of a mandate-driven, top-
down system, where neither teachers nor principals
think they are involved in district decisions on instructional matters, teachers don't have any choice but to
position themselves as implementers of programs and
procedures. And, although they are often the people
responsible for developing the programs and, in this
sense, might be said to control the content of such
things as the MAP tests, they act on mandate, and
there doesn't seem to be much two-way communication between the administrators who conceive the program and the teachers who develop and then
implement them.

It was in this context that the critical-thinking discussion
project was begun. Its goal was to create environments in which
students would think critically and creatively about what they were
doing and take greater responsibility for their learning. But, as
Tony says, "it was imposed in an authoritarian context that presup-
posed that teachers could not make the same kinds of critical moves
within the system." In other words, teachers were being asked to

empower and trust students in ways that they themselves were not
being empowered or trusted. People in a highly managed system,
which was designed to make them achieve clearly specified and
limited goals, were being asked to reorient their behavior toward
open-ended tasks, critique, and responsibility for making countless
unspecifiable decisions heretofore made by superiors. Thus, the policy environment that was created to meet one set of goals does not
yet seem to support the newer, more robust goals.

Will it ever do so? Pittsburgh is much better off than NUPS,
in a number of important ways; but, simply because it *is* a more
coherent district, we can see more clearly something that was difficult to see amidst all the confusion of NUPS. The tension between
institution and practice, between a rationality of administrative effectiveness and a rationality of learning and excellence, between a
language of getting things done and a language of reaching understanding, exists in Pittsburgh, as it does in North Urban. It is a
tension between two very different ways of thinking, each anchored
in its own school of thought, going back at least to the Enlighten-
ment. Policy, at its best, stems largely from the first tradition; practice, at its best, stems largely from the second.

Richard Wallace's greatest accomplishments so far lie in the
areas of policy, management, and leadership. He has not yet
brought about major changes in practice, but he has introduced
something into the current system that has great potential to transform practice, if he can couple it with new kinds of policy and
management that support it as well as the old kinds have supported
a basic-skills training agenda. What he has introduced is a vision
of a much higher level of literacy, for a much broader range of
students, than has been aspired to in any but a few other urban
school districts in the United States. To bring that vision into reality, he has asked students, teachers, and administrators to converse
about fundamental ideas that have transformed the world, and to
help them learn how to do that, he created the Schenley and Brookline training centers, public spaces where adults can become the
kinds of excited learners they want their students to become.

Can such a conversation be forced on people from the top of
an organization? Can it be sustained by a traditional system for
testing and accountability? Can it spread sufficiently to alter the

traditional culture of urban public schooling, which has swallowed up so many similar efforts in the past? Can Richard Wallace institutionalize it to the point where it survives his retirement? Can other school districts, larger and more troubled, follow the Pittsburgh model? Should they? These are the questions we are asking as we leave Pittsburgh—and the United States—behind and head north to Canada, to visit a school district once called the best in the world.

CHAPTER SEVEN

A Higher Literacy in Toronto

Etobicoke, Ontario, is a long, narrow part of Toronto that began not too long ago as a tiny borough and grew quickly to become a major bedroom community. The Etobicoke school system is one of six systems, or "boards," that make up the Toronto school system. For most of its relatively short life, its population has been upper middle class and suburban, but when the district absorbed another town along the shore of Lake Ontario, it brought in a large number of working-class, blue-collar people. Up at the north end, the so-called new Canadians—largely Jamaican, West Indian, Pakistani, and East Indian—have spilled over from neighboring areas, so that today the Etobicoke school system, just slightly smaller than Pittsburgh's system, has three distinct sections: the north, which is serving a great many children of color whose first language is not English; the central area, which is serving white middle-class students; and the southern area, which is serving lower-middle-class and working-class whites.

Etobicoke also has a separate, publicly funded Catholic school system, which serves more than one-quarter of the children in the town. The Catholic system has grown enormously in the last few years because many of the new Canadians are Catholics. All the schools are financed through the sales tax and property taxes.

Toronto is an ethnically diverse, economically booming city of over two million people. It population has doubled since 1953, when it became the first city in North America to establish a metropolitan system of government. The city accounts for 18 percent of the value of all Canadian manufacturing per year, 30 percent of Canada's construction activity, and 50 percent of its annual merchandise exports. It is home to seven thousand manufacturing companies, including four hundred high-tech companies. Almost half of Canada's top five hundred businesses are here. At the same time, more than 94 percent of the firms in the area are small businesses with fewer than fifty employees. Toronto is Canada's financial center, sometimes described as a well-developed small industrial nation.

It is impossible to obtain the kind of demographic information about the Toronto boards that one would ordinarily find for an American school district: they don't collect it. When Sam Stringfield and I meet with the Etobicoke board's statistician, we ask him for statistics on percentages of minorities, children in poverty, and children on welfare, and he looks at us as if we are asking for information about Jupiter or Mars.

"Why would you want that kind of information?" he asks.

"It would help us compare this board with American school districts serving similar clientele," Sam says.

The statistician just shakes his head.

"We don't collect that kind of information about people," he says.

"How do you know which children need special services?" Sam asks.

"The teachers know. When they see a student who is having difficulty, they refer him to the assessment teachers. They see to it he gets tutoring. That's how we do it. What do you do?"

Sam explains that we try ahead of time to identify children liable to have problems, by looking at information about their parents' income, education level, race, and so on. On the basis of these statistics, we provide extra money to schools for remediation.

"So you can predict ahead of time who is not going to benefit from your education system?" the statistician asks. "And you know how they won't benefit, and what remediation they're going to need?"

"Yes."

"Hmm. Interesting."

Ontario vigorously pursues a policy of multiculturalism. Ontarians talk of "the great Canadian mosaic," contrasting it with the American metaphor of the melting pot, a concept that they think does not work. Every effort is made to celebrate everyone's culture and to offer instruction in every language for as long as the new Canadians need it during their transition to Canadian life. In Etobicoke, special classes are available in Urdu, Greek, Mandarin Chinese, Punjabi, and Polish. They are taught nights and Saturdays and are supported by a separate budget.

In the 1950s, Ontario had a strong ministry of education. Provincial inspectors regularly went into the districts to inspect schools, and they exerted considerable control over the boards. In the 1960s, the ministry took a more laissez-faire approach to schooling. The thrust was to adapt schooling to local needs and allow more community control. The ministry's guidelines for curriculum and instruction were more general and vague in the 1960s than they had been in the past; but, after 1975, the ministry reasserted a strong policy role, declaring its intention to radically reform the province's entire educational system.

It moved to centralize a number of functions that had been delegated to local boards. In three key reports, it spelled out the basic goals of education in Ontario and provided guidelines for meeting them. A similar movement was under way in the United States. However, whereas the U.S. movement focused on mandating minimum competencies and basic skills, the emphasis in Ontario was on robust educational outcomes. Although the ministry was as assertive as many departments of education in the United States, it coupled its mandate for change with a challenge to educators in the boards and schools: they, not the ministry, would develop the curriculum, instruction, and assessment tools necessary to meet the guidelines. Ontario developed a vision at the top and proceeded to stimulate bottom-up changes consonant with that vision. Here is what one Toronto administrator told us:

We have a strong belief that, in order for children to really understand the basics, they have to have a problem-solving ability of their own. So we encourage creative thinking and critical thinking, and we provide all sorts of opportunities for kids to write and to speak with their teachers and with their peers, to come to grips with their own understanding of things. It isn't just a matter of taking it in and spitting it out. We continue to emphasize basics. What is different is that, rather than getting *back* to basics, we think we're getting *forward* to basics. That means that, rather than returning to the traditional rote teaching methods, and all the achievement testing that goes along with that, we look forward to more creative teaching methods, based on a student's experience, and helping students to create meaning out of their lives.

To understand what has happened in Ontario, it is necessary to turn to those key ministry reports: *Education in the Primary and Junior Divisions, The Formative Years,* and *Ontario Schools: Intermediate and Senior Divisions* (Ontario Ministry of Education, 1975a, 1975b, 1984) (full information on these publications is in the Bibliography at the end of this book). After getting advice from thousands of teachers, parents, administrators, and citizens, the ministry synthesized central ideas, placed them in the framework of the best available knowledge about learning and education, and then tried to describe, in these three publications, the kinds of learning experiences most likely to enable all children to fulfill their potential. From the beginning, the ministry distinguished between its own guidelines and "detailed courses of study," which it deemed inappropriate. According to *The Formative Years* (p. 2), "The major responsibility for planning curriculum rests with the school. Only by accepting this responsibility can it respond to the special needs and characteristics of the children in its care." More specifically, the ministry gave individual teachers *and students* responsibility for choosing the strategies, resources, and activities most likely to bring about a high level of learning. This approach was in marked contrast with policies dominant in the United States at that time, policies that reflected little confidence in teachers and did not assign any such responsibility to students.

The Formative Years goes on to say (p. 4), "It is the policy of the Government of Ontario that every child have the opportunity to develop as completely as possible in the direction of his or her talents and needs." Thus, the curriculum, which includes both what students learn and how they learn, must enable each child "to acquire the basic skills fundamental to his or her continuing education" (pp. 6–7).

Listed under these basic skills in *Education in the Primary and Junior Divisions* (p. 7) (also known here as "the guidelines") are such things as "the ability to comprehend ideas through reading, listening, and viewing; the ability to communicate ideas through writing, speaking, and other visual and nonverbal media; the ability to understand and employ mathematical operations and concepts; and the ability to apply rational or intuitive processes to the identification, consideration, and solution of problems." In addition, each individual should develop "skills of inquiry, analysis, synthesis, and evaluation. . . . Children who acquire such reasoning skills will be able to continue learning throughout their lives" (p. 7). Thus, the basic skills in Ontario include reasoning, problem solving, and thinking, as well as the skills, dispositions, and habits associated with thoughtfulness, even at the prekindergarten and elementary levels. "To develop and maintain confidence and a sense of self-worth" (p. 7) is a goal expressed in terms of enhancing students' desires "to understand and examine personal interests, abilities, and goals in keeping with the needs of an ever-changing environment" and in terms of developing "such attributes as intellectual curiosity, awareness, sensitivity, perseverance, and the desire for excellence" (p. 7). Other goals are "to gain the knowledge and acquire the attitudes that [the student] needs for active participation in Canadian society" (p. 7) and "to develop the moral and aesthetic sensitivity necessary for a complete and responsible life" (p. 7). Included here are opportunities to develop an "appreciation of cultural heritage and the arts," as well as "an appreciation of the ethics of society and the conduct prescribed by such ethics" (p. 7).

The ministry did not stop with these general statements. It followed them up with material on how children learn, drawing on both behaviorist and cognitive psychologies, with a preference for approaches based in cognitive field development as better explanations of how children acquire complex behaviors, such as communication, concept formation, and problem solving.

When we asked an administrator to tell us how learning happens best, we got this reply:

> Learning happens best when a teacher is able to engage a student in important dialogue; when the teacher listens carefully, not only to the big messages, but to the vibrations of what that youngster is all about, and says to himself or herself, "This youngster is capable of great things." I don't mean by that, you're capable of being a great politician, or whatever. Maybe you're capable of being a great lathe operator or artist, or whatever—but a teacher who sees a potential in students that is much greater than what they are today and engages students in that voyage.

As we have seen, Americans' statements about educational objectives tend to atomize subjects and lay them out as bits of knowledge and skill. The ministry's documents, by contrast, describe broad concepts to be mastered. For instance, they suggest that children should learn about concrete relationships, the concept of space (one's body space, for instance) and different kinds of space, and area as a measure of surface. They stress the necessity of experience with three-dimensional objects, as well as the need to understand invariance and relationships, the concepts of identity and stability of substance, ideas of time, historical concepts and perceptions, and moral and ethical notions appropriate to the different grade levels and ages of children. The ministry also asserts that certain assumptions about children and learning are basic to the recommended curriculum:

- Children are curious. Their need to explore and manipulate should be fulfilled through handling real things that involve more than one sense. The more all the senses are involved, the more effective the experience.

- Most human activity is a purposeful search for pattern. This includes organizing new information and relating it to previously developed concepts. Incongruity between old patterns and new experiences stimulates questioning, observation, manipulation, and application in a variety of new situations. Maintaining the right balance between novel and familiar experiences in learning situations is one of the most vital tasks in the art of teaching.
- Learning experiences gain power if they are part of organized and meaningful wholes.
- Children have an intrinsic need for mastery over situations, a need that they express by using their experiences to search out the significant patterns in reality and thus reduce uncertainty.
- Children find self-fulfillment in successful learning and are not motivated merely by external rewards and approval. . . .
- Play is an essential part of learning. It is free from the restrictions of reality, external evaluations, and judgment. Children can try out different styles of action and communication without being required to make premature decisions, or being penalized for errors. . . .
- Children learn through experience with people, symbols, and things.
- The symbolic process for children develops through a sequence of representation. Initially, children must understand that a real object can be represented by such symbols as a spoken word, gesture, dramatic movement, toy, model, picture; ultimately they must understand that an object can be represented by the printed word. The development of symbolism underlies the communication, recording, and coding of experience in a

condensed and systematic form [Ontario Ministry
of Education, 1975a, pp. 15–16].

Given such goals and assumptions and such ideas about how children learn, the guidelines say a thing or two about how to teach.
For instance, "content is more than subject matter or a set of facts
and opinions such as those contained in a textbook. . . . It is assumed that the source for content will be the environment—people,
things, and symbols. Both the teacher and child should be involved
in choosing content" (p. 17). Moreover, content "must be gauged
against the following questions" (p. 18):

Will it give children an opportunity for direct inquiry,
independent study, and creative ability in the context
of their own interests, abilities, and developmental
needs? Will it fulfill their needs to explore and to manipulate? Will it satisfy the search for pattern? Will it
relate to what the children already know? Will it be
sufficiently novel to stimulate questions, observations,
and manipulations? Will the children be able to see
what they are learning as part of an organized and
meaningful whole? Will it spring from real experiences in the children's environment? Is it appropriate
to each child's level of development? Will the children
be able to know when they've been successful? Will it
provoke questions, involvement, a desire for further
exploration? Will it encourage learning through play?
Will it provide experiences with qualitative relationships? Will the content provide opportunities for various techniques of investigation? Will it be socially
useful? Will this content lead to a reasoned knowledge
of and pride in Canada?

The guidelines go on to say that in teaching and learning there
must be empirical knowledge, symbolic activities, esthetic activities,
ethical development, and integrative activities that synthesize learning across disciplinary lines.

With respect to skills, the guidelines suggest that children can learn skills from one another by example and imitation, as well as through teachers' instruction. They discourage spending "excessive time working prematurely on skills in return for little, if any, improvement" (p. 19).

According to the guidelines (p. 22), "The teachers' task is to anticipate the various skills and subskills required by the topic under study and to help childen select and sequence those that are congruent with their own purposes and stage of development." They further point out that skills are best learned when the child sees that they are necessary for a particular task. Skills are refined and improved through practice in a variety of situations. Intervention and practice must be flexibly organized for individuals and groups, not necessarily applied to a whole class.

The guidelines suggest a number of different groupings of children: individuals working on assignments, inquiry research, and practice; work groups chosen by the children; larger teaching groups; and class groups. The teacher's job is to help these groups develop and to guide children through the day in various groups.

With respect to time, the guidelines suggest that learning from real-life situations, "from exploration and from inquiry, imposes rhythms of time that cannot be tied to a time table" (p. 23). Further, "there is no evidence that any particular learning experience should take place at a fixed time during the day. It is practically impossible to predict the time each child needs for various tasks or experiences; balance between areas of the curriculum and kinds of learning should be examined on a weekly or monthly basis, not in terms of a single day's activities; and responsibility for planning activities and using time should be shared with the children" (p. 24).

The guidelines also say that space should be changed. There should be subdivisions of large and small areas. There should be movable work space, work benches, and storage space. There should be water supplies, surfaces for painting, different levels, open space, outdoor areas, and so on.

With respect to other kinds of activities for teachers, the guidelines say (p. 26), "Questioning is an important tool or resource in the hands of a competent teacher. Becoming aware of the many kinds of questions that exist and their differing uses can help a teacher avoid the trap of asking too many questions of fact. Some factual questions are needed, but more profitable in the long run are those that lead the child toward higher levels of learning, such as inferring, analyzing, or generalizing."

The guidelines established for students in prekindergarten through grade 6 are extended to grades 7 through 12 in *Ontario Schools: Intermediate and Senior Divisions.* "The major purpose of a school is to help each student develop his/her potential as an individual and as a contributing, responsible member of society who will think clearly, feel deeply, and act wisely," that report begins (p. 2), again using language that is rare in American policy documents of this kind. The goals of education in Ontario are clearly spelled out. It is the shared responsibility of students, teachers, and parents to help each student do the following things:

- Develop a responsiveness to the dynamic processes of learning, which include observing, sensing, inquiring, creating, analyzing, synthesizing, evaluating, and communicating
- Develop resourcefulness, adaptability, and creativity in learning and living
- Acquire the basic knowledge and skills needed to comprehend and express ideas through words, numbers, and other symbols
- Develop physical fitness and good health
- Gain satisfaction from participating and sharing the participation of others in various forms of artistic expression
- Develop a feeling of self-worth, fostered by realistic self-appraisal, confidence and conviction in the pursuit of excellence, self-discipline, and the satisfaction of achievement, and reinforced by encouragement, respect, and supportive evaluation
- Develop an understanding of the role of the individual within the family and the role of the family within society

- Acquire skills that contribute to self-reliance in solving practical problems in everyday life
- Develop a sense of personal responsibility in society at the local, national, and international levels
- Develop esteem for the customs, cultures, and beliefs of a wide variety of societal groups
- Acquire skills and attitudes that will lead to satisfaction and productivity in the world of work
- Develop respect for the environment and a commitment to the wise use of resources [adapted from Ontario Ministry of Education, 1984, pp. 3–4].

These goals show up everywhere in Ontario, especially in documents dealing with the curriculum. Curriculum policy is based on a report called *Schools General: Foundations for Curriculum in the Elementary and Secondary Schools in Ontario.* Policies are spelled out in separate publications for each subject, each of which begins with references to *The Formative Years* and its goals, rationalizing its recommendations in terms of the spirit of the earlier documents.

Again and again, the curricular policy documents stress the importance of thinking, solving problems, inquiring, working with others, using language in all its forms, working in a multicultural environment, and being active, independent learners. Some samples are shown in Exhibit 7.1.

Ontario has created a coherent, forceful set of policies in curriculum, instruction, and assessment that call explicitly for critical and creative thinking, problem solving, active learning, and thoughtfulness in all aspects of schooling, for all children. In this, the province is fifteen years ahead of any American state. How are the policies working?

One fine spring morning, Tony, Sam, and I walk from our hotel across a field to Broadacres Elementary School, which is in an area surrounded by high-rise apartments and condominiums. We're greeted by Mary Lowe, the principal, a slightly graying woman in her early forties, who offers us coffee and takes us to her office.

Exhibit 7.1. Sample Curricular Policy Documents.

Dramatic Arts

Students should be involved in various types of writing that are pertinent to the dramatic experience. These include anecdotal reports; character sketches; critical reviews; directors', designers', or stage managers' notes; reports of interviews; production notes; prompt books; scripts, written either in groups or individually; student journals, logs, or diaries; and writings in role.

There will be a balance of two kinds of knowledge: that gained through dramatic activities and that acquired by planning and reflecting on those activities. Part of the purpose of all courses in dramatic arts is for students to gain affective understanding (felt knowledge) of what they may already know cognitively (rational knowledge).

The focus of all work will be on the analyzing, interpreting, and synthesizing of experience.

History and Contemporary Studies

Why study contemporary society?

Today's society is complex and changing rapidly. Adolescents and young adults face an often bewildering network of forces, groups, issues and events. The courses in contemporary studies will help students to organize, analyze, and develop an understanding of these elements.

Today's society is an information society.

Today's society requires a renewed emphasis on thinking and communication skills. The methods used to process information also help students to develop thoughtful, creative, open-minded approaches to situations and problems. The skills acquired in contemporary-studies courses should help students to become self-directed, self-motivated problem solvers, who are able to communicate clearly and effectively.

Chemistry

The topics and research approach chosen should develop (a) students' aptitudes, abilities, and interests; (b) students' ability to apply the techniques and principles of scientific inquiry, problem-solving procedures, divergent thinking, and both oral and written communication skills; (c) a co-operative attitude and interpersonal skills on the part of students.

Students are expected to bear the major responsibility for planning and implementing their investigations.

Students might do an in-depth literature search to answer a hypothesis or question of a chemical nature. The result would be a well-organized essay involving an extensive compilation of data and a complete bibliography. In such cases students would probably make a class presentation of their work.

Exhibit 7.1. Sample Curricular Policy Documents, Cont'd.

Science in the Primary and Junior Divisions

Listed below are some questions that teachers can use to help themselves implement the spirit of *Science Is Happening Here.*
How do I:

- encourage children to identify and pursue their own questions and interests?
- participate along with children in exploration and investigation?
- encourage the children to observe, question, discuss, and experiment?
- facilitate the development of language through science experiences?
- maintain a flexible learning environment that will accommodate the needs, abilities, and interests of all the children?

Intermediate Geography

All studies should be rooted in well-developed skills and should provide students with opportunities to gather information, to translate that information into formats that are easily understood, and to communicate the information to others.

Opportunities to achieve affective objectives are an important part of every unit. As an example, participation in worthwhile community projects can help students gain valuable insights into human nature and social realities. Programs that combine the acquisition of knowledge and skills with opportunities to develop and apply personal value systems present an ideal balance in geography.

The school halls are a veritable gallery of children's art, not simply taped to the walls but framed attractively. It is spectacular art. No two works are the same, and it is all over the place. It is the most attractive school I've ever seen.

Ms. Lowe's office—wood-paneled, like most of the offices we visit in the district—contains books (Kenneth Goodman's *What's Whole in Whole Language?* is on her desk) and dozens of stuffed bears. Many of them look as if they have received considerable attention over the years—there are missing eyes or ears and fur worn smooth.

Ms. Lowe tells us that Broadacres is made up of 50 percent "advancement" (gifted) students (they don't use our word) and 50 percent home-school students. The school draws on a community that includes luxury apartments and subsidized housing. Ms. Lowe is totally committed to active learning. She believes that all her teachers share that commitment, whether they are teaching advancement or home-school students (all must teach both). They support active learning, but not all of them are as comfortable with it as they need to be, and some teachers are farther ahead than others. She quotes Michael Fullan, dean at the University of Toronto, to the effect that it is better to practice active learning first, knowing that understanding of it will follow, than to try to develop the complete understanding before practice. I ask her what the keys are to managing active learning.

"Teachers have to learn to be good observers in active learning," she says. "They really have to be able to watch each child and know what's going on. I can take a very traditional teacher in my school, as long as he or she cares about children. That's the real key. But I could never take an active-learning teacher, even though I prefer the active-learning approach, if that teacher didn't really love children."

Sam asks her what "whole language" means to her, and she explains that you have to begin with children's language and children's experience and build from there to the inherited experience in the traditional curriculum. She believes in reading to kids, immersing them in literature, but she also believes in a balanced, integrated approach that ensures that children do become accomplished readers and do not fall between the cracks.

We talk a bit about the dilemma that active learning poses because it is so child-centered and because the child's pace may differ from the school's or from the parents' expectations.

"If a student doesn't read by the end of the second grade, we find ourselves under a lot of pressure from parents," Ms. Lowe says. "But what are we to do? If you hold him back, his self-esteem drops. If you cram him before he's ready, it won't take. We know it won't take. If you wait for the child to mature and develop and finally catch fire as a reader, you know you're probably doing the right thing, but you find it very anxiety-producing. Parents begin to panic and everyone begins to wonder if the child has gotten 'behind.' "

This is a critical problem for advocates of child-centered learning, and it's a very difficult test of traditional school materials and procedures, which assume that children develop in more or less uniform and predictable ways. If you believe that the most important thing about reading is to get a child to want to read for his or her own purposes, not to read in some mechanical and meaningless fashion, then you have to wait as you immerse the child, month after month, in a richly textured language environment. Some children take longer than others. The faith is that, sooner or later, they will read it, but if the delay starts crossing class borders, from second to third grade, from third to fourth, from fourth to fifth, everyone starts going crazy. The mounting pressure on the child to read probably only makes it more difficult to do so.

If everyone would wait and relax, this would not be a problem, according to theory. But as you move up, grade after grade, the capacity to read well is the key to success. In these schools, students are expected to do a good deal of independent study, and teachers assume that when children are reading, they understand what they're reading. There is constant tension between the need to establish a sequential curriculum and the need to let each child move along at his or her own pace. There is also constant tension between the need to teach children particular things and the need to let them follow their interests.

I go to Marg Harrison's class. Ms. Harrison appears to be in her thirties, with frosted hair and extremely bright eyes. She is wearing a large, colorful, unusual-looking sweater. Everything about her suggests creativity, and so does her classroom, which is an extremely rich learning environment filled with students' work, plants, animals, project centers, books the children have written, other books, works of art, games, and assorted interesting learning materials.

Ms. Harrison calls herself an inquiry-oriented teacher. She says she became an inquiry-oriented teacher when a bill was passed that required the schools to prepare for diversity.

"So I've prepared myself," she says.

She has become quite the expert on inquiry-based instruction. She's done it for enough years to have built up a large repertoire of responses to children's ideas. She knows how to deepen students' interests and guide them from one activity to another, each more challenging. She has a large blackboard with Bloom's taxonomic levels on it. Under each level is a series of reading, writing, and inquiry assignments that students can tackle whenever they feel ready.

During class, students wander up and pick cards individually from the board and then wander off again to start projects. As I talk with Ms. Harrison and watch her work, it is clear that she is a great teacher. She knows the strengths, weaknesses, and interests of all her students intimately, and she knows how to guide them individually in what they are doing. Students move in and out of small groups and large group discussions easily, without a lot of noise. Their displayed work is of very high quality. I notice an interesting and quite sophisticated project on the solar system and the universe, for instance, with the following definition: "A black hole is a monstrous, never-ending star that has sucked itself inside out."

As we talk, a student teacher from York University begins a unit on metric measures. The children look around for things that are close to one meter long. Then they run around measuring one another and numerous objects in the room and out in the halls. The measuring is done inexactly, so that students come up with somewhat different dimensions. These discrepancies become the subject of further discussion.

I notice that, whatever Ms. Harrison or her student teacher does, they do many things at once. If they are looking at a map of the provinces, for example, one of them will ask, "Can you name them from memory, in order? What are their abbreviations? Does anyone hear any long vowels? Which province names have long and short vowels?" When questions arise about the vowels in the name *Saskatchewan*, a student goes to the dictionary and reports back to the class on what a dot over a vowel means in terms of correct pronunciation. No lesson is ever about any one particular subject; everything seems to be an opportunity to explore ideas, language, grammar, geography, history, or mathematics.

As this goes on, I talk with Ms. Harrison about mathematics, which in our experience is often a weakness in active-learning classrooms. She says that the district's "math inventories"—concept guides and tests—are a big help. They were developed by outstanding teachers in the area, and she uses them faithfully. The district also has guidelines for social studies and language arts, from which she feels free to choose whatever she wants to focus on. Ms. Harrison sees such guidelines as menus from which she can choose, not as mandates or specifics that she must address literally. The school board's job, in her view, is to lay out the menu; the ministry's job is to lay out the general guidelines for the board; and her job is to choose how to match the interests and capacities of her children with the spirit of the guidelines and any other appropriate curricular materials.

I asked another teacher at Broadacres what it was like to change from the old way of teaching to active learning.

"It took two years of soul searching," the teacher replied, "and working late at night, and working very closely with a lot of dedicated people who were willing to give me a hand and help. It was scary. You go home at night thinking, 'Well, I didn't stand at the blackboard and write copious things for the children to copy.' And it . . . that's scary for a while. And there are times when right now they're so active in what's happening in the individual projects, they don't need me at the moment. And . . . and that takes a while, too, to . . . to get used to the fact that they don't need you at times. At times, they need you desperately, and you try to spread yourself between group after group."

"Is it harder to teach this way?"

"No. *Harder* isn't the right word. It's not harder. It's . . . there's more work. It's more fun. It's more rewarding."

"So if you're no longer a lecturer, what are you?"

"Oh, I . . . I think I'm a teacher, in the true sense of the word. I think I teach children to learn and to love learning as much as I love learning. I'm . . . over twenty-nine and still taking courses. And . . . and I hope these guys will for the rest of their lives, too. And I believe I teach kids to like themselves. That's important."

An administrator, responding to my question about whether teachers are permitted to select textbooks, said, "We leave the decision regarding textbooks and learning-resource materials to the teachers, and we supply the resources that enable them to direct those resources at the individual child."

"Does this approach have any benefits with regard to motivating teachers? Preventing burnout?"

"It gives the teacher the ultimate responsibility for what goes on in his or her own classroom. And I can't think of any better way of keeping a teacher charged up with the responsibilities and the challenges of learning. We also find in that process that not only the children but also the teachers are learning. They have to keep on learning with the kids, as partners, in order to continue to be able to make those appropriate decisions."

I wander to another third- and fourth-grade class, where I find students planning their rain forest projects. The classroom itself looks like a rain forest of various colors of paper. This is an extremely rich learning environment.

I sit in with a group of students who have decided that they want to make a life-sized papier-mâché elephant. One member of the group is a tall black boy. Another is a blue-eyed blond boy. There are also an Asian girl, an Indian girl, and a redheaded boy who looks like Huck Finn. They work well together, asking questions and driving each other to greater and greater heights of imagination.

When the teacher comes around to hear about their project, she listens and asks questions, but she does not discourage their plans. Instead, she suggests that they go and measure the area where the elephant will be, to see if a life-sized model will fit. She also asks questions about where elephants fit into rain forests, which sends some kids back to check the literature.

I leave that class and run into Tony Petrosky, who has been observing "communications" work—what we would call special education or remedial instruction.

"It's not like in the states," Tony says. "Here, it's genuine tutorials. First, I watched a teacher with three advancement students. She comes in a half-day every day and uses the other half-day to go to workshops or to other schools. She was dealing with writing problems."

That teacher found out that one of the students hated to print, and so she taught him cursive writing and got him to start writing on a computer. He was writing stories when Tony came in. The teacher showed Tony her plan for helping the student, and Tony was impressed: numerous sophisticated writing exercises, miscue analysis of his reading, fine-motor exercises to increase his control; no drills, no worksheets; lots of probing, questioning, responding, coaching. Here are Tony's notes on another "communications" session with regular students:

> The communications teacher uses an I.Q. test because the district requires it, but her portfolio of information on each kid was full of observations of him writing, reading, miscue analysis, spelling—not standardized test scores. She insists on working with three to four students at a time, and she feels that as long as the children aren't literally brain-damaged, she can bring their skills up to snuff in three months—one year or two at most, but that's not, according to her, the big problem. The big job she has, as she sees it, is making sure students that come to her leave with their self-confidence and esteem intact, because it's those self-images and expectations, she believes, that determine whether students will be remediated. She avoids recommending holding students back, because that does almost irreparable damage to their sense of self-as-learner, but she has had to do that for two students who transferred from French schools, and both of those are now suffering the effects of that holding back. I tell her how we remediate in the States, and she is aghast.

Tony is impressed with the way all teachers collect many kinds of information about their students, very little of it statistical, and he wonders if they are able to do what they do because they do *not* think about the objectives:

> Since they don't collect the data on students from standardized tests, they think differently about education. The report instrument developed at Broadacres is a good example of a descriptive instrument that gives a good deal of information about students' work in language and math and uses almost no test data.

There is no test paranoia here like I've seen in the States. Teachers don't use textbooks. They teach through projects. They don't spend time preparing students to take tests, the way Pittsburgh does with its prep a week before the CAT [California Achievement Test] or the way it tests students continually with its MAP tests.

Take a comparative look at the kinds of information a teacher would get from Broadacres' approach and what she would get from MAP tests:

- The Pittsburgh instruments reflect a very skills-subskills orientation; the Broadacres approach is a whole-language, developmental orientation.
- The Pittsburgh MAP relies on numerical scores; the Broadacres approach relies on descriptive information and observation.
- Objectives-based in Pittsburgh; project-based in Broadacres. The project-based approach allows for (or makes it easier for) higher-order thinking work, collaborative learning, individual research, because of the nature of the problems it describes and poses. The objectives-based approach breaks up the work students do, so teachers think of what students might do in a much more fragmented and atomistic fashion—for example, "inferential skills" or "literal skills," instead of a project that includes a range of skills student must use as they work out problems in natural contexts.

According to a brochure for parents, Broadacres has already committed itself to active-learning programs in communication. The school offers whole-language programs, a "celebration of writing" through its Young Authors' Conferences, and a "writing process" approach to writing instruction, integrated learning, problem solving, and thinking skills. The resource center is intended to be the school's main focus. The school is also aiming to expand its

active-learning programs in mathematics, through the addition of
more manipulative exercises and more construction and measuring
activities, which enable a learner to feel confident about mathematics. Other activities to be added will help students use their knowledge and understanding of math in all the other subjects, to enhance
their ability to reach creative solutions to problems and see relationships, working independently toward higher understanding.

The teachers and the principal want to reinforce the school's
language-arts program by adding a "Books Alive" reading club,
which will use four volunteers for every seven students, each volunteer giving a half-day per week to do shared reading of at least two
novels per month. The school also wants to develop an active-
learning program in basic French and expand its active-learning
program into environmental studies. Teachers want to address such
topics as acid rain and its effects on plants. They want to recycle
school waste, beautify the courtyard, and have students learn about
general plant husbandry, conservation, and solar energy. They also
want to set up a greenhouse and coordinate the school's environmental activities with those of community groups and with such
resources as the local arboretum.

The school is aiming to establish an "artists in the school"
program, bringing in graphic artists, people from the field of drama,
and musicians. The school is also proposing to develop active-
learning programs that will make better use of computers and au-
diovisual technology. Through outreach to the community and involvement of a wide range of citizens, Broadacres is trying to develop
active-learning programs for multiculturalism and sex equity. The
brochure for parents reads as follows:

> We believe that curriculum is everything that our
> children experience and participate in throughout the
> day. The formal curriculum, which consists of mathe-
> matics, language arts, environmental studies, French,
> music, the visual arts, and physical education, must
> therefore reflect and contain our goals of sex equity
> and multiculturalism. Whatever the subject, the con-
> tributions, rich heritage, and abilities of all humans

are integrated and utilized. When situations arise
where intolerance is evident, class meetings are held,
and discussions analyze the reasons for prejudice, as
well as societal and legal restrictions. We make clear
to our children that each of them is respected and
cherished as a full human being, irrespective of gender
or membership in a particular ethnic or racial
grouping.

I am talking with an administrator, and I ask, "What is the
connection between active learning and the fact that the ethnic and
racial groups get along better here?"

"Well, first of all, the students interact with each other.
They're taught a certain [number] of social skills—how to be cul-
turally sensitive, as well as how to analyze what other people are
saying. They're taught how to react to what's being said, and not
to the person [who's] saying it. And this will help them later on in
life to deal with other adults from different backgrounds."

"In other words, a kid's ability to relate to all sorts of folks,
peers or otherwise."

"And in different settings."

"And doing this in different settings is part of what he knows
is expected of him, as a skill that he has to develop?"

"Most certainly. Very definitely. So the future of schools is
to learn how to handle newcomers coming from a variety of backgrounds, a variety of languages, a variety of religious beliefs, in a
way that allows them to feel that they have a place here, will be
successful. So we in the system spend a lot of time working on the
attitudes and beliefs of our teachers, and that's making a very big
difference in terms of how we deal with these youngsters. Once we
start to see that this is important to us, this is not a passing phase,
then we work on awareness in terms of . . . well, what backgrounds
are these kids coming from? What does it mean for a youngster
who's grown up in Israel, with all the powerful socialization of that
society, to, overnight, find himself here, at the age of fourteen?
Doesn't really want to be here. Had seen his future quite clearly in
Israel, planned out for him, with all the loyalties that entails. And
he's here—a stranger in a foreign land—and we sometimes forget

that not everybody who's here wants to be here, and many people think that what they've left has much value. So we really need to spend time learning about those backgrounds, learning about what it feels like to be here with all those mixed feelings, and helping the youngster—first, with the language, and, secondly, with socialization."

The Broadacres approach to evaluation is as ambitious as the school's approach to everything else. According to one of its internal documents, "Evaluation should not take place only in written form. Other forms of evaluation, such as observation or demonstration, are equally valid or could be more appropriate. A balanced evaluation program includes as many forms of evaluation as possible which are appropriate to the student's development and level of achievement. . . . Because evaluation is an integral part of any educational program or process, it is essential that we constantly examine our evaluation techniques with a view to changing and improving them."

The school draws heavily on locally developed resource documents for evaluation that are far more robust, comprehensive, interesting, and sophisticated than the evaluation materials one typically sees in American school districts.

Broadacres is very concerned with the way it reports information to parents and the community. It has a number of informational booklets, and the staff worries about ineffective informational systems. Staff members want to develop a teacher-preparation center at Broadacres to serve teachers from all around the district, turning the entire school into a clinic. They want to develop a series of videotapes on what they are doing and make them available to home and school associations, and they want to institute regular newsletters written by students in the various grades. For the benefit of the community, they already have evening office hours, drop-in sessions for parents, curriculum nights, open-door policies, volunteer programs for senior citizens, and parent-teacher interviews. They want to develop new volunteers, new in-service training, a regular column in the local newspaper, more home visits, a regular telephone line to teachers, and 7:30 A.M. breakfasts at the school.

To follow through on the implementation of its guidelines, the Ontario Ministry of Education did not develop a standardized test for the whole province. Instead, it relied on the boards to develop the appropriate plans and evaluation systems. In 1983, the ministry reviewed forty-two randomly selected schools to determine the degree to which the ideas in *The Formative Years* and *Education in the Primary and Junior Divisions* had been carried out (Terry, 1985). As a consequence of the review report, a guide was developed for the 1986–87 school year, so that boards could do their own internal reviews, provide their teachers with regular feedback, develop strategies for enhancing the role of the principal as a curriculum leader, and establish clear policies (consistent with the ministry's guidelines) for curriculum review, development, and implementation.

The guide was carefully separated from issues of instructional evaluation and was designed simply to provide appropriate feedback about implementation of the guidelines. It employs a five-point scale, which encompasses traditional approaches to education, increasing child-centeredness, learners' independence, increasing amounts of problem solving by students, increasing integration of school subjects, increasing involvement of students in decision making, and increasing use of reading, writing, and discussion across the curriculum (see the resource section at the back of the book).

The contrasts at each pole of each five-point scale are clear. Under *evaluation,* for instance, at one extreme we have learners' progress evaluated primarily by standardized tests, in conjunction with teachers' grade-level tests; at the other extreme we have learners' progress evaluated not only through teachers' observations and assessments of daily work and projects but also through a full range of techniques (including checklists, observation guides, teacher-made tests, anecdotal comments, and standardized tests used only as a reference). Along the way are intervals of increasing sophistication.

Under *grouping,* at one extreme we have the learner group, which is the class, and it is primarily taught as a single large group; and at the other extreme we primarily have individuals and many small groups, and the size of the group is determined by factors related to the learner. At one extreme the basis of group organization is mainly administrators' needs; at the other extreme the basis of group organization is a combination of achievement, ability, and interest, and there are frequent self-selection opportunities for learners.

Under the *nature of learning* activity, learning activities at one extreme call for the learner to recall or find facts; at the other extreme they require recalling, finding, and interpreting facts, applying information to new situations, reorganizing information into other forms, and exploring open-ended situations, whose outcomes are not always predetermined.

At one extreme under *planning*, we have planning done primarily by the teacher, who works independently; at the other, the teacher has frequent consultations with colleagues, including the principal, to plan common classroom experiences and approaches. Meetings for goals, aims, and general philosophy are considered, and the learner is involved, formally and informally, through whole-class, group, and individual discussions with the teacher.

Under *routines,* at one extreme we have routines established and enforced by the teacher; activities are initiated and terminated by the teacher, and formal systems (for example, raising of hands) are required of learners. At the other, we have routines developed cooperatively by teachers and learners; activities are initiated and terminated by learners with the teacher's guidance, and interaction occurs informally at the discretion of the learners, within established routines.

Under *time,* at one extreme we have the day organized into small designated blocks; at the other, large blocks of time may be put to various uses from day to day.

We wanted to know how it could be determined that this child-centered, active-learning approach really produced results. An administrator offered an explanation.

"The bottom line is, we don't have graffiti on our walls. The bottom line is that we have an increasing number of students who are graduating out of our high schools with higher and higher skills. The bottom line is that our businesses are telling us that we're doing better, or not doing better. The bottom line is that parents are telling us we're satisfied, or not satisfied. The bottom line is that we're still getting the best people in our classes as teachers.''

"In other words, the bottom line, as far as you're concerned, is not just a simple score on a test."

"A simple score on a test, in a multicultural, multiracial society, is the kiss of death to opportunity for all people."

"Why?"

"Because it negates the past of people! Would you give a test tomorrow morning in this school, or in an elementary school, when you know that in that classroom you're going to have children who two days ago were in Managua, in the middle of a civil war? Would you give a test—the same test—to a child who is sitting next to this youngster, who has grown up in an upper-middle-class neighborhood, who has only known English, and whose parents are university professors? Would you give the same test to a child who also comes from a middle-class background, but who hasn't had breakfast, and whose parents just had a fight and are about to split? The same test? The same morning? And would you say that this is an objective way of finding out what kids know? That it's reasonable? That it's the bottom line? Even business doesn't do that! Even business doesn't treat their employees that way. Why do we treat kids that way?"

An educator said, "I think the major difference between Ontario and America—and I'm not sure of the reason behind it—is that we have not got hung up on these measurement issues. We're much more back on how you accomplish it, and what it looks like. So we—the combination of the government and the citizenry, if you like—have not insisted on measurement as the solution. It's just that we have more of a habit, if you like, of looking at the broader curriculum because it's been legitimized for so many years in the policies.''

"But if you don't insist on measurement as the solution, what do you insist on?"

"Well, we insist on the quality of teachers. The quality of teaching. Then we insist on the curriculum policy and its implementation, and then we look for what results it yields. And, I must say, that is a struggle. How do you measure some of these things?

Some of the more measurable goals, for example—reading achievement, math achievement, science achievement—are not necessarily
all the important goals, if you shift over to how a student accesses
information, reasoning skills, critical-thinking skills, independent
thinking, self-concept, and those things. So we're not any farther
ahead on those, in terms of measurement, necessarily. But we think
those are so important that we would rather struggle with the measurement problem than be satisfied with the achievement results of
lesser goals."

　　Most Etobicoke parents seem pleased with their schools. A
recent survey (Etobicoke Board Research and Evaluation Department, 1987) found that 96 percent feel welcome at their children's
elementary schools, 86 percent feel welcome at secondary schools,
92 percent rated their elementary schools excellent (87 percent so
described their secondary schools), and 94 percent said their children like school (87 percent for secondary school). Among parents
of elementary students, 63 percent said they have adequate involvement in decisions affecting their children, and the proportion was
the same for parents of secondary students; 81 percent of the elementary school parents and 63 percent of the secondary parents said the
school is helping their children develop good values.
　　Lest all of this sound too rosy, Terry (1985) found uneven
implementation of the ministry's policies and guidelines. Although
Terry found positive learning atmospheres in all the schools, the
implementation of the child-centered, experience-based curriculum,
even after ten years, had taken place fully in fewer than 25 percent
of the schools; the rest were moving in that direction, but slowly.
In about one-quarter of the schools, a good balance had been
achieved between whole-class teaching, smaller groupings, and individualized instruction. Researchers also observed a positive balance between teacher-directed instruction and pupils' exploration
and discovery. Nevertheless, traditional pedagogy (characterized as
"the sage on the stage") continued to prevail in most classrooms.
About 25 percent or fewer of the schools had fully integrated the
curriculum across subject areas. Between 25 percent and 50 percent
of the schools had literature-based reading programs that were balanced, child-centered, and integrated into nurturing learning envi-

ronments, with imaginative and varied learning opportunities. According to Terry (1985) six factors heavily influenced the course of the guidelines' implementation:

1. *Clarity:* It wasn't clear to many people what the nature of the curriculum should be, even though they understood the philosophy behind the policies.
2. *The adoption process:* More attention was paid to the upper divisions than to the primary and junior divisions.
3. *Central administrators' support and involvement:* The less support and involvement, the slower the implementation.
4. *Principals' support and involvement:* Where principals did not know how to be strong curriculum leaders, implementation was slow.
5. *Teachers' isolation:* Where teachers' normal isolation from one another was not overcome with collaborative work and opportunities to observe and provide mutual help, implementation lagged.
6. *Underestimation of the task:* It is very difficult to transform habits and practices many generations old.

Tony, Sam, and I focused on some points about Ontario and Etobicoke while ignoring others. The outstanding virtue of the place, from our point of view, is its policy framework. In Ontario, the provincial government explicitly and relentlessly is asking for thoughtfulness. The ministry has developed policy documents that are themselves models of thoughtfulness and that have transformed the curriculum, instruction, and assessment. The trustees, central administrators, principals, and teachers we talked with are impressively literate and interested in ideas to an unusual degree. Etobicoke's teachers have developed a rich and diverse curriculum in response to the ministry's guidelines; general, top-down mandates have stimulated imaginative, bottom-up applications. The district has moved away from "the sage on the stage" and toward a truly child-centered, experienced-based, learning-focused system that is supported, not thwarted, by the government. The elementary schools we visited are the best we have seen. They are supported in their innovativeness, not thwarted, by the district. Their students outperform American students on the few common indicators available (Lapointe, Mead, and Phillips, 1989). Etobicoke is a coherent, well-run district that seems to have learned how to organize itself around constant improvement.

As far as we could tell, minorities and poor children receive as much challenge as majority students. Condescending, patronizing, "dumbing down" remedial materials are rare. Multiculturalism, supported firmly by policy, pervades the curriculum and positively influences the attitudes of teachers and students alike. Clearly, urban education need not be as flagrantly poor and inequitable as it so often is in American cities. Clearly, large-scale systemic change toward a higher level of literacy for a broader range of students is possible, and state and district policy, especially if based on a coherent and robust vision of the future, can play a major role in bringing about and sustaining the higher literacy.

But Etobicoke and Toronto and Ontario are not without their detractors and difficult problems. Although they are among the highest-paid teachers in North America, the elementary teachers went on strike in 1987. Although most parents support the changes that have taken place, a vocal minority do not believe that education has improved for their children. While we were there, a group of parents spent an evening with a trustee, ridiculing the schooling and demanding more rote learning, more drill, more recitation, and more standardized testing. One critic told us that professional educators, having gained so much power from this movement, were now too far ahead of the public and were dangerously isolated. We also heard that principals may not have received enough training to get them deeply enough involved in the new philosophy.

Active learning places extremely difficult logistical and diagnostic demands on teachers. Without constant diligence, teachers can miss signals that their students are not performing up to capacity, and teachers may let them drift. Independent study is not for everyone; some students need far more structure than others. Staff development has to be continuous, and it has to be absolutely first-rate.

But Etobicoke's school population is shrinking. Layoffs and cutbacks are inevitable. Some people told us that seniority rules will operate to prune out the younger, more appropriately trained teachers and administrators, protecting older educators who never bought the new philosophy. In any case, it is hard to sustain substantive change when people are pitted against one another for jobs, and when staff turnover is high.

Articulation from level to level seemed problematic. Middle schools, as usual, seemed caught between the child-centered approach of the early grades and the pressure for a more college-oriented approach in the later grades. After having abandoned the practices of junior high schools many years ago, some middle schools are reinstituting junior high schedules and practices. The high schools we visited were good but not markedly better than good high schools in the United States.

It is hard to see how Ontario can continue to pay the costs of public, Catholic, and French schools and take on even more systems as various groups apply for public funding. Sooner or later, the province will run out of money.

Finally, Toronto demonstrates that, even at its best, the process of changing schools to develop a higher level of literacy for a broader range of students, takes a long time. After fifteen years of concentrated effort Toronto's schools have much positive progress to show, but they are also a long way from having transformed the entire system. Perhaps that is the work of a generation.

CHAPTER EIGHT

Cultivating
a Literacy
of Thoughtfulness

Tony Petrosky, Sam Stringfield, Rona Wilensky, Alan Davis, some other researchers, and I visited more districts and many more schools than I have mentioned in the preceding chapters, and we looked at far more material than we could ever include in this book. I have tried to use each chapter to focus on only a few of the many possible positive or negative points that could be made about any school or district, any set of policies. Now it is time to sum up, across all the schools and districts and states we visited, all the research we reviewed and all the conversations we had with thoughtful people about the issues raised in this study.

We know how to develop a literacy of thoughtfulness. There are no secrets here. If you want young people to think, you ask them hard questions and let them wrestle with the answers. If you want them to analyze something or interpret it or evaluate it, you ask them to do so and show them how do it with increasing skill. If you want them to know how to approach interesting or difficult problems, you give them interesting or difficult problems and help them develop a conscious repertoire of problem-solving strategies. If you want them to think the way scientists or historians or mathematicians do, you show them how scientists and historians and mathematicians think, and you provide opportunities for them to practice and compare those ways of thinking.

In every school we visited, someone knew what to do and practiced it to some degree. Great teachers have always known how to make students think about and apply their knowledge. But seldom did we see the *majority* of teachers in a school practicing or stimulating a literacy of thoughtfulness. None of the school districts we studied in the United States was committed to fostering, *on a wide scale,* the kinds of activities known to lead to a literacy of thoughtfulness.

There is some hope in this observation. First of all, the large-scale cultivation of a literacy of thoughtfulness is not a problem on which we need much more research before we can act, as so many other problems seem to be. We know more than enough about the substance of this literacy to get started. The bulk of the effort has more to do with democracy, community building, and political will. Second, we can hope for success because the educational system is still quite young; it is still evolving. We do not know that we cannot cultivate a literacy of thoughtfulness, because we have not yet attempted it; neither policymakers nor educators have really asked for it yet. There is no reason to believe that, if enough people wanted to move education in this direction, we could not do it.

Schools and districts that are farthest along in developing more thoughtfulness among students have also created more thoughtful environments and conditions for the adults in the system. These schools and districts are distinguished by a different kind of conversation, a style of communication that builds community. Although disagreements exist, they are in the open and are the subject of intense and sustained inquiry and debate. Good schools are symbolically rich places, where vivid and interesting conversations are taking place up and down the hierarchy. Adults are visibly engaged in inquiry, discovery, learning, collaborative problem solving, and critical thinking. Poor schools, by comparison, are symbolically impoverished; people are mum or secretive, isolated from one another or afraid to speak their minds. Anyone who hopes to excite and challenge young people without exciting and challenging their teachers hopes in vain. How an approach to cultivating thinking or problem solving will fare in any particular school or district is a function of the conversations going on (or not going on) around and within it. We have seen in the foregoing chapters how certain kinds of policy and certain kinds of leadership can create or destroy the working conditions that stimulate the right kinds of conversations among adults and generate richly textured literacy environments for children. Again, we know what works; carrying it out on a large scale is a political problem, not a substantive one.

In most schools, the language of the classroom is primarily a language about the process of teaching something; it is not itself a language of learning. We came to call this language "talkinbout," because we saw so many people talking about reading but not actually reading, talking about writing but not actually writing, and so on. "Talkinbout" is an abstract language, an adult reconstruction after the fact of an experience that the student is not allowed to have firsthand. It is a rumor about learning.

The language of teachers' guides and curricular materials is a form of "talkinbout": a peculiarly stiff, jargon-ridden language of process, of how to do things. It is not a language of expression or reflection. It is a language of work and technique, oriented toward achieving some narrowly (and often trivially) defined success, rather than toward achieving deeper understanding. It is about effectiveness, not truthfulness or rightness in the moral sense. It leaves little room for critical or creative thinking, little latitude for judgment.

Ironically, the primary conditions for thoughtfulness—mystery, uncertainty, disagreement, important questions, ambiguity, curiosity—exist in every classroom. You see them in the faces of the children; you hear them in the halls. Potential learning opportunities are everywhere, but these fertile conditions are either ignored or perceived as barriers to teaching, as threats to order.

If you want to change individuals, you usually have to make them conscious of things that are right in front of their faces, things that they cannot see while everyone else can. You often have to help them learn how to listen to themselves, how to recognize contradictions in what they are saying, patterns of expression that reveal underlying assumptions and ideas. So it is with changing organizational cultures: you start with language. You have to help the people in the organization listen to themselves and raise questions about what they hear. Are they speaking "talkinbout," or are they sharing a language of learning? What does each kind of language sound like and feel like? What kinds of responses does each kind generate? As soon as people begin to focus on their language, a literacy of thoughtfulness has gained a toehold, and community building has begun. As soon as that happens, the potential learning opportunities that seemed invisible or threatening become visible and easy to exploit.

Schools and districts that are making progress on a literacy of thoughtfulness must overcome numerous disincentives and perceived barriers. None of the barriers is an absolute deterrent, but the total combination constitutes a formidable challenge.

We asked teachers and administrators what they saw as the principal constraints on giving students more opportunities to think, solve problems, and learn to use their minds more effectively. The case studies in the previous chapters document their answers in context, but six issues came up so often that they deserve summary comments here.

The most frequently given reason for not moving toward an instruction more conducive to thoughtfulness was time. We were told that there simply is not enough time in the day to challenge every student or provide personalized opportunities for learning. Teachers who were sympathetic to the idea of providing more challenges said that they did not have the time to prepare well for discussions, collaborative activities, or interdisciplinary lessons; they did not have the time to respond thoughtfully to 145 essays or projects. Others pointed out that the day is too fragmented for sustained intellectual activities. How can thirty teenagers discuss an important idea in forty-five minutes? Many pointed out that the school schedule—a Byzantine document prepared with so much labor and compromise that no one dares change it—dominates decision making in the school and in the district.

These are understandable objections. Time, not substance, has come to be the fundamental unit of education. We do not ask what a high school graduate knows about mathematics; we ask how many years of mathematics she has had, a year being the total number of forty-five-minute periods during which she was seated in class. This turns out to be about 132 hours, or sixteen and one-half work days. Some year. We award credits and degrees for time spent in a seat. Curricula are laid out in terms of scope-and-sequences pegged to class time. Reading skill is expressed in terms of time; tests are timed. Nowhere more than here are the contemporary institutions of education's roots—planted in early-twentieth-century time-study notions of industrial efficiency—so exposed.

Ultimately, the ways in which time serves to structure the work of teachers and students will have to change, if we want a literacy of thoughtfulness on a large scale. This will require a profound revolution in our thinking about schooling and learning, and perhaps about time itself. We need not wait for such a revolution, however, as the case studies demonstrate. Even in today's schools, much can be done to structure and use time differently. Teachers can "block time"—that is, put two or three class periods back to back and treat them as one long, team-taught period, within which there is enough time for thoughtful work. Principals can simply declare, as they have in some schools, that there are two periods, morning and afternoon. Teachers' contracts and job descriptions can be reconceived, to give teachers necessary preparation time. Interactive videodisc and computer technologies can be used in ways that free teachers' time. As we saw in Toronto, cooperative learning frees teachers for more individual diagnosis and treatment of learning problems.

We saw huge differences in the efficiency with which teachers and schools used their time. Time and learning opportunities are wasted profligately in schools. Bells ring, announcements intrude over the public-address system, students are pulled out for various activities or wander in late or act out and interrupt others. Teachers take attendance, pass out materials, ask students to pass in materials, and devote enormous energies to controlling students' behavior. The lecture mode, known to be one of the least efficient ways of imparting information, dominates far too many classrooms. Some schools have done "time audits" to determine how they are now using time and how they can do better.

Have time considerations driven out substance because of policies, rules, and regulations? Probably, to some degree. Policy, as we argued in Chapter Five, addresses education as an institutional process, an administrative matter. It is loaded with assumptions about time as a measure of quality. We certainly believe that a thorough review and discussion of how policy says, explicitly or implicitly, that time is more important than substance would be a worthwhile undertaking in a school, a district, or a state. Some states are already doing away with the so-called Carnegie Unit (the amount of time a student spends in a given course) as an index of education completed; perhaps others will follow their example.

Ultimately, educational policy rests on a complicated social agreement: that all the learning necessary to prepare young people for life will take place within twelve years. Twelve is an arbitary number; there could be any other approved number of years, or there could be no approved number at all. Perhaps a national commitment to lifelong education in a literacy of thoughtfulness would relieve some of the enormous pressure that students, parents, and teachers now feel to keep on schedule. Fortunately, thoughtfulness, as we have defined it, is neither a skill nor a commodity, and so it does not require a schedule.

Time is also a function of what is called coverage, the second most frequently given reason why there is not more thoughtfulness in the schools. Teachers feel that they must cover an already sprawling and constantly expanding list of topics within and across subject matter areas. Some of the demands of coverage stem from policy mandates, but many appear to derive from simple accumulation, over the years, of ideas, texts, lesson plans, and publishers' promotions, as well as from the steady expansion of knowledge about almost everything.

To be sure, the curriculum has become too broad for anyone to master all of it, and too shallow for anyone to know anything in depth. This is an inevitable result of the goals-and-objectives, scope-and-sequence approach to organizing knowledge, which breaks any item into dozens of subitems and subsubitems. It is what happens when you apply an administrative rationality to a knowledge base that is conceived as a collection of facts and to a teaching technology that is conceived as a means of transmitting facts: you get this huge pile of unrelated, decontextualized facts. Test after test of factual recall reveals that this curriculum does not work. Students cannot remember much, and what they do recall is superficial and useless. We have long since reached the limits of what we can "shoe-horn" into such a curriculum and what we can get out of it.

No doubt we need a revolution in our thinking about knowl-edge, just as we do in our thinking about time. But as we have seen in the case studies, some people find both the time and the room in the curriculum. In some schools, teachers are saying "Less is more." Since no human being can learn all the facts there are to know, teachers concentrate on enabling students to learn fewer things in greater depth, with greater connectedness. They make the question, not the fact, the fundamental unit of the curriculum; they emphasize context and application. Then they make sure that stu-dents learn how to learn, how to find any information they may need, now or in the future. If you know how to find information, you needn't try to memorize so many facts.

In our studies of curriculum, we found that programs and practices that develop a literacy of thoughtfulness are diverse, frag-mented, and widely varying in quality. Many thinking-oriented programs have been developed and championed by individual teachers, on their own initative and with encouragement and mate-rials from their professional associations. Textbooks and work-books for critical thinking, higher-order thinking skills, reasoning, problem solving, and other such activities have emerged steadily in the last few years. In their new editions, textbook publishers regu-larly add end-of-chapter questions calling for thought.

Two general approaches to instruction in thinking dominate the scene as the 1990s begin. One aims to teach elements of thinking and problem solving directly, either as subjects in themselves or, more popularly, as dimensions of any subject matter. The other aims to develop a comprehensive literateness, assuming that thoughtfulness will necessarily evolve along the way.

In the first camp, one finds many teachers trying to move their students through the stages of Bloom's taxonomy—synthesis, analysis, interpretation, and evaluation. We have seen productive applications of the taxonomy, and we have seen applications that make no sense at all. One also finds in this camp programs that have grown from philosophy courses (especially formal and infor-mal logic), research in cognitive psychology, research in artificial intelligence, and studies of experts and expert systems. Leaders in this diverse field include Robert Ennis, Robert Sternberg, Ray Nickerson, Alan Collins, Richard Paul, Edward de Bono, John Baron, Joan Baron, David Perkins, Robert Swartz, Reuven Feuerstein, and Matt Lipman, to name some of the most visible. Their ideas overlap in some areas and diverge radically in others. Around the work of each has grown secondary work, as well as materials that in turn have spawned tertiary work, rumors, and back-pocket programs and approaches that their leaders themselves would probably repudiate if they saw them in action.

In the second camp, one finds people whose roots lie more in the humanities than in the sciences, more in progressive educational philosophy, language, sociolinguistics, reading, writing, and literacy studies. For these theorists and educators, a whole-language approach to instruction, or an experience-based, child-centered approach, or a constructivist, hands-on, active-learning approach, is primary; thinking, problem solving, and creativity are things that naturally happen in an environment designed to encourage the construction and negotiation of meaning. Leaders in this camp include Theodore Sizer, Donald Graves, the Montessorians, Ken and Yetta Goodman, Ken Macrorie, James Moffett, James Britton, Nancy Martin, and a host of Deweyans, alternative educators, and structural reformers. Like those in the first group, people in this group hold views that are not necessarily compatible; like the first group, this one has also spawned secondary and tertiary experts, as well as programs and "rumor mills" of widely varying quality.

By and large, efforts to teach thinking directly—either in separate courses or through infusion of thinking into the entire curriculum—do not call for structural changes in schooling as we now know it. The precepts of many of the best thinkers in the field can be interpreted as calling for major changes in curriculum and pedagogy, but they need not be so interpreted, nor have they been in any of the districts we studied. Holistic approaches to developing thoughtfulness, by contrast, pose a potential threat to the current structural organization of schooling because they require particular environments and ecologies. They need not *compel* radical change, but they call the status quo more dramatically into question.

Cutting across both camps are profoundly different schools of thought about the nature of knowledge, the nature of learning, and the kinds of curricula and pedagogy most likely to develop a higher level of literacy for a broader range of students. These different ways of thinking are woven into the fabric of American life and are as old as the republic itself. They can be traced to radically different views about human nature and about the role of government in unleashing our human potential for good or restricting our potential for evil. Some Americans believe neither that children should think for themselves nor that governmental institutions should show them how. Some believe that when approaches to thoughtfulness involve students in creating or expressing their own values, schools have overstepped their bounds. Some argue that programs such as those I have described in this book constitute a form of state-supported secular religion. Attempts to censor books in the curriculum surface regularly, coming about equally from the left and the right of the political spectrum. Threats of lawsuits over curricular matters are common. Everyone seems to have something that he or she insists *must* be taught, and something that he or she insists must *not* be taught. Perhaps we should not be surprised that the results of our compromises are largely incoherent and irrelevant.

The solutions to the coverage issue are both substantive and political. Communities, through a democratic, learning-oriented conversation, can decide what knowledge and habits of mind will best prepare students for the world they live in and will inherit, and they can support their decisions through strong, sometimes courageous political leadership; or they can let things drift on in a muddle.

A third reason why so little disciplined thinking or problem solving takes place in classrooms is the belief, widely shared, that most students do not have the intelligence required by a literacy of thoughtfulness. Unlike the Japanese, who believe that performance is related to how hard one works, Americans tend to believe that performance is related to intelligence, and that intelligence is primarily a product of genetic inheritance. The bell-shaped curve of intelligence distribution seems to guarantee that only a small percentage of students will be intelligent enough to be interested or engaged in such abstract operations as problem solving and critical thinking. Thus is the goal of thoughtfulness for all students believed to be against nature.

But it is not against nature, as we have seen and as an enormous body of research and experience testifies. We know that almost all children can learn whatever they are motivated to learn and whatever they are given appropriate opportunities to learn (see Education Commission of the States, 1990, for a synthesis of the research). Intelligence, creativity, and talent are not scarce resources; for all practical purposes, they appear to be limitless. How a country exploits or fails to exploit this fact is a political matter.

A fourth constraint on thoughtfulness, often cited in our interviews, is that most students do not want to be engaged learners. Their priorities are elsewhere—music, television, play. What need do children have for critical and creative thinking or problem solving, anyway? Thoughtfulness is for adults. Moreover, numerous educators seem to believe that thinking is developmentally inappropriate before grade 9.

To both of these objections we can only point out what our case studies and the broader body of research document: that students of all ages can learn and practice various kinds of critical and creative thinking appropriate to their ages and become deeply engaged in their learning. Of course, just like the rest of us, they will resist changes in the status quo at first, but once they get into active learning, they appear not only to love it but also to improve their tolerance and use of the periods in which they are required to be passive learners.

We also learned, as so many others have, that expectations for minority and disadvantaged students are low. Sometimes it was said that schoolwork runs against the grain of such students' cultures or family upbringing. Sometimes we were told that if you ask too much of a disadvantaged student, you will further erode his or her self-esteem. Sometimes it was said that minorities, especially adolescent boys, resist academics as a matter of racial pride or as an act of social protest, and that they often taunt their academically inclined classmates. Sometimes it was said that minorities do not need much more than basic skills, because they will most probably be doing low-level work after they leave school.

Some people told us that minorities have unique learning styles and do not like to conceptualize the way Anglos do. Some said that institutionalized racism undermines the motivation of minority children, so that they give up early, knowing they cannot get ahead. Some told us that minority and poor parents do not provide the kind of support that Anglo and affluent parents provide, and so their children cannot be expected to compete. Some also told us that competition itself, even for grades, is foreign to the cultures of some minority children. Some people told us that minority parents prefer drill, rote, memorization, and tightly disciplined instruction for their children, distrusting progressive approaches that undermine parental authority.

Schools that are making progress in cultivating a literacy of thoughtfulness have explicitly addressed the problem of lower expectations for different groups of students. This is a sensitive matter. Most educators, caring deeply about poor and minority children, believe that they are acting commonsensically in their students' best interests and are unconscious of the ways in which they communicate lower expectations. They are hurt and angered by any suggestion that they harbor a bias. The human-relations training required to deal with this problem is long and difficult. Moreover, the problem is complicated by the fact that many students have developed low expectations for themselves and act accordingly.

Here, again, a revolution in how mainstream Americans view and treat people of different classes, races, cultures, and language groups would no doubt speed the spread of a literacy of thoughtfulness for everyone. So would the elimination of institutionalized forms of racism and classism, which remain latent in the structures of present-day schooling. But, again, we do not have to wait for the revolution. We have to give students and teachers opportunities to prove to themselves, happily, that they have been wrong. We know a great deal about how to do that. Success breeds success. As students succeed at things that neither they nor their teachers really believed they could do, amazing things begin to happen.

A fifth constraint on thinking and problem solving in the classroom is that most teachers do not know how to do what is necessary, because they did not see any active learning in their own elementary and secondary education. They probably spent most of their undergraduate years listening to lectures. The average teacher probably did not engage in active learning in schools of education until his or her clinical experience—if he or she had one, and if it was done well. These are big *ifs*.

The kind of literacy that we are talking about calls for a very different notion of what a teacher is and does. David Cohen (1988) and many others have amply documented the reasons why the old notion of what teachers are is extremely difficult to change. Models of thoughtful learning environments are rare. Teachers seldom get the chance to observe one another. Teachers' inservice training seldom exemplifies the precepts of active, hands-on learning or discovery. Indeed, teachers' inservices are woefully superficial and notoriously boring. Teachers' professional meetings are conducted largely in the lecture mode, and workshops tend to involve little real intellectual work.

The top businesses in America devote 2 percent of their budgets to constant human resources development. School districts, by comparison, devote almost nothing. We saw one approach to this difficulty in Pittsburgh, at the Schenley Teacher Center. Louisville has also created such a center. Without powerful ways of enabling large numbers of teachers to learn and practice techniques conducive to thoughtful, active learning by students, we will not get very far.

A sixth constraint on activities conducive to more active learning, critical thinking, and creativity is the widespread belief that these activities either cannot be evaluated or cannot be evaluated in ways compatible with current accountability systems. We have seen in earlier chapters that the first belief is dead wrong. There are many ways to evaluate possession of the knowledge and capacity to think critically and creatively, to reason, to solve various kinds of problems, and, in manifold ways, to demonstrate degrees and kinds of thoughtfulness (Brown, 1989a, 1989b). Unfortunately, many teachers and administrators do not know about their options and do not believe that they can develop their own alternative measures. Fortunately, assessment agencies in California, Vermont, Connecticut, Michigan, Illinois, New York, and New Jersey, to name some leaders among the states, are developing alternative measures and beginning to share them widely. The second belief is justified in schools and school districts that are subjected to high-stakes basic-skills testing in an atmosphere of mistrust. Like so many of the other barriers we have discussed, however, this is a problem of politics, not of know-how.

Policy environments make a difference. Policy environments consist of many types of policy, the rules and regulations attached to them, and the understandings or misunderstandings that have grown around them. Efficiency policies (which explicitly or implicitly address the financing, costs, and logistics of mass education), equity policies, accountability and quality-control policies (including teacher and student assessment, certification, and recertification policies), and content policies (curriculum) interact with one another and with strategic plans, union relationships, local and state politics, community relationships, tradition, and professional codes and standards, to create a policy environment that is more or less supportive of thoughtfulness. Our studies of policy led us to the following conclusions.

"Thoughtfulness policy" (policy about critical and creative thinking, problem solving, inquiry, and so on), whether at the state or local level, is weak. Goals or other kinds of statements dealing with these matters are absent, poorly stated, or buried in the rubble of a thousand other goals, all of which are apparently of equal value. Seventeen states now mention some aspect of the literacy of thoughtfulness in their goal statements. Many of them have only recently done so; perhaps this is a trend. The point here, of course, is that if you do not ask for it, you are unlikely to get it. If you do ask for it, you have a chance.

Thoughtfulness policy is usually framed in terms of skills and subskills. The terms *thinking skills* and *higher-order thinking skills* are most common. Skills can be incorporated into the current teaching technology (a transmission model, featuring lecture, recitation, teachers' dominance, and students' passivity), with no requirement for significant changes in teaching or schooling; this will have to change. Some of the more recent goal statements and vision statements in certain states (Vermont, Kansas, and California, for example) are moving in the right direction, with robust descriptions of a higher literacy that cannot be achieved without radical alteration in the current teaching technology.

State and local policies are silent about active learning, a necessary ingredient of any critical- and creative-thinking effort. Policy says what to teach and how many hours to teach it, but not how to teach it, and assumes that the transmission model is adequate for teaching anything, and the number of hours of exposure to a subject is the best measure of learning. Policies in curriculum, testing, accountability, certification, teacher evaluation, and inservice training all implicitly or explicitly reinforce a transmission model of teaching. As we saw in Chapter Seven, policy documents can address the "how" in ways that shape classroom behavior.

Policy is often contradictory or confused and leads to contradictory or confused implementations. The school-finance law we looked at in Chapter Five, for instance, requires local districts to create assessments unique to the districts' particular needs while creating assessments that are the same as everyone else's. Recent reform packages reflect the "horse trading" necessary to pass any complex legislation. Liberal and conservative sentiments and incompatible educational philosophies coexist at the policy level, sending mixed signals and leaving ample room for multiple interpretations and implementations.

Many problems attributed to policy are either not related to policy at all or are so indirectly related that policy is simply not the appropriate level at which to address them. People forget that policymakers are often the last ones to know anything; they react more than they act. Moreover, different teachers and principals interpret their freedom within policy constraints in different ways. One teacher will say that she is oppressed by her state's basic-skills tests, but a teacher down the hall will tell you that the tests are not a problem. One principal will be to interpret policy mandates so strictly that there is no time for any innovation or thoughtful dialogue, while another in the same district is "restructuring" his school as if the policy mandates did not exist. Thus, policy both is and is not a constraint on change toward more thoughtfulness. Much depends on leadership and on how leaders create and sustain environments conducive to thoughtfulness.

Policy affects the quality and quantity of discourse in schools and school districts. Policy is itself a form of discourse that shapes how questions are asked, problems are defined, and progress is gauged. It creates terms, analogies, technical vocabularies, and typical forms of response. Policy statements are understood and acted on in various ways. They may be accurately understood, in spirit or in letter, but not acted on, for many reasons. They may be accurately understood but acted on in wrong ways. They may be misunderstood and acted on in the right (intended) way, or they may be misunderstood and fiercely fought against. Policy guidelines must pass through bureaucracies and media reports, both of which can distort them in strange and wondrous ways.

Again and again, we saw that the difference between a school or a district that offered conditions hospitable to thoughtfulness and a school or a district that did not was a difference in the kind, quality, and coherence of the conversations that were taking place there. *What good policy can do is stimulate, legitimate, and sustain healthy conversations and literate discourse. It can assemble people to inquire into the most fundamental matters, to argue about them and use the very skills and dispositions they want to develop in students: problem solving, reasoning, analysis, questioning, collaborating, democratic decision making, and all the rest.* Bad policy either does nothing to the system, in which case its natural entropy grows, or it stimulates unhealthy conversations and resistance. It shuts discourse down, rather than opening it up.

Visiting schools, we were struck by the enormous fragmentation of the educational enterprise. Education is physically fragmented, classroom to classroom and building to building. Articulation from grade to grade is poor, and teachers of one grade do not know what their students studied in previous grades or what they will study in the next. We have preschools, schools for kindergarten through grade 2, intermediate schools, middle schools, junior high schools, and high schools. Time, too, is fragmented into bits, and space is fragmented into smaller spaces. Students may be transferring into or out of a school all year long; whole classrooms turn over in many urban schools. In any given classroom, students may be pulled out for special programs, band, athletics, or anything else. Students may be sick or chronically tardy or cutting classes. Teachers and principals come and go, as do superintendents and school board members. How can anything be sustained in such a system? Is it even a system, in the strict sense, or are we just imagining that it is?

Communication in and among schools is fragmented and uneven. People are remarkably isolated from one another. In large districts, communication up and down the hierarchy may be Kafkaesque. Communication between a school and parents and the larger community is often poor, sometimes nonexistent. Substantive communication among people teaching different subjects or different kinds of students seldom takes place; people haven't been educated to talk to one another. Communication between elementary teachers and middle school teachers, or between middle school teachers and high school teachers, or between high school teachers and college professors, is usually strained or thwarted by everyone's consciousness of a pecking order in the profession. Communication between people focused on institutional matters and people focused on learning is difficult, as we have seen. The language of bureaucracy—the instrumental rationality that is supposed to hold the institution together and guide it—fosters alienation, not communication. It separates people and deals with them individually, not in groups. It creates the illusion that everyone is "on the same page," when in fact no one knows what's going on. The irony of administrative discourse is that it aims to create coherence but, at best, it only colludes with the natural incoherence of the system.

Our educational system is fragmented—conceptually, socially, and politically. Americans do not agree about their educational goals, as the current national effort to define those goals demonstrates. Even when we find some agreement about ends, we often fight about means for achieving them. We do not agree about the nature of learning. Behaviorists and constructivists and a host of other theorists and researchers press interesting, valuable, and often conflicting ideas on us as this area of inquiry explodes with new knowledge. Practitioners carry on, with little awareness of what is happening in the study of learning. We do not agree about instruction or curriculum, either within or across subject areas (reading and writing, for instance). Union leaders and managers see things differently; so do ethnic groups, conservative and liberal politicians, and people in different economic classes.

To contemplate all this fragmentation and dissonance, all

this potential for incoherence, one cannot help thinking that it's a miracle to have done as well as we have. But that observation holds for this vast and diverse country as a whole. Democracy itself is hard, seemingly impossible work. The task of transforming our educational system so that it develops a far more empowering literacy for a far broader range of people than ever before is actually the task of carrying forward the democratic promise that has always drawn this country on toward new frontiers and futures. What is at stake is not this country's economic competitiveness in world markets, although that is the most visible cause of our current anxiety about schooling; it is our capacity to move the democratic experiment another step ahead. The events of 1989 and 1990 make it clear that the world needs our leadership in democratic nation building more than it needs our economic leadership.

To transform our educational system so that it better enables each individual to develop his or her talents to the fullest will require new kinds of policy and leadership. We have seen, in earlier chapters, what does not work and what holds promise. Clearly, the general task is to move away from fragmentation and toward more integration; away from the isolation of teacher or school or district and toward the idea of a community of learners; away from the politics of confrontation and toward a politics of collaboration; away from a largely vertical, authoritarian organizational structure and toward a flatter, more democratic structure; away from an emphasis on minimal, basic skills and toward an emphasis on challenging everyone in the system; away from a system with little clarity of purpose and toward a system drawn into the future by a compelling vision of what this nation will achieve in the world as it both understands more deeply and enacts the values and ideals on which it was founded.

What we need are policies and leaders to create conversations of the kind we saw in Pittsburgh and Toronto, to change the level and kinds of discourse going on in and around schools, and to stimulate inquiry, questioning, problem solving, and a focus on learning for everyone in the system, not just students. It is not necessary to totally transform everything that is going on in schools today; it is necessary only to move toward more thoughtfulness. To judge from our own and others' studies, devoting four times as much school time directly to critical and creative thinking and problem solving—through more writing, discussion, project work, and cooperative learning—would bring the average amount of time spent on thoughtful, active learning to about a day and a half a week, or two days at the most. That may not seem like much, but it is an achievable goal, and it could make a huge difference.

Policymakers can do much to facilitate such a change. The most powerful thing they can do is to *ask for* more thoughtful, active learning. For decades, they have asked for minimal or basic skills, and that is what they have received. In Ontario, they asked for more, and they are getting more. In Connecticut, Maine, Vermont, South Carolina, and California, policymakers and community leaders are spelling out more robust visions of education for their young people, and they are likely to get more robust learning because they asked for it. In a system as fragmented as this one, you cannot get anywhere without clear, forceful signals about what you want.

Having asked for more active, thoughtful learning, policymakers can improve the likelihood of getting it by creating policy environments friendly (or at least not hostile) to it. Trust is essential, as we have seen; where it does not exist, the first duty of policymakers and leaders is to create it. There is no point in implementing anything in an atmosphere of mistrust. The best way to get people to trust one another is to put them into situations that force them to learn together and depend on each other to solve important problems. The more people have to work together to accomplish things, the more likely it is that trust can be developed and sustained. Policies and processes that force collaboration, teamwork, and shared responsibility can, with the right kind of leadership, bring about sufficient trust to get good things done.

We are saying that students at all ages must take increasing responsibility for their learning. That is the only way to get them deeply engaged and committed to their education. It is a natural way to teach them responsibility and reinforce the values that undergird all genuine learning: courage, honesty, persistence, and respect for knowledge and for those who know more. It is the only way to develop knowledge and habits of mind that will endure. It is the best cure for discipline problems. Policy must be very clear about all this and must protect the kinds of activities that follow from these assumptions.

As sensible as all this sounds, and as solidly as these assumptions are grounded, they still stir fear and resistance. Many of us harbor deep ambivalence toward children. Many of us worry about the authority of adults over young people, and about the need to contain the natural and necessarily naïve enthusiasms of the young. If truth be told, many of us would rather see children sitting passively and quietly in rows, learning obedience and self-denial above all else. Policy that is wishy-washy on the matter of requiring students to use their minds more actively and fully will not get the job done. What is striking about the Ontario guidelines is their confidence and authority. "We know that this is how young people learn best," they say in effect, "and here is what we're going to do"—no apologies, no maybes.

Of the documents we examined from state departments of education, too few even made assertions about how young people learn best, let alone went on from such premises to lay out logical ways to proceed. Perhaps this is because, in this country, we are fond of telling ourselves that education is not very scientific, and that we do not really know much about it. Perhaps learning theories have become too embedded in political ideologies, and so we don't mention them, in an attempt to be politically neutral and objective about schooling. Whatever the reasons, our failure to clearly state what we believe and know about learning, and to back it up with strong supportive policy, only contributes to the general wishy-washiness of the system. What is called for is political courage and backbone.

Although we have enormous evidence and common sense to back us up on this point, we have also found it politically difficult to assert vigorously that all children can learn whatever they are motivated to learn and whatever they are given appropriate opportunities to learn. To be sure, the basic structures of schooling were established when this was not widely believed; it appeared that only a few students had the intelligence to excel at schoolwork, just as it appeared that only a few people could excel at being millionaires or rulers of vast empires. It appeared that poor people and minorities—and, in fact, the majority of the young people who swarmed into schools during the Great Depression—lacked the interest, intelligence, and willpower to tackle academic work. It appeared that a high I.Q. was the key to academic success, and only a few people had high I.Q.s. It appeared that children had to learn how to compete, so that they could fit into a dog-eat-dog, competitive world. There had to be winners, and there had to be losers; schools had to sort people into the economic and social strata that were best for them. Allowing that it all made sense at one time and was consistent with the economic and social realities of the early twentieth century, it has not made sense for the past fifty years, and it does not fit the economic and social realities we have faced during that period. But with all our greater knowledge about human talents and learning, with all that has deepened our understanding, we have yet to assert vigorously, through our policies and practices, the counterview to the wasteful, prejudiced one that so deeply influenced our country and its educational system in its formative years. Again, this has not been a question of insufficient knowledge; it has been a question of political will.

I hope the case studies have raised issues and ideas that the reader will want to pursue. I have avoided offering a magic formula or formal recommendations, preferring to let the reader's own context be the guide. The case studies themselves and the books listed in the Bibliography contain hundreds of recommendations and ideas. To the inevitable question "What should I do differently tomorrow, now that I have read this book?" I have no better answer than this: Get three friends, and ask them three questions raised by the case studies. Follow your answers with tougher and tougher questions, until you all start seeing things differently. You will know what to do.

Resource:
Guidelines
for Program Review
from the Ontario
Ministry of Education

Learner progress is evaluated

Entirely by the teacher, i.e., assignments are handed in and returned	Primarily by the teacher with limited opportunity for learner participation, e.g., assignments evaluated with learner present	Mainly by the teacher with some learner participation, e.g., teacher asks for learner input re. clarification	Jointly by the teacher and learner, e.g., teacher asks for learner input; learner may select some items for evaluation	Jointly by the teacher and learner with opportunities for input from learner's peers, e.g., conferencing

Learner progress is evaluated

Primarily by standardized tests in conjunction with teacher/grade level tests	Primarily through teacher-made tests supported by standardized or grade-level tests	Primarily through teacher-made tests used in conjunction with assessment of term projects. Standardized tests form part of the total evaluation.	Through teacher assessment of daily work and projects in conjunction with teacher-made tests. Standardized tests are used primarily for reference.	Through teacher observation and assessment of daily work and projects. A full range of techniques is used: checklists, observation guides, teacher-made tests, anecdotal comments, etc. Standardized tests are used as reference.

The purpose for learner evaluation is to

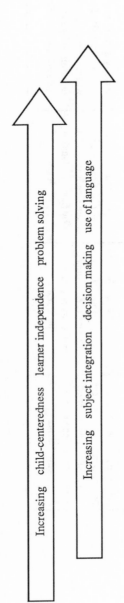

| Arrive at a mark or grade | Arrive at a mark or grade and to identify learners who need extra drill and practice | Collect information for instructional grouping | Collect information for instructional grouping for program modification | Collect information regarding learners' progress with a view to setting new goals with individuals, groups, and the class |

Increasing   child-centeredness   learner independence   problem solving

Increasing   subject integration   decision making   use of language

The learner group is the class

Primarily taught as a single large group	Primarily divided into two or three groups where group size is determined by factors independent of the learner	Primarily divided into two or three groups where group size is determined by factors related to the learner	Primarily divided into several small groups where size is determined by factors related to the learner	Primarily numerous small groups and individuals where size of group is determined by factors related to the learner

The basis for group organization is

Mainly for administrative need	Mainly achievement or ability of learners	A combination of achievement or ability and interests of learners	A combination of achievement or ability and interests, with occasional self-selection opportunities by learners	A combination of achievement or ability and interests, with frequent self-selection opportunities by learners

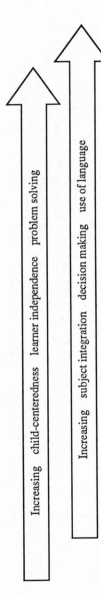

Increasing   child-centeredness   learner independence   problem solving

Increasing   subject integration   decision making   use of language

Learning activities are such that

The total activity/assignment is obligatory	The total assignment/activity is obligatory with limited options	Assignments contain obligatory items balanced with optional items	Assignments contain teacher-generated options from which learners select	Assignments contain activities planned by the teacher and learner cooperatively as well as activities generated by the learner under the teacher's guidance

Learning activities call for

Primarily written responses	Written responses with some provision for illustrations	A combination of written and illustrative responses with limited opportunities for 3-dimensional-responses such as model building, drama, and manipulation of material	A combination of written and illustrative responses with frequent opportunities for 3-dimensional-responses as well as Seeking information from conventional classroom and resource center materials, i.e., books and filmstrips	A combination of written and illustrative responses and frequent opportunities for 3-dimensional-responses as well as Seeking information from a full range of sources (totally integrated activity)

Learning activities call for the learner to

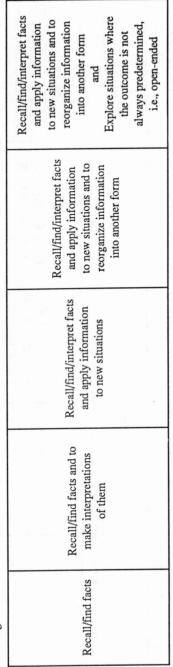

| Recall/find facts | Recall/find facts and to make interpretations of them | Recall/find/interpret facts and apply information to new situations | Recall/find/interpret facts and apply information to new situations and to reorganize information into another form | Recall/find/interpret facts and apply information to new situations and to reorganize information into another form and Explore situations where the outcome is not always predetermined, i.e., open-ended |

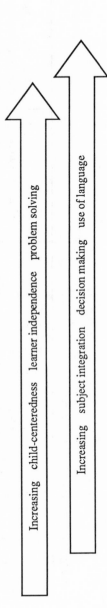

Increasing   child-centeredness   learner independence   problem solving

Increasing   subject integration   decision making   use of language

Use of the seating arrangement is such that learners

Are at tasks working totally on their own	Are interacting in pairs or with those sitting adjacent	Are interacting in groups	Are interacting in groups of various sizes as well as working individually	Are interacting in flexible arrangements based on their perceived needs under the guidance of the teacher

Learners' seating arrangements are tables which are normally

In rows	In pairs	In another linear configuration, e.g., horizontal rows with tables touching	In a configuration where learners face others	In a flexible arrangement to meet the needs of individual learners and of the program

Learning stations

| Are the learners' tables | Are primarily the learners' tables with limited interest centers | Are learners' tables with some interest centers and a small-group instructional area | Are tables with activity centers on the perimeter of the room and a small-group meeting area | Include a variety of work surfaces and areas, e.g., tables, easels, areas outside the classroom, activity centers, counters, ledges, and open floor space to accommodate individuals and small and large groups |

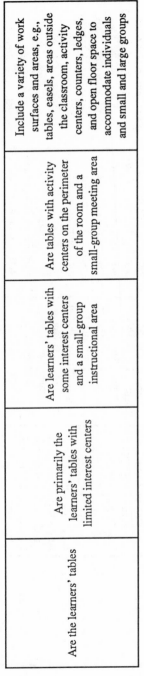

Increasing child-centeredness learner independence problem solving

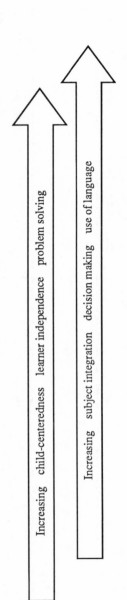

Increasing subject integration decision making use of language

Planning is based primarily on

Sequential progression through texts and/or commercial teachers' guidebooks	Etobicoke/Ministry guidelines and resource documents	Etobicoke/Ministry guidelines and resource documents with some reference to learners' needs	Observation and evaluation of learning progress in conjunction with curriculum guides and resource documents with some reference to the interests of the learner	Observation and evaluation of learning progress in conjunction with curriculum guides and resource documents and The interests of the learner

Planning is done

Primarily by the teacher working independently	Primarily by the teacher with occasional consultation with colleagues, including the principal, to plan shared experiences, e.g., excursions, informal program or learner related matters such as how to manage a particular child	By the teacher with frequent consultations with colleagues, including the principal, to plan common classroom experiences, e.g., unit of study, grade or school experience, case conference	By the teacher with frequent consultations with colleagues, including the principal, to plan common classroom experiences and approaches as well as meetings where goals, aims, and general philosophy are considered. and The learner is involved on an occasional informal basis	By the teacher with frequent consultations with colleagues, including the principal, to plan common classroom experiences and approaches and meetings where goals, aims, and general philosophy are considered. and The learner is involved, formally and informally, through whole class, group, and individual discussion with the teacher

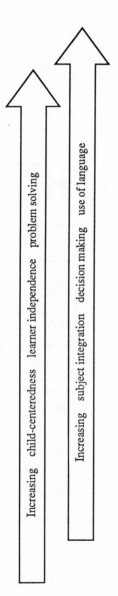

Increasing   child-centeredness   learner independence   problem solving

Increasing   subject integration   decision making   use of language

Resources, equipment, and materials in the classroom include

Texts, charts, pictures, and globes (secondary sources)	Texts, charts, pictures, and globes (secondary sources) and Audio-visual materials such as records, tapes, films, filmstrips, and videotapes	Texts, charts, pictures, and globes and audio-visual materials such as records, tapes, films, filmstrips, and videotapes including Tradebooks and computers	Texts, charts, pictures, globes, audio-visual materials, tradebooks, computers and Games, puzzles, arts/crafts materials and small construction materials	Texts, charts, pictures, globes, audio-visual materials, tradebooks, computers, games, puzzles, arts/crafts materials and small construction materials and Blocks (small or floor) sand/water tables, drama props, and "found" material

During the teaching/learning period the learners used

Texts, charts, pictures, and globes (secondary sources)	Texts, charts, pictures, and globes and Audio-visual materials such as records, tapes, films, filmstrips, and videotapes	Texts, charts, pictures, and globes and audio-visual materials such as records, tapes, films, filmstrips, and videotapes including Tradebooks and computers	Texts, charts, pictures, globes, audio-visual materials, tradebooks, computers and Games, puzzles, arts/crafts materials and small construction materials	Texts, charts, pictures, globes, audio-visual materials, tradebooks, computers, games, puzzles, arts/crafts materials and small construction materials and Blocks (small or floor) sand/water tables, drama props, and "found" material

The resource center is used

Primarily for book exchange	For book exchange and for book talks	For book exchanges, book talks, and teaching learners how to use the resource center, i.e., library skills	Book exchanges, book talks, and teaching learners how to use the resource center, i.e., library skills and For small groups of learners to visit to use the space and materials for a topic under study	For individuals, small groups, and large groups, as an extension of the classroom

Access to the resource center is

Only through scheduled periods	Through scheduled periods and occasional open, unscheduled periods	Through a balance between scheduled periods and open, unscheduled periods	Through some scheduled and a significant number of open, unscheduled periods	Through open, unscheduled periods

Routines are

Established and enforced by the teacher with activities initiated and terminated by the teacher. Formal systems required of learners, e.g., raising of hands.	Established and enforced by the teacher with activities initiated and terminated by the teacher. Some formal systems in place for learners. Learner interaction at set times.	Established and initiated by the teacher in consultation with the learners and provide for formal and informal interaction throughout the day	Developed cooperatively by the teacher and learners. Activities are initiated and terminated by learners with teacher guidance. Interaction occurs informally at the discretion of the learners within established routines.

The day is organized

Into numerous small designated time blocks (10 – 30 minutes)	Into numerous small designated time blocks with one major designated time block (60 – 75 minutes)	Into two large designated time blocks (45 – 75 minutes) with other small designated blocks of time	Around large designated blocks of time	Around large blocks of time which could vary from day to day

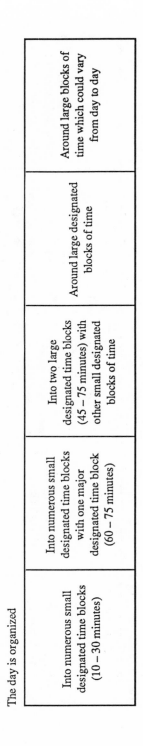

Decisions about the use of time are made

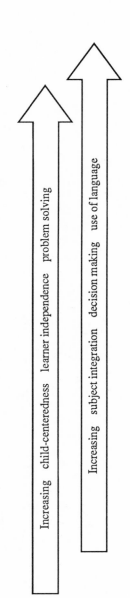

By the teacher following a preset schedule	By the teacher following a preset schedule. The learners have the use of spare time after work completion.	By the teacher modifying a preset schedule to accommodate the needs of the learners	By the teacher establishing with the learners a flexible schedule to accommodate the needs and interests of the learners	By the learner under the guidance of the teacher using a contract or other similar organizational system

Increasing   child-centeredness   learner independence   problem solving

Increasing   subject integration   decision making   use of language

Bibliography

The following works were consulted as background for the case studies or cited in the text.

Adler, M. J. *The Paideia Proposal: An Educational Manifesto*. New York: Macmillan, 1982.

Adler, M. J. *Reforming Education*. New York: Macmillan, 1988.

Airasian, P. W. "State-Mandated Testing and Educational Reform: Context and Consequences." *American Journal of Education*, 1987, *174* (5), 394–412.

American Association of School Administrators. *Teaching Thinking and Reasoning Skills: Problems and Solutions*. AASA Critical Issues Report no. 20. Arlington, Va.: American Association of School Administrators, 1987.

American Library Association. *American Library Association Presidential Committee Final Report on Information Literacy*. Chicago: American Library Association, 1989.

Anderson, B., and Cox, P. *Configuring the Education System for a Shared Future: Collaborative Vision, Action, Reflection*. Denver, Colo.: Education Commission of the States and the Regional Laboratory for Educational Improvement, 1988.

Anyon, J. "Social Class and School Knowledge." *Curriculum Inquiry*, 1981, *11* (1), 3–42.

Applebee, A. N., Langer, J. A., and Mullis, I.V.S. *Writing: Trends Across the Decade, 1974–84*. Princeton, N.J.: Educational Testing Service, 1985.

Arter, J. A., and Salmon, J. R. *Assessing Higher-Order Thinking Skills: A Consumer's Guide.* Portland, Ore.: Northwest Educational Laboratory, 1987.

Baron, J. B. "Performance Testing in Connecticut." *Educational Leadership,* 1989, *46* (7), 8.

Baron, J. B., and Sternberg, R. J. (eds.). *Teaching Thinking Skills: Theory and Practice.* New York: W. H. Freeman, 1987.

Barth, R. S. "On Sheep and Goats and School Reform." *Phi Delta Kappan,* 1986, *68* (4), 293–296.

Barth, R. S. *Improving Schools from Within: Teachers, Parents, and Principals Can Make a Difference.* San Francisco: Jossey-Bass, 1990.

Bastian, A., Fruchter, N., Gittell, M., and others. "Toward Democratic Education." *Tikkun,* 1985, *1* (2), 45–52.

Benne, K., and Tozer, S. (eds.). *Society as Educator in an Age of Transition: Part II.* Chicago: National Society for the Study of Education, 1987.

Bennett, W. J. *James Madison High School.* Washington, D.C.: U.S. Department of Education, 1987.

Bennett, W. J. *American Education: Making it Work.* Washington, D.C.: U.S. Department of Education, 1988.

Berryman, S. "Breaking Out of the Circle: Rethinking Our Assumptions About Education and the Economy." Paper presented at the 43rd national conference and exposition of the American Society for Training and Development, Washington, D.C., June 1987a.

Berryman, S. "Shadows in the Wings: The Next Educational Reform." Paper presented at the Educational Policy Forum sponsored by the American Educational Research Association and Institute for Educational Leadership, Washington, D.C., Mar. 1987b.

Beyer, B. K. "Improving Thinking Skills—Defining the Problem." *Phi Delta Kappan,* 1984a, *65* (6), 486–490.

Beyer, B. K. "Improving Thinking Skills—Practical Approaches." *Phi Delta Kappan,* 1984b, *65* (7), 556–560.

Bloom, B. S. *Taxonomy of Educational Objectives: Cognitive Domain.* New York: Longman, 1964.

Bloom, B. S. *Human Characteristics and School Learning.* New York: McGraw-Hill, 1976.

Bloome, D. "Reading as a Social Process in a Middle School Classroom." In D. Bloome (ed.), *Literacy and Schooling.* Norwood, N.J.: Ablex, 1987.

Boomer, G. "Of Parrots and Pathfinders: What Are the Basics We Should Be Teaching?" Paper presented to the Federation of School Community Organizations, Sydney, Australia, Sept. 1987.

Boomer, G. "Standards and Literacy: Two Hundred Years on the Road to Literacy: Where to from Here?" Paper presented at the annual meeting of the Victorian State Board of Education, Victoria, British Columbia, May 1988.

Booth, W. C. "Cultural Literacy and Liberal Learning: An Open Letter to E. D. Hirsch, Jr." *Change,* 1988, *20,* 13-21.

Brann, E.T.H. *Paradoxes of Education in a Republic.* Chicago: University of Chicago Press, 1979.

Britton, J. *Language and Learning.* London: Penguin, 1970.

Broudy, H. S. *The Real World of the Public Schools.* San Diego: Harcourt Brace Jovanovich, 1972.

Brown, R. "Testing and Thoughtfulness." *Education Leadership,* 1989a, *46* (7), 31-33.

Brown, R. "You Can't Get There from Here." In *Three Presentations: From the Fourth National Conference on Assessment in Higher Education.* Washington, D.C.: American Association for Higher Education, 1989b.

Bruner, J. *Actual Minds, Possible Worlds.* Cambridge, Mass.: Harvard University Press, 1986.

Calfee, R. *Indicators of Literacy.* Rutgers, N.J.: Center for Policy Research in Education, Rutgers University, 1988.

California Assessment Program. "Authentic Assessment in California." *Educational Leadership,* 1989a, *46* (7), 6.

California Assessment Program. *A Question of Thinking.* Sacramento: California State Department of Education, 1989b.

Carnegie Forum on Education and the Economy. *A Nation Prepared: Teachers for the 21st Century.* New York: Carnegie Corporation, 1986.

Cash, W. J. *The Mind of the South.* New York: Random House, 1941.

Cazden, C. *Classroom Discourse: The Language of Teaching and Learning*. Portsmouth, N.H.: Heinemann, 1988.

Chance, W. " . . . *the best of educations": Reforming America's Public Schools in the 1980's*. Chicago: John D. and Catherine T. MacArthur Foundation, 1986.

Chipman, S. F. *What Is Meant by "Higher-Order Cognitive Skills"?* Arlington, Va.: Personnel and Training Research Programs, Office of Naval Research, 1987.

Clinton, B. "The Common Aganda: Liberating Undreamed-of Talent." *The Journal of State Government*, 1987, *60* (2), 61–63.

Cohen, D. K. "Education Technology, Policy and Practice." *Educational Evaluation and Policy Analysis,* Summer 1987, pp. 153–156.

Cohen, D. K. *Teaching Practice: Plus ça change.* . . . East Lansing: National Center for Research on Teacher Education, Michigan State University, 1988.

Cohen, M. *Restructuring the Education System: Agenda for the 1990's*. Washington, D.C.: National Governors' Association, 1988.

Cole, M., and Griffin, P. (eds.). *Contextual Factors in Education*. Madison: Wisconsin Center for Education Research, 1987.

College Entrance Examination Board. *Our Voices, Our Visions: American Indians Speak Out for Educational Excellence*. New York: College Entrance Examination Board, 1989.

Collins, A. "Different Goals of Inquiry Teaching." *Questioning Exchange*, 1988, *2* (1), 39–45.

Comber, G., Maisttellis, N., and Zeiderman, H. *Touchstones*. Annapolis, Md.: C.2.M. Press, 1985.

Common, D. L. "Who Should Have the Power to Change Schools: Teachers or Policy-Makers?" *Education Canada*, Summer 1983, 40–45.

Connecticut State Board of Education. *Connecticut's Common Core of Learning*. Hartford: Connecticut State Board of Education, 1987.

Corcoran, T. B., Walker, L. J., and White, L. J. *Working in Urban Schools*. Washington, D.C.: Institute for Educational Leadership, 1988.

Costa, A. (ed.). *Developing Minds: A Resource Book for Teaching*

Thinking. Alexandria, Va.: Association for Supervision and Curriculum Development, 1985.

Costa, A., and Lowery, L. *Techniques for Teaching Thinking*. Pacific Grove, Calif.: Midwest Publications, 1989.

Cremin, L.A. *The Transformation of the School: Progressivism in American Education, 1876–1957*. New York: Knopf, 1961.

Darling-Hammond, L. "Between a Rock and a Hard Place: The Humanities and School Reform." *Basic Education: Issues, Answers and Facts*, 1987–88, *3* (2), entire issue.

Darling-Hammond, L., and Berry, B. *The Evolution of Teacher Policy*. Santa Monica, Calif.: RAND Corporation, 1988.

de Bono, E. *New Think: The Use of Lateral Thinking in the Generation of New Ideas*. New York: Basic Books, 1967.

de Bono, E. "The CoRT Thinking Program." In A. Costa (ed.), *Developing Minds: A Resource Book for Teaching Thinking*. Alexandria, Va.: Association for Supervision and Curriculum Development, 1985.

de Castell, S., and Luke, A. "Literacy Instruction: Technology and Technique." *American Journal of Education*, 1987, *95*, 413–441.

de Castell, S., Luke, A., and Egan, K. *Literacy, Society, and Schooling: A Reader*. Cambridge, England: Cambridge University Press, 1986.

de Haven-Smith, L. *Philosophical Critiques of Policy Analysis*. Gainesville: University of Florida Press, 1988.

deLone, R. H. *Small Futures: Children, Inequality, and the Limits of Liberal Reform*. New York: Harcourt Brace Jovanovich, 1979.

Dewey, J. *How We Think*. Lexington, Mass.: Heath, 1933.

Dewey, J. *Democracy and Education*. New York: Free Press, 1966.

Dorris, M. *The Broken Cord*. New York: Harper & Row, 1989.

Dougherty, V., deLone, R. and Odden, A. *Current Practice: Is It Enough?* Denver, Colo.: Education Commission of the States, 1989.

Drucker, P. F. *The New Realities: In Government and Politics/In Economics and Business/In Society and World View*. New York: Harper & Row, 1989.

Duckworth, E. *The Having of Wonderful Ideas and Other Essays on Teaching and Learning*. New York: Teachers College Press, 1987.

Dyrenfurth, M. J. *Literacy for a Technological World*. Columbus: Ohio State University Press, 1984.

Education Commission of the States. *A Summary of Major Reports on Education*. Denver, Colo.: Education Commission of the States, 1983.

Education Commission of the States. *The Evolving Reform Agenda: Three-Year Plan of the Education Commission of the States, 1987–1990*. Denver, Colo.: Education Commission of the States, 1987a.

Education Commission of the States. *School Reform in Perspective*. Denver, Colo.: Education Commission of the States, 1987b.

Education Commission of the States. *School Reform in 10 States*. Denver, Colo.: Education Commission of the States, 1988.

Education Commission of the States. *All Kids Can Learn: A Research Synthesis*. Denver, Colo.: Education Commission of the States, 1990.

Eisner, E. "Creative Education in American Schools Today." *Educational Horizons*, 1985a, *63* (4), 10–15.

Eisner, E. (ed.). *Learning and Teaching the Ways of Knowing*. Chicago: National Society for the Study of Education, 1985b.

Etobicoke Board Research and Evaluation Department. *Summary of the Parent Survey Results for Etobicoke Public Schools*. Etobicoke, Ontario: Etobicoke Board of Education, 1987.

Fallows, J. "America's Changing Economic Landscape." *Atlantic Monthly*, Mar. 1985, pp. 47–68.

Farr, R. "Textbook Selection and Curriculum Change." *Journal of State Government*, 1987, *60* (7), 86–91.

Feuerstein, R. "Effects of Instrumental Enrichment on the Psychoeducational Development of Low-Functioning Adolescents." *Journal of Educational Psychology*, 1979, *71* (6), 751–763.

Feuerstein, R. "Can Evolving Techniques Better Measure Cognitive Change?" *Journal of Special Education*, 1981, *15* (2), 201–219.

Fisher, D. L. *Functional Literacy and the Schools*. Washington, D.C.: U.S. Department of Health, Education, and Welfare, 1978.

Flakus-Mosqueda, P. *Critical Thinking in American Schools: Results of a Survey of Selected Teachers*. Denver, Colo.: Education Commission of the States, 1988.

Fraatz, J. *The Politics of Reading.* New York: Teachers College Press, 1987.

Freire, P. *Pedagogy of the Oppressed.* New York: Seabury Press, 1970.

Fullan, M. *The Meaning of Educational Change.* Toronto, Ontario: OISE Press, 1982.

Fullan, M., and Park, P. *Curriculum Implementation.* Toronto, Ontario: Ontario Ministry of Education, 1981.

Glasser, W. *Control Theory in the Classroom.* New York: Harper & Row, 1986.

Goodlad, J. *A Place Called School.* New York: McGraw-Hill, 1984.

Goodlad, J. (ed.). *The Ecology of School Renewal: Part I.* Chicago: National Society for the Study of Education, 1987.

Goodman, K. S. *What's Whole in Whole Language?* Portsmouth, N.H.: Heinemann, 1986.

Gordon, E., and Wilkerson, D. *Compensatory Education for the Disadvantaged: Programs and Practices, Preschool Through College.* New York: College Examination Entrance Board, 1966.

Goswami, D., and Stillman, P. R. (eds.). *Reclaiming the Classroom: Teacher Research as an Agency for Change.* Upper Montclair, N.J.: Boynton Cook, 1987.

Graves, D. H. *Writing: Teachers and Children at Work.* Portsmouth, N.H.: Heinemann, 1983.

Gray, D. "Socratic Seminars: Basic Education and Reformation." *Basic Education: Issues, Answers and Facts,* 1988, *3* (4), entire issue.

Green, J. (ed.). *What Next? More Leverage for Teachers.* Denver, Colo.: Education Commission of the States, 1986.

Green, J. *The Next Wave.* Denver, Colo.: Education Commission of the States, 1987.

Griesemer, J. L., and Butler, C. *Education Under Study: An Analysis of Recent Major Reports on Education.* (2nd ed.) Chelmsford, Md.: Northeast Regional Exchange, 1983.

Grittner, F. M. (ed.). *Learning a Second Language.* Chicago: National Society for the Study of Education, 1980.

Groening, M. *School Is Hell.* New York: Random House, 1987.

Gutman, A. *Democratic Education.* Princeton, N.J.: Princeton University Press, 1987.

Habermas, J. *The Theory of Communicative Action.* Vol. 1. (Thomas McCarthy, trans.) Boston: Beacon Press, 1984.

Helge, D. *A National Study Regarding At-Risk Students.* Bellingham, Wash.: National Rural Development Institute, 1990.

Hiebert, E. H., and Calfee, R. "Advancing Academic Literacy Through Teachers' Assessment." *Educational Leadership,* 1989, *46* (7), 50–54.

Hill, D. "Order in the Classroom." *Teacher,* 1990, *1,* 70–77.

Hill, P. T., Wise, A. W., and Shapiro, L. *Educational Progress: Cities Mobilize to Improve Their Schools.* Santa Monica, Calif.: RAND Corporation, 1989.

Hirsch, E. D. *Cultural Literacy: What Every American Needs to Know.* Boston: Houghton Mifflin, 1987.

Hispanic Policy Development Project. *Make Something Happen.* Washington, D.C.: Hispanic Policy Development Project, 1984.

Hodsoll, F. *Toward Civilization.* Washington, D.C.: National Endowment for the Arts, 1988.

Holmes, B. J., and Green, J. *A Quality Work Force: America's Key to the Next Century.* Denver, Colo.: Education Commission of the States, 1988.

"Human Capital: The Decline of America's Work Force." *Business Week,* Sept. 19, 1988, pp. 100–141.

Hunter, M. C. *Improved Instruction.* El Segundo, Calif.: Tip Publications, 1976.

Hunter, M. C. *Mastery Teaching.* El Segundo, Calif.: Tip Publications, 1982.

Institute for Educational Leadership. *School Boards: Strengthening Grassroots Leadership.* Washington, D.C.: Institute for Educational Leadership, 1986.

Jackson, P. W. (ed.). *Contributing to Educational Change: Perspectives on Research and Practice.* Berkeley, Calif.: McCutchan, 1986a.

Jackson, P. W. *The Practice of Teaching.* New York: Teachers College Press, 1986b.

Jennings, B. "Interpretation and the Practice of Policy Analysis." In F. Fischer and J. Forester (eds.), *Confronting Values in Policy Analysis.* Newbury Park, Calif.: Sage, 1987.

Johnston, W. B. *Workforce 2000: Work and Workers for the 21st Century.* Indianapolis, Ind.: Hudson Institute, 1987.

Joyce, B. "School Renewal as Cultural Change." *Educational Leadership,* 1989, *46,* 70–77.

Kahn, D. *Implementing Montessori Education in the Public Sector.* Cleveland Heights, Ohio: North American Montessori Teachers' Association, 1990.

Kaplan, G. *Who Runs Our Schools? The Changing Face of Educational Leadership.* Washington, D.C.: Institute for Educational Leadership, 1989.

Keating, D. P. *Adolescents' Ability to Engage in Critical Thinking.* Madison, Wis.: Wisconsin Center for Education Research, 1988.

Keniston, K., and the Carnegie Council on Children. *All Our Children.* New York: Carnegie Corporation, 1977.

Kennedy, E. *Indian Education: A National Tragedy—A National Challenge.* Washington, D.C.: U.S. Government Printing Office, 1969.

Kirsch, I. S., and Jungeblut, A. *Literacy: Profiles of America's Young Adults.* Princeton, N.J.: National Assessment of Educational Progress, 1986.

Kurfiss, J. G. *Critical Thinking: Theory, Research, Practice, and Possibilities.* ASHE-ERIC Higher Education Report no. 2. Washington, D.C.: Association for the Study of Higher Education, 1988.

Langer, E. J. *Mindfulness.* Reading, Mass.: Addison-Wesley, 1989.

Langer, J. A. "Literacy Instruction in American Schools: Problems and Perspectives." *American Journal of Education,* 1984, *92,* 107–132.

Lapointe, A., Mead, N., and Phillips, G. *A World of Differences: An International Assessment of Mathematics and Science.* Princeton, N.J.: Educational Testing Service, 1989.

Leithwood, K. A., Holmes, M., and Montgomery, D. J. *Helping Schools Change: Strategies Derived from Field Experience.* Ontario, Canada: Ontario Institute for Studies in Education, 1979.

Lemann, N. "The Origins of the Underclass." *Atlantic Monthly,* June 1986, pp. 31–55.

Link, F. R. (ed.). *Essays on the Intellect.* Alexandria, Va.: Association for Supervision and Curriculum Development, 1985.

Lipman, M. "Critical Thinking—What Can It Be?" *Educational Leadership,* 1988, *46* (1), 38–43.

Livingston, C., Castle, S., and Nations, J. "Testing and Curriculum Reform: One School's Experience." *Educational Leadership,* 1989, *46* (7), 23–25.

Lloyd-Jones, R., and Lunsford, A. *The English Coalition Conference: Democracy Through Language.* Urbana, Ill.: National Council of Teachers of English, 1989.

Lowery, L. *Thinking and Learning: Matching Developmental Stage with Curriculum and Instruction.* Pacific Grove, Calif.: Midwest Publications, 1989.

MacIntyre, A. *After Virtue.* Notre Dame, Ind.: University of Notre Dame Press, 1981.

MacIntyre, A. *Whose Justice? Which Rationality?* Notre Dame, Ind.: University of Notre Dame Press, 1988.

Mackie, R. (ed.). *Literacy and Revolution.* New York: Continuum, 1981.

Macrorie, K. *Twenty Teachers.* New York: Oxford University Press, 1984.

McTighe, J., and Cutlip, G. "The State's Role in Improving Student Thinking." *Educational Horizons,* Summer 1986, 186–189.

Martin, N., D'Arcy, P., Newton, B., and Parker, R. *Writing and Learning.* London: Schools Council Publications, 1976.

Marzano, R. J. "Policy Constraints to the Teaching of Thinking." *Journal of State Government,* 1987, *60* (2), 64–67.

Marzano, R. J., and Arrendondo, D. E. *Tactics: A Program for Teaching Thinking.* Denver, Colo.: Mid-Continent Regional Educational Laboratory, 1986.

Marzano, R. J., and Hutchins, C. L. *Thinking Skills: A Conceptual Framework.* Denver, Colo.: Mid-Continent Regional Educational Laboratory, 1985.

Maxwell, W. (ed.). *Thinking: The Expanding Frontier.* Philadelphia: Franklin Institute Press, 1983.

Miller, G. A. "The Challenge of Universal Literacy." *Science,* Sept. 1988, pp. 1293–1298.

Moffett, J. *Teaching the Universe of Discourse.* Boston: Houghton Mifflin, 1968.

National Center on Education and the Economy. *To Secure Our*

Future: The Federal Role in Education. Rochester, N.Y.: National Center on Education and the Economy, 1989.

National Center on Education and the Economy. *High Skills or Low Wages!* Rochester, N.Y.: National Center on Education and the Economy, 1990.

National Commission on Excellence in Education. *A Nation at Risk.* Washington, D.C.: U.S. Government Printing Office, 1983.

National Education Association. *Response: Status of the American Public School Teacher, 1985–86.* Washington, D.C.: National Education Association, 1987.

National Governors' Association. *Time for Results: The Governors' Report on Education.* Washington, D.C.: National Governors' Association, 1986.

New Jersey Basic Skills Council. *Thinking Skills: An Overview.* Trenton: New Jersey State Board of Higher Education, 1986.

Nicholls, J. *The Competitive Ethos and Democratic Education.* Cambridge, Mass.: Harvard University Press, 1989.

Nickerson, R. S. *The Teaching of Thinking.* Hillsdale, N.J.: Erlbaum, 1985.

Norris, S. P. "Synthesis of Research on Critical Thinking." *Educational Leadership,* 1985, *42* (8), 40–45.

Norris, S. P., and Ennis, R. H. *Evaluating Critical Thinking.* Pacific Grove, Calif.: Midwest Publications, 1989.

Ontario Ministry of Education. *Education in the Primary and Junior Divisions.* Toronto: Ontario Ministry of Education, 1975a.

Ontario Ministry of Education. *The Formative Years.* Toronto: Ontario Ministry of Education, 1975b.

Ontario Ministry of Education. *Ontario Schools: Intermediate and Senior Divisions Programs and Diploma Requirements 1984.* Toronto: Ontario Ministry of Education, 1984.

Passow, A. H. *Issues of Access to Knowledge: Grouping and Tracking.* Chicago: National Society for the Study of Education, 1988.

Pauker, R. A. *Teaching Thinking and Reasoning Skills.* AASA Critical Issues Reports. Arlington, Va.: American Association of School Administrators, 1987.

Paul, R. W. "Critical Thinking: Fundamental to Education in a Free Society." *Educational Leadership,* 1984, *42* (1), 4–14.

Paul, R. "Dialogical Thinking: Critical Thought Essential to the

Acquisition of Rational Knowledge and Passions." Paper presented at the fourth international Conference on Critical Thinking and Educational Reform, Sonoma, Calif., 1986.

Paul, R. W. *Critical Thinking, Moral Integrity, and Citizenship: Teaching for the Intellectual Virtues.* Rohnert Park, Calif: Center for Critical Thinking and Moral Critique, Sonoma State University, 1988.

Pellicer, L. O. *High School Leaders and Their Schools.* Vol. 1: *A National Profile.* Reston, Va.: National Association of Secondary School Principals, 1988.

Perkins, D. N. *The Mind's Best Work.* Cambridge, Mass.: Harvard University Press, 1981.

Pipho, C. "States Put 'Excellence' into Orbit." *Phi Delta Kappan,* 1983, *65* (1), 5-6.

Pipho, C. "States Warm to Excellence Movement." *Phi Delta Kappan,* 1984, *65* (7), 516-517.

Powell, A., Farrer, E., and Cohen, D. K. *The Shopping-Mall High School.* Boston: Houghton Mifflin, 1985.

Presseisen, B. *Thinking Skills: Meaning, Models, and Materials.* Philadelphia: Research for Better Schools, 1984.

Presseisen, B. *Critical Thinking and Thinking Skills: State of the Art Definitions and Practice in Public Schools.* Philadelphia: Research for Better Schools, 1986.

Presseisen, B. (ed.). *At-Risk Students and Thinking: Perspectives from Research.* Washington, D.C.: National Education Association, 1988.

"The Productivity Paradox." *Business Week,* June 6, 1988, pp. 100-113.

Ralph, J. H., and Fennessey, J. "Science or Reform: Some Questions About the Effective Schools Model." *Phi Delta Kappan,* 1983, *65,* 689-694.

Ravitch, D. *The Troubled Crusade.* New York: Basic Books, 1983.

Research and Policy Committee of the Committee for Economic Development. *Children in Need.* New York: Committee for Economic Development, 1987.

Resnick, L. B. *Education and Learning to Think.* Washington, D.C.: National Academy Press, 1987.

Rhodes, R. W. "Holistic Teaching/Learning for Native American Students." *Journal of American Indian Education*, 1988, *27* (2), 21–29.

Schlechty, P. C. *Schools for the 21st Century: Leadership Imperatives for Educational Reform.* San Francisco: Jossey-Bass, 1990.

Schlefer, J. "Making Sense of the Productivity Debate: Reflections on the MIT Report." *Technology Review*, 1989, *92* (5/6), 28–40.

Scribner, J. D. (ed.). *The Politics of Education.* Chicago: National Society for the Study of Education, 1977.

Shepard, L. A. "Why We Need Better Assessments." *Educational Leadership*, 1989, *46* (7), 4–9.

Shulman, L. S. "Knowledge and Teaching: Foundations of the New Reform." *Harvard Educational Review*, 1987, *57*, 1–21.

Sinclair, R. L., and Ghory, W. J. *Reaching Marginal Students: A Primary Concern for School Renewal.* Berkeley, Calif.: McCutchan, 1987.

Sizer, T. *Horace's Compromise.* Boston: Houghton Mifflin, 1984.

Southern Regional Education Board. *Meeting the Need for Quality: Action in the South.* Atlanta: Southern Regional Education Board, 1983.

Sternberg, R. J. *How Can We Teach Intelligence?* Philadelphia: Research for Better Schools, 1983.

Swartz, R. J., and Perkins, D. N. *Teaching Thinking Issues and Approaches.* Pacific Grove, Calif.: Midwest Publications, 1989.

Tanner, L. N. (ed.). *Critical Issues in Curriculum.* Chicago: National Society for the Study of Education, 1988.

Task Force on Education for Economic Growth. *Action for Excellence: A Comprehensive Plan to Improve Our Nation's Schools.* Denver, Colo.: Education Commission of the States, 1983.

Terry, E. *Education in the Junior Division: A Look at Forty-Two Schools.* Provincial Review Report no. 5. Toronto: Ontario Ministry of Education, 1985.

Timar, T., and Kirp, D. "Education Reform in the 1980's: Lessons from the States." *Phi Delta Kappan*, 1989, *70* (6), 505–511.

Tinder, G. *Community: Reflections on a Tragic Ideal.* Baton Rouge: Louisiana State University Press, 1980.

Toulmin, S. *The Uses of Argument*. Cambridge, England: Cambridge University Press, 1958.

Tyson-Bernstein, H. *Conspiracy of Good Intentions: America's Textbook Fiasco*. Washington, D.C.: Council for Basic Education, 1988.

Useem, E. L. *Low-Tech Education in a High-Tech World: Corporations and Classrooms in the New Information Society*. New York: Free Press, 1986.

Venezky, R. L., Kaestle, C. F., and Sum, A. M. *The Subtle Danger: Reflections on the Literacy Abilities of America's Young Adults*. Princeton, N.J.: Educational Testing Service, 1987.

Walberg, H., and Lane, J. (eds.). *Organizing for Learning: Toward the 21st Century*. Reston, Va.: National Association of Secondary School Principals, 1989.

Walsh, D., and Paul, R. W. *The Goal of Critical Thinking: From Educational Ideal to Educational Reality*. Washington, D.C.: American Federation of Teachers, 1987.

Wells, S. *Teachers Discuss Reform*. Denver, Colo.: Education Commission of the States, 1987.

Westbury, I., and Purves, A. C. *Cultural Literacy and the Idea of General Education*. Chicago: National Society for the Study of Education, 1988.

Wiggins, G. "The Futility of Trying to Teach Everything of Importance." *Educational Leadership*, 1989a, *47* (3), 44–59.

Wiggins, G. "Teaching to the (Authentic) Test." *Educational Leadership*, 1989b, *46* (7), 41–47.

Wilensky, R., and Kline, D. M. *Renewing Urban Schools: The Community Connection*. Denver, Colo.: Education Commission of the States, 1988.

Wilkinson, W. G. *A Plan to Restructure Schools in Kentucky*. Frankfort, Ky.: Office of the Governor, 1988.

William T. Grant Foundation Commission on Work, Family and Citizenship. *The Forgotten Half: Non-College Youth in America*. Washington, D.C.: William T. Grant Foundation Commission on Work, Family and Citizenship, 1988.

Wolf, D. P. "The Art of Questioning." *Journal of State Government*, 1987, *60* (2), 81–85.

Wolf, D. P. *Reading Reconsidered: Literature and Literacy in High School.* New York: College Entrance Examination Board, 1988.

Wolf, D. P. "Portfolio Assessment: Sampling Student Work." *Educational Leadership,* 1989, *46* (7), 35–39.

Wolf, D., Davidson, L., and Davis, M. *Beyond A, B, and C: A Broader and Deeper View of Literacy.* Cambridge, Mass.: School of Education, Harvard University, 1987.

Zuboff, S. *In the Age of the Smart Machine: The Future of Work and Power.* New York: Basic Books, 1988.

Index

Ability grouping, 113, 114
Absorption, in fairness model, 145–146
Accountability, in North Urban schools, 99, 124–125
Active Learning, 76, 108, 169, 212; in Canada, 215, 217–219, 221–223, 226–227, 230; and literacy of thoughtfulness, 239, 241, 244–245, 249
Adler, M. J., 143–145, 167
Aims, M., 10–11
Alexander, 164
Alnes, J., 56
Apple, M., 33
Aristotle, 167
Arkansas, school reform effort in, 150
Art classes, 82, 222
Ashton, P., 109–111
Aspen Institute of Humanistic Studies, 32, 143–144, 183
Assertive Discipline Program, 103–104

Baca, P., 92–94, 97–98
Bailey, T., 5
Barnes, Ms., 28–29
Baron, J. B., 239
Basal readers, 79, 86

Basic skills: back to, 1–30; curriculum of, 140, 141; forward to, 205; and higher-order skills, 9, 206; and outcomes vision, 100–101; political role of, 9–10, 172, 173, 176
Bass, Ms., 43
Berryman, S., 4
Bilingualism, 60–63, 68
Black students: compliance of, 55–56; in Daviston, 36–58; in Pittsburgh, 190–192; rural and urban, 55–56; in Southland County, 1–30
Bledsoe, Ms., 38–43
Bloom, B. S., 216–217, 238
Brant, M., 114–115
Britton, J., 239
Brown, R., 243
Bruner, D., 114–116, 120
Bruner, J., 182
Bruster, B., 104–106
Burden, Ms., 17–18
Bureau of Indian Affairs (BIA), 60
Bush, G., 126
Busing, 101, 138

California, progress in, 243, 244, 249
California Achievement Tests (CAT), 183, 221

Capacity, and fairness, 144–145
Cash, W. J., 54
Cazden, C., 22
Chance, W., 9, 33
Classroom environment: in Canada,
    216, 219; in Southland County,
    25
Clinton, B., 150
Cohen, D. K., 22, 243
Collins, A., 239
Columbia University, education
    and employment center at, 5
Columbus, C., 192
Comber, G., 167
Committee to Support the Philadel-
    phia Public Schools, 33
Communication: fragmented, 247;
    in Pittsburgh schools, 175–176,
    195–196
Community: educational focus in,
    155–156; and fairness, 148–149;
    sense of, and literacy, 56
Compensatory education policy,
    139–142
Competence, minimum, 9, 115, 204
Connecticut, progress in, 243, 249
Control Data Corporation, 56
Courts, and policy making, 137–142
Curriculum: coverage in, 237–240;
    policy documents on, 213–214

Davis, A., 64–67, 74–79, 83–87, 232
Davis, D., 106–108
Davis, J., 164–170, 186
Daviston: described, 36; district of-
    fices of, 36–38; expectations in,
    37; hand-me-down literacy in,
    36–58; High School in, 37–51
de Bono, E., 239
deLone, R. H., 33–34, 183–185
Democracy, and literacy of thought-
    fulness, 248
Denver, worker skills wanted in, 4
Desegregation, 101, 131–135, 181,
    195
Dewey, J., 75, 239
Dione, Mr., 102–104, 106
Direct instruction, 174, 196, 198, 199
Discussion: in Southland County,

18–19, 22, 27; teachers trained in,
    164–201
Dorris, M., 68
Driver, J., 13–15, 18, 19

Edna McConnell Clark Founda-
    tion, 122–123
Education: Canadian goals for,
    211–212; climates, 148; frag-
    mented, 246–248. See also School
    reform
Education Commission of the
    States (ECS), 6, 183, 241
Education policy, 6, 83, 229, 236,
    246; environments, 160–163, 244,
    249; executive, 149; judicial, 137–
    142; legislative, 157–159; and li-
    teracy of thoughtfulness, 244;
    and policy makers, 160; and state
    school boards, 157, 159
Eighth-grade classes: in Daviston,
    45; in North Urban schools, 111–
    115, 116; in Southland County,
    25–27
Eleventh-grade classes: in Daviston,
    38–40; on reservation, 62–63
Ellison, R., 41
Empowerment: from discovery, 106;
    from early education, 11
English as a Second Language
    (ESL), 62
English classes: in Daviston, 38–41;
    in North Urban schools, 116,
    120, 130; on reservation, 65–66,
    81; in Southland County, 23–24
Ennis, R., 239
Equality, 148
Equity, 138, 139, 222
Eresh, J., 178, 180
Etobicoke Board Research and
    Evaluation Department, 228
Evaluation: in Canada, 224–228;
    and literacy of thoughtfulness,
    243–244
Expectations: in Daviston, 37; and
    fairness, 143; and literacy of
    thoughtfulness, 241–242; in
    North Urban schools, 122–123,
    135; in Pittsburgh, 180, 182; rais-

ing, 151–152; on reservation, 62–
64

Fairness: absorption model of, 145–
146; capacity model of, 144–145;
and community, 148–149;
institution-practice tension in,
147–148; and policy, 142–149;
and responsibility for learning,
146–148
Ferris, Ms., 20–22
Feuerstein, R., 115, 239
Fifth-grade class, in Pittsburgh, 192
First-grade class, on reservation, 87
Florida, school reform effort in, 150
Ford Foundation, 168
Fourth-grade classes: in Canada,
219; on reservation, 83–85
Francis, Ms., 111–115, 118–120
Fullan, M., 215

G., Mrs., 25–27
Gifted education, 107–111
Glasser, W., 194
Global economy: and governor's
concerns, 150, 151–152; and
Southland County, 1–2, 3–4
Goodlad, J., 22
Goodman, K. S., 11, 214, 239
Goodman, Y., 239
Gordon, E., 139
Governor, and policy making, 7,
149–157
Graham, B., 150
Graves, D. H., 34, 76, 239
Green, Ms., 23–25

Habermas, J., 157, 162
Harris, J., 6–10, 54, 57
Harrison, M., 216–218
Harvard University: arts education
collaboration by, 170; Graduate
School of Education at, 32, 35
Helge, D., 29
Herman, S., 175–177
Higher-order thinking skills: and
basic skills, 9, 206; in Daviston,
37, 42–43; on reservation, 79–82
Hill, D., 104

History syllabus, 170–172
Hobbes, T., 185–186
Hoffman, N., 32–33
Holmes, Dr., 111
Hopkins, A., 112–113, 116–118
Hughes, L., 40
Hunter, M. C., 174, 198–199

Illinois, progress in, 243
Indonesia, learning in, 152–153
Inquiry-based instruction, 216–217
Instrumental rationality, 161–162
Intelligence, and literacy of
thoughtfulness, 240–241, 250–251
Iowa Test of Basic Skills, 103

Jackson, H., 126–127, 131–132
Jackson, P. W., 162
Japan, performance in, 240
Johnson, B., 12, 13
Jones, Mrs., 51–52
Jungeblut, A., 32

Kafka, F., 247
Kahn, D., 11
Kansas, progress in, 244
Kennedy, E., 61
Kettering Foundation, 56
Kierkegaard, S., 167
Kindergarten: on reservation, 76–77,
86–87; in Southland County, 10–
11, 28, 30
King, M. L., 133
Kirsch, I. S., 32
Knight, S., 122–126

Langer, J. A., 34–35
Language: of authority, 54–55;
classroom, 40; of learning, 162;
of legislation, 157; for literacy of
thoughtfulness, 234–235; Native
American, 60–62; of policy, 161–
162; and poor students, 139–142;
talkinbout, 234–235. *See also*
Whole-language approach
Lansing, M., 123–126
Lapointe, A., 230
Learning: assumptions about, 207–
209; language of, 162; pleasures

of, 152–153; responsibility for,
146–148; 249–250; styles of, 15–
16, 139–142
Legislative policy making, 157–160
LeMahieu, P., 172–175, 176
Lemann, N., 12
Lipman, M., 34, 239
Literacy of thoughtfulness: in adult
environments, 233–234; in Canada, 202–231; and community
sense, 56; concepts of, 31–35;
conditions for, 234; constraints
on, 235–244; coverage constraints
on, 237–240; cultivating, 232–
251; and evaluation, 224–228,
243–244; hand-me-down, 36–58;
higher, 33, 90; and intelligence,
240–241, 250–251; knowledge
about, 232–233; language for,
234–235; in North Urban district,
92–136; as quest for meaning,
90–91; recommendations on,
248–251; on reservation, 59–91;
in rural south, 1–30, 36–58; and
student interests, 241–242;
teacher training for, 164–201,
242–243; time constraints on,
235–237, 246, 249
Louisville, teaching center in, 243
Lowe, M., 212, 214–215

McClaine, R., 178–179, 180
MacIntyre, A., 147, 162
McNamara, R., 195
Macrorie, K., 239
Magnet programs: in North Urban
schools, 135–136; in Pittsburgh,
179, 183–186
Maine, progress in, 249
Maisttellis, N., 167
Marshall, Mr., 120
Martin, N., 239
Masefield, J., 40
Math classes: in Daviston, 43, 45; in
North Urban schools, 111–114,
118–120; on reservation, 66–67,
81–82; in Southland County, 25–
27
Mead, N., 230

Meers, W., 38, 44
Michigan, progress in, 243
Miller, M., 18–19
Moffett, J., 55, 239
Montessori principles: in kinder-
garten, 11; in North Urban
schools, 135–136, 145–146; and
thinking, 239
Muller, P., 82
Multiculturalism, 204, 227, 230
Music and art classes, on reserva-
tion, 82

National Center on Education and
Employment, 5
National Education Association, 44
Native Americans. *See* Reservation
New Hampshire, University of, 34
New Jersey, progress in, 243
New York, progress in, 243
Nickerson, R. S., 239
Nicoleau, G., 34, 57
North Urban Public Schools
(NUPS): accountability in, 99,
124–125; aspects of reform in,
92–136; Assertive Discipline Program of, 103–104; background
on, 92–95; compensatory education in, 140–141; curriculum passages in, 129–130; described, 95–
101; desegregation of, 101–102,
133–135; elementary schools of,
135–136; expectations at, 122–
123, 135; and fairness policy,
142–143, 147; Fletcher Middle
School of, 111–126; gifted-and-
talented program of, 105, 107,
109–111; and governor, 150;
"high" classes at, 102–108, 114–
115, 121; intermediate school of,
102–108; and judicial policy,
137–138, 140–141; and legislature, 158; Lyndon Baines Johnson High School of, 126–133;
management of, 96–97; objectives in, 98, 99, 103, 113; Pittsburgh compared with, 194–195,
200; and policy making, 160–161,
162; school board of, 93–94, 96,

97, 99, 101–102, 103, 122, 133–
134, 135, 137–138; sounding
board in, 131–132; spillover effect in, 103, 107–108; student
body in, 93–94, 134–135; teacher
survey at, 136
Northern Arizona, University of, 69
Northwest Regional Educational
Laboratory, 1

Objectives: concept of, 14–15; in
Daviston, 43; in North Urban
schools, 98, 99, 103, 113; in Pittsburgh schools, 170–171, 173, 176,
197; sample, 16; state-mandated,
7, 14–16, 17, 19, 23
"Odyssey of the Mind," 105, 110
Ontario Ministry of Education,
204–212, 225–226, 229, 249, 250,
253–267. See also Toronto
Orwell, J., 92, 97–99, 115, 125

Paideia Group, 167
Paul, R. W., 239
Peck, J., 93–94, 97, 100–101, 133,
134
Perkins, D. N., 239
Petrosky, A., 12, 15, 22–23, 25–27,
38, 39, 43, 46–51, 54–55, 97, 166,
183, 195, 196–199, 212, 219–221,
229, 232
Phidias, 165
Philip, 164
Phillips, G., 230
Philosophy for Children, 34, 110–
111
Pierce, Ms., 25
Pipho, C., 6
Pittsburgh: administrators in, 175–
177, 179–183, 194–196, 198; aspects of teacher development in,
164–201, 248; background on,
168–169; board members in, 172–
175, 176, 182; Brookline Center
in, 169, 175, 200; Center for Advanced Studies in, 169; classroom
observations in, 185–193; communication in, 175–176, 195–196;
curriculum reform in, 174; dis-

trict evolution in, 172–183; Division of Arts Education in, 170;
efforts in, 193–201; expectations
in, 180, 182; high schools in,
164–172, 183–185, 187–189, 192–
193; impact in, 189; Langely
High School in, 187–189;
magnet classes in, 179, 183–186;
Monitoring Achievement in
Pittsburgh (MAP) in, 173, 176,
178, 180, 183, 195–199, 221; objectives in, 170–171, 173, 176,
197; principals in, 177–180, 198;
Rogers Middle School in, 185–
186; Schenley High School in,
164–172, 183–185; Schenley
Teacher Center in, 164–172, 175,
187, 200, 243; and state officials,
177; students in, 183–186; Syllabus Examination Project (SEP)
in, 169, 170–172, 173–174, 176,
177–180, 193; teachers in, 164–
167, 169, 174, 177, 188–189, 198;
union in, 181
Pittsburgh, University of, 12
Plato, 167
Plutarch, 164–165, 168
Policy: aspects of making, 137–163;
attitudes about, 161; Canadian
framework for, 229–230; from
courts, 137–142; on curriculum,
213–214; equity, 138–139; and
fairness, 142–149; and governors,
7, 149–157; impact of, 246;
institution-practice tension
from, 198–200, 216; judicial, 137–
142; legislative, 157–160; makers
of, 160–163; recommendations
on, 236–237, 244–246, 249;
thoughtfulness, 244
Probing: in Daviston, 40, 52; in
Southland County, 21–22

Questioning strategies: guidelines
on, 210–211; in North Urban
schools, 116, 118, 119; in Southland County, 17, 24

Reading class, in Daviston, 46, 81, 84
Recitation format, 28, 40, 63, 65, 116, 191, 192, 230; in Southland County, 22-23, 25
Reflection, in Southland County, 24-25
Reservation: aspects of language and culture on, 59-91; as bilingual and bicultural, 59-62, 87-91; curriculum for, 68-71, 80-82, 88; expectations on, 62-64; high school on, 62-64; intermediate school on, 64-67, 83-87; learning styles on, 68-71; primary school on, 71-87, 91; and state policy, 83; whole-language approach on, 72-74, 83, 85, 87, 91
Rhodes, R. W., 69-71
Riley, B., 150
Roberts, H., 37-38
Rockefeller Foundation, 170
Rural education, 29, 55

S., Mrs., 47-51
St. John's model, 167, 196
Sandoval, E., 123-124
Schlefer, J., 4
School culture, 83
School reform: bottom-up, 204-206, 229-230; in Daviston, 42-43, 53-54; and educators, 154-155; elements in, 6-7; legislatures and, 157-160; in Southland County, 2, 4, 6, 30; top-down nature of, 7-9, 53-54
Science classes: in Pittsburgh, 189-190; on reservation, 67, 82; in Southland County, 19-20, 21
Second-grade class, on reservation, 77-78
Shakespeare, W., 178
Simon, P., 187
Sixth-grade classes: in Pittsburgh, 189-190; on reservation, 65-67; in Southland County, 15-16
Sizer, T., 22, 239
Smith, E., 56
Social studies classes: in North Ur-

ban schools, 116-118, 127-130; in Pittsburgh, 192; on reservation, 62-63, 81; in Southland County, 15-16, 24-25
South Africa, compliant students in, 56
South Carolina, school reform effort in, 150, 249
Southern states, history's impact in, 52-55
Southland County: back to basics in, 1-30; background on, 1-3; described, 12-15; Elementary School in, 15-22, 23-25, 28-29; High School in, 46-51; Junior High School in, 22-23, 25-27; and state department of education, 6-11; summary on, 29-30
Staff development, 182, 198, 230
Standardized testing, 158, 174, 220, 225, 227, 230
Standards, educational, basic level of, 10
State University of New York at Albany, Center for the Learning and Teaching of Literature at, 34
Sternberg, R. J., 239
Stringfield, S., 1-3, 12, 15, 51-52, 183, 203, 212, 215, 229, 232
Students: and interest in learning, 241-242; learning styles of, 15-16, 139-142; responsibility of, 249-250
Swartz, R. J., 239

Teachers: competency test for, 7, 13, 16-17, 20, 28; discussion training for, 164-201, 242-243; opinions of, 136, 188-189, 198; staff development needed for, 56-57
Teaching: assumptions about, 209-211; institution-practice tension in, 147-148, 162, 198-200, 216
Terry, E., 225, 228-229
Thinking lessons: approaches to, 238-240; in North Urban schools, 120
Thinking skills: creative thinking, 60, 158, 205, 234, 249; critical

thinking, 33, 167, 169–173, 196,
199, 205, 238, 240–241, 249;
higher-order, 9, 37, 99, 221, 238
Third-grade classes: in Canada, 219;
in Daviston, 51–52; in Pittsburgh, 190–192; on reservation,
59–60, 78–79, 83; in Southland
County, 17, 20–21, 25
Thoughtfulness. *See* Literacy of
thoughtfulness
Tinder, G., 148–149
Toronto: active learning in, 215,
217–219, 221–223, 226–227, 230;
aspects of education in, 202–231;
assessed, 228–231, 236, 248; background on, 202–204; Broadacres
Elementary School in, 212, 214–
224; community outreach in,
222; evaluation in, 224–226, 227–
228; and ministry guidelines,
204–212, 225–226, 229; multiculturalism in, 204, 222–223, 227,
230
Toronto, University of, 215
Tracking, 113, 114
Trust, policies for, 249

Unions, and school reforms, 8–9,
53, 181
U.S. Secretary of Education, 57
Urban schools. *See* North Urban
Public Schools; Pittsburgh;
Toronto

Values, enhancing, 153
Vann, R., 36–38
Vermont, progress in, 243, 244, 249

Walden, M., 104–106, 108
Wallace, R., 168, 175–177, 179–183,
193–196, 200–201
Washington, B., 92–93
Watkins, W., 19–20
Watson, B., 184
Whole-language approach: in Can-
ada, 215, 221; in kindergarten,
11; in North Urban schools, 135,
141; on reservation, 72–74, 83, 85,
87, 91; and thinking, 239
Wilensky, R., 102, 107, 109, 111,
112, 118–122, 232
Wilkerson, D., 139
Williams, Mr., 62–63
Wilson, Mr., 127–130
Wilson, Ms., 15–17, 19
Wilson, N., 92, 99, 102, 110
Wisconsin, University of, 33
Wolf, D. P., 35
Workers, desired skills of, 4–6
Writing classes: in Canada, 219–
220; and math classes, 25–27; on
reservation, 76–78, 80–81; in
Southland County, 46–51

York University, 217

Zeiderman, H., 167
Zigmund, B., 79–80, 82–83, 87
Zuboff, S., 4